U0106567

Bilingual Classics

OUR
VILLAGE

Mary Russell Mitford

CONTENTS

INTRODUCTION

by Anne Thackeray Ritchie

I.

There is a great deal of admirable literature concerning Miss Mitford, so much of it indeed, that the writer of this little notice feels as if she almost owed an apology to those who remember, for having ventured to write, on hearsay only, and without having ever known or ever seen the author of "Our Village." And yet, so vivid is the homely friendly presence, so clear the sound of that voice "like a chime of bells," with its hospitable cheery greeting, that she can scarcely realise that this acquaintance exists only in the world of the might-have-beens.

For people who are beginning to remember, rather than looking forward any more, there certainly exists no more delightful reading than the memoirs and stories of heroes and heroines, many of whom we ourselves may have seen, and to whom we may have spoken. As we read on we are led into some happy bygone region, —such as that one described by Mr. du Maurier in "Peter Ibbetson," —a region in which we ourselves, together with all our friends and acquaintances, grow young again; —very young, very brisk, very hopeful. The people we love are there, along with the people we remember. Music begins to play, we are dancing, laughing, scampering over the country once more; our parents too are young and laughing cheerily. Every now and then perhaps some old friend, also vigorous and hopeful, bursts into the book, and begins to talk or to write a letter; early sights and sounds return to us, we have NOW, and we have THEN, in a pleasant harmony. To those of a certain literary generation who read Miss Mitford's memoirs, how many such familiar presences and names must appear and reappear. Not least among them that of her biographer, Mr. Harness himself, who was so valued by his friends. Mrs. Kemble, Mrs. Sartoris, Charles Allston Collins, always talked of him with a great respect and tenderness. I used to think they had a special voice with which to speak his name. He was never among our intimate friends, but how familiar to my recollection are the two figures, that of Mr. Harness and Miss Harness, his sister and housekeeper, coming together along the busy Kensington roadway. The brother and sister were like characters out of some book, with their kind faces, their simple spiritual ways; in touch with so much that was interesting and romantic, and in heart with so much that suffered. I remember him with grey hair and a smile. He was not tall; he walked rather lame; Miss Harness too was little, looking up at all the rest of the world with a kind round face and sparkling eyes fringed with thick lashes. Mary Mitford was indeed happy in her friends, as happy as she was unfortunate in her nearer relations.

With much that is sad, there is a great deal of beauty and enjoyment in Miss Mitford's life. For her the absence of material happiness was made up for by the presence of warm-hearted sensibility, of enthusiasm, by her devotion to her parents. Her long endurance and filial piety are very remarkable, her loving heart carried her safely to the end, and she found comfort in her unreasoning life's devotion. She had none of the restlessness which is so apt to spoil much that might be harmonious; all the charm of a certain unity and simplicity of motive is hers, "the single eye," of which Charles Kingsley wrote so sweetly. She loved her home, her trees, her surrounding lanes and commons. She loved her friends. Her books and flowers are real and important events in her life, soothing and distracting her from the contemplation of its constant anxieties. "I may truly say," she once writes to Miss Barrett, "that ever since I was a very young girl, I have never (although for some years living apparently in affluence) been without pecuniary care, —the care that pressed upon my thoughts the last thing at night, and woke in the morning with a dreary sense of pain and pressure, of something which weighed me to the earth."

Mary Russell Mitford was born on the 16th of December

1787. She was the only child of her parents, who were well connected; her mother was an heiress. Her father belonged to the Mitfords of the North. She describes herself as "a puny child, with an affluence of curls which made her look as if she were twin sister to her own great doll." She could read at three years old; she learnt the Percy ballads by heart almost before she could read. Long after, she used to describe how she first studied her beloved ballads in the breakfast-room lined with books, warmly spread with its Turkey carpet, with its bright fire, easy chairs, and the windows opening to a garden full of flowers, —stocks, honeysuckles, and pinks. It is touching to note how, all through her difficult life, her path was (literally) lined with flowers, and how the love of them comforted and cheered her from the first to the very last. In her saddest hours, the passing fragrance and beauty of her favourite geraniums cheered and revived her. Even when her mother died she found comfort in the plants they had tended together, and at the very last breaks into delighted descriptions of them.

She was sent to school in the year 1798 to No. 22 Hans Place, to a Mrs. St. Quintin's. It seems to have been an excellent establishment. Mary learnt the harp and astronomy; her taste for literature was encouraged. The young ladies, attired as shepherdesses, were also taught to skip through many mazy movements, but she never distinguished herself as a shepherdess. She had greater success in her literary efforts, and her composition "on balloons" was much applauded. She returned to her home in 1802. "Plain in figure and in face, she was never common-looking," says Mr. Harness. He gives a pretty description of her as "no ordinary child, her sweet smiles, her animated conversation, her keen enjoyment of life, and her gentle voice won the love and admiration of her friends, whether young or old." Mr. Harness has chiefly told Miss Mitford's story in her own words by quotations from her letters, and, as one reads, one can almost follow her moods as they succeed each other, and these moods are her real history. The assiduity of childhood, the bright enthusiasm and gaiety of her early days, the growing anxiety of her later life, the maturer judgments, the occasional despairing terrors which came to try her bright nature, but along with it all, that innocent and enduring hopefulness which never really deserted her. Her elastic spirit she owed to her father, that incorrigible old Skimpole. "I am generally happy everywhere," she writes in her youth—and then later on: "It is a great pleasure to me to love and to admire, this is a faculty which has survived many frosts and storms." It is true that she adds a query somewhere else, "Did you ever remark how superior old gaiety is to new?" she asks.

Her handsome father, her plain and long-enduring mother, are both unconsciously described in her correspondence. "The Doctor's manners were easy, natural, cordial, and apparently extremely frank," says Mr. Harness, "but he nevertheless met the world on its own terms, and was prepared to allow himself any insincerity which seemed expedient. He was not only recklessly extravagant, but addicted to high play. His wife's large fortune, his daughter's, his own patrimony, all passed through his hands in an incredibly short space of time, but his wife and daughter were never heard to complain of his conduct, nor appeared to admire him less."

The story of Miss Mitford's 20,000 pounds is unique among the adventures of authoresses. Dr. Mitford, having spent all his wife's fortune, and having brought his family from a comfortable home, with flowers and a Turkey carpet, to a small lodging near Blackfriars Bridge, determined to present his daughter with an expensive lottery ticket on the occasion of her tenth birthday. She had a fancy for No. 2224, of which the added numbers came to 10. This number actually came out the first prize of 20,000 pounds, which money started the family once more in comparative affluence. Dr. Mitford immediately built a new square house, which he calls Bertram House, on the site of a pretty old farmhouse which he causes to be pulled down. He also orders a dessert-service painted with the Mitford arms; Mrs. Mitford is supplied with a carriage, and she subscribes to a circulating library.

A list still exists of the books taken out by her for her daughter's use; some fifty-five volumes a month, chiefly trash: "Vicenza," "A Sailor's Friendship and Soldier's Love," "Clarentina," "Robert and Adela," "The Count de Valmont," "The Three Spaniards," "De Clifford" (in four volumes) and so on.

The next two or three years were brilliant enough; for the family must have lived at the rate of three or four thousand a year. Their hospitality was profuse, they had servants, carriages, they bought pictures and furniture, they entertained. Cobbett was among their intimate friends. The Doctor naturally enough invested in a good many more lottery tickets, but without any further return.

The ladies seem to take it as a matter of course that he should speculate and gamble at cards, and indeed do anything and everything he fancied, but they beg him at least to keep to respectable clubs. He is constantly away. His daughter tries to tempt him home with the bloom of her hyacinths. "How they long to see him again!" she says, "how greatly have they been disappointed, when, every day, the journey to Reading has been fruitless. The driver of the Reading coach is quite accustomed to being waylaid by their carriage." Then she tells him about the primroses, but neither hyacinths nor primroses bring the Doctor away from his cards. Finally, the rhododendrons and the azaleas are in bloom, but these also fail to attract him.

Miss Mitford herself as she grows up is sent to London more than once, to the St. Quintin's and elsewhere. She goes to the play and to Westminster Hall, she sees her hero, Charles James Fox, and has the happiness of watching him helped on to his horse. Mr. Romilly delights her, but her greatest favourite of all is Mr. Whitbread. "You know I am always an enthusiast," she writes, "but at present it is impossible to describe the admiration I feel for this exalted character." She speaks of his voice "which she could listen to with transport even if he spoke in an unknown language!" she writes a sonnet to him, "an impromptu, on hearing Mr. Whitbread declare in Westminster Hall that he fondly trusted his name would descend to posterity."

> The hope of Fame thy noble bosom fires,
> Nor vain the hope thy ardent mind inspires;
> In British breasts whilst Purity remains,
> Whilst Liberty her blessed abode retains,
> Still shall the muse of History proclaim
> To future ages thy immortal name!

There are many references to the celebrities of the time in her letters home, —every one agrees as to the extreme folly of Sheridan's entertainments, Mrs. Opie is spoken of as a rising authoress, etc. etc. etc.

Miss Austen used to go to 23 Hans Place, and Miss Mitford used to stay at No. 22, but not at the same time. Mrs. Mitford had known Miss Austen as a child. She may perhaps be forgiven for some prejudice and maternal jealousy, in her later impressions, but Mary Mitford admired Jane Austen always with warmest enthusiasm. She writes to her mother at length from London, describing everything, all the people and books and experiences that she comes across, —the elegant suppers at Brompton, the Grecian lamps, Mr. Barker's beauty, Mr. Plummer's plainness, and the destruction of her purple gown.

Mrs. Mitford writes back in return describing Reading festivities, "an agreeable dinner at Doctor Valpy's, where Mrs. Women and Miss Peacock are present and Mr. J. Simpson, M.P.; the dinner very good, two full courses and one remove, the soup giving place to one quarter of lamb." Mrs. Mitford sends a menu of every dinner she goes to.

In 1806 Dr. Mitford takes his daughter, who was then about nineteen, to the North to visit his relations; they are entertained by the grandparents of the Trevelyans and the Swinburnes, the Ogles and the Mitfords of the present day. They fish in Sir John Swinburne's lake, they visit at Alnwick Castle. Miss Mitford kept her front hair in papers till she reached Alnwick, nor was her dress discomposed though she had travelled thirty miles. They sat down, sixty-five to dinner, which was "of course" (she somewhat magnificently says) entirely served on plate. Poor Mary's pleasure is very much dashed by the sudden disappearance of her father, —Dr. Mitford was in the habit of doing anything he felt inclined to do at once and on the spot, quite irrespectively of the convenience of others, —and although a party had been arranged on purpose to meet him in the North, and his daughter was counting on his escort to return home (people posted in those days, they did not take their tickets direct from

Newcastle to London), Dr. Mitford one morning leaves word that he has gone off to attend the Reading election, where his presence was not in the least required. For the first and apparently for the only time in her life his daughter protests. "Mr. Ogle is extremely offended; nothing but your immediate return can ever excuse you to him! I IMPLORE you to return, I call upon Mamma's sense of propriety to send you here directly. Little did I suspect that my father, my beloved father, would desert me at this distance from home! Every one is surprised." Dr. Mitford was finally persuaded to travel back to Northumberland to fetch his daughter.

The constant companionship of Dr. Mitford must have given a curious colour to his good and upright daughter's views of life. Adoring her father as she did, she must have soon accustomed herself to take his fine speeches for fine actions, to accept his self-complacency in the place of a conscience. She was a woman of warm impressions, with a strong sense of right. But it was not within her daily experience, poor soul, that people who did not make grand professions were ready to do their duty all the same; nor did she always depend upon the uprightness, the courage; the self-denial of those who made no protestations. At that time loud talking was still the fashion, and loud living was considered romantic. They both exist among us, but they are less admired, and there is a different language spoken now to that of Dr. Mitford and his school.[1] This must account for some of Miss Mitford's judgments of what she calls a "cynical" generation, to which she did little justice.

II.

There is one penalty people pay for being authors, which is that from cultivating vivid impressions and mental pictures they are apt to take fancies too seriously and to mistake them for reality. In story-telling this is well enough, and it interferes with nobody; but in real history, and in one's own history most of all, this faculty is apt to raise up bogies and nightmares along one's path; and while one is fighting imaginary demons, the good things and true are passed by unnoticed, the best realities of life are sometimes overlooked....

But after all, Mary Russell Mitford, who spent most of her time gathering figs off thistles and making the best of her difficult circumstances, suffered less than many people do from the influence of imaginary things.

She was twenty-three years old when her first book of poems was published; so we read in her letters, in which she entreats her father not to curtail ANY of the verses addressed to him; there is no reason, she says, except his EXTREME

---

[1]   People nowadays are more ready to laugh than to admire when they hear the lions bray; for mewing and bleating, the taste, I fear, is on the increase.

MODESTY why the verses should be suppressed, —she speaks not only with the fondness of a daughter but with the sensibility of a poet. Our young authoress is modest, although in print; she compares herself to Crabbe (as Jane Austen might have done), and feels "what she supposes a farthing candle would experience when the sun rises in all its glory." Then comes the Publisher's bill for 59 pounds; she is quite shocked at the bill, which is really exorbitant! In her next letter Miss Mitford reminds her father that the taxes are still unpaid, and a correspondence follows with somebody asking for a choice of the Doctor's pictures in payment for the taxes. The Doctor is in London all the time, dining out and generally amusing himself. Everybody is speculating whether Sir Francis Burdett will go to the Tower. [1] "Oh, my darling, how I envy you at the fountain-head of intelligence in these interesting times! How I envy Lady Burdett for the fine opportunity she has to show the heroism of our sex!" writes the daughter, who is only encountering angry tax-gatherers at home.... Somehow or other the bills are paid for the time, and the family arrangements go on as before.

Besides writing to the members of her own home, Miss Mitford started another correspondent very early in life; this was Sir William Elford, to whom she describes her outings

[1] Here, in our little suburban garden at Wimbledon, are the remains of an old hedgerow which used to grow in the kitchen garden of the Grange where Sir Francis Burdett then lived. The tradition is that he was walking in the lane in his own kitchen garden when he was taken up and carried off to honourable captivity. —A.T.R.

and adventures, her visits to Tavistock House, where her kind friends the Perrys receive her. Mr. Perry was the editor of the "Morning Chronicle;" he and his beautiful wife were the friends of all the most interesting people of the day. Here again the present writer's own experiences can interpret the printed page, for her own first sight of London people and of London society came to her in a little house in Chesham Place, where her father's old friends, Mrs. Frederick Elliot and Miss Perry, the daughters of Miss Mitford's friends, lived with a very notable and interesting set of people, making a social centre, by that kindly unconscious art which cannot be defined; that quick apprehension, that benevolent fastidiousness (I have to use rather far-fetched words) which are so essential to good hosts and hostesses. A different standard is looked for now, by the rising generations knocking at the doors, behind which the dignified past is lying as stark as King Duncan himself!

Among other entertainments Miss Mitford went to the fetes which celebrated the battle of Vittoria; she had also the happiness of getting a good sight of Mme. de Stael, who was a great friend of the Perrys. "She is almost as much followed in the gardens as the Princess," she says, pouring out her wonders, her pleasures, her raptures. She begins to read Burns with youthful delight, dilates upon his exhaustless imagination, his versatility, and then she suggests a very just criticism. "Does it not appear," she says, "that versatility is the true and rare characteristic of that rare thing called genius—versatility and playfulness;" then she goes on to speak of two highly-reputed novels just come out and ascribed to Lady Morley, "Pride and Prejudice" and "Sense and Sensibility."

She is still writing from Bertram House, but her pleasant gossip continually alternates with more urgent and less agreeable letters addressed to her father. Lawyers' clerks are again calling with notices and warnings, tax-gatherers are troubling. Dr. Mitford has, as usual, left no address, so that she can only write to the "Star Office," and trust to chance. "Mamma joins in tenderest love," so the letters invariably conclude.

Notwithstanding the adoration bestowed by the ladies of the family and their endearing adjectives, Mr. Harness is very outspoken on the subject of the handsome Doctor! He disliked his manners, his morals, his self-sufficiency, his loud talk. "The old brute never informed his friends of anything; all they knew of him or his affairs, or whatever false or true he intended them to believe, came out carelessly in his loose, disjointed talk."

In 1814 Miss Mitford is living on still with her parents at Bertram House, but a change has come over their home; the servants are gone, the gravel turned to moss, the turf into pasture, the shrubberies to thickets, the house a sort of new "ruin half inhabited, and a Chancery suit is hanging over their heads." Meantime some news comes to cheer her from America. Two editions of her poems have been printed and sold. "Narrative Poems on the Female Character" proved a real success. "All who have hearts to feel and understandings to discriminate, must wish you health and leisure to complete your plan," so write publishers in those golden days, with complimentary copies of the work....

Great things are happening all this time; battles are being fought and won, Napoleon is on his way to St. Helena; London is in a frenzy of rejoicings, entertainings, illuminations. To Mary Mitford the appearance of "Waverley" seems as great an event as the return of the Bourbons; she is certain that "Waverley" is written by Sir Walter Scott, but "Guy Mannering," she thinks, is by another hand: her mind is full of a genuine romantic devotion to books and belles lettres, and she is also rejoicing, even more, in the spring-time of 1816. Dr. Mitford may be impecunious and their affairs may be threadbare, but the lovely seasons come out ever in fresh beauty and abundance. The coppices are carpeted with primroses, with pansies and wild strawberry blossom, —the woods are spangled with the delicate flowers of the wood sorrel and wood anemone, the meadows enamelled with cowslips.... Certainly few human beings were ever created more fit for this present world, and more capable of admiring and enjoying its beauties, than Miss Mitford, who only desired to be beautiful herself, she somewhere says, to be perfectly contented.

III.

Most people's lives are divided into first, second and third volumes; and as we read Miss Mitford's history it forms no exception to the rule. The early enthusiastic volume is there, with its hopes and wild judgments, its quaint old-fashioned dress and phraseology; then comes the second volume, full of actual work and serious responsibility, with those childish parents to provide for, whose lives, though so protracted, never seem to reach beyond their nurseries. Miss Mitford's third volume is retrospective; her growing infirmities are courageously endured, there is the certainty of success well earned and well deserved; we realise her legitimate hold upon the outer world of readers and writers, besides the reputation which she won upon the stage by her tragedies.

The literary ladies of the early part of the century in some ways had a very good time of it. A copy of verses, a small volume of travels, a few tea-parties, a harp in one corner of the room, and a hat and feathers worn rather on one side, seemed to be all that was wanted to establish a claim to fashion and inspiration. They had footstools to rest their satin shoes upon, they had admirers and panegyrists to their heart's content, and above all they possessed that peculiar complacency in which (with a few notable exceptions) our age is singularly deficient. We are earnest, we are audacious, we are original, but we are not complacent. THEY were dolls perhaps, and lived in dolls' houses; WE are ghosts without houses at all; we come and go wrapped in sheets of newspaper, holding flickering lights in our hands, paraffin lamps, by the light of which we are seeking our proper sphere. Poor vexed spirits! We do not belong to the old world any more! The new world is not yet ready for us. Even Mr. Gladstone will not let us into the House of Commons; the Geographical Society rejects us, so does the Royal Academy; and yet who could say that any of their standards rise too high! Some one or two are happily safe, carried by the angels of the Press to little altars and pinnacles all their own; but the majority of hard-working, intelligent women, "contented with little, yet ready for more," may they not in moments of depression be allowed to picture to themselves what their chances might have been had they only been born half a century earlier?

Miss Mitford, notwithstanding all her troubles (she has been known to say she had rather be a washerwoman than a literary lady), had opportunities such as few women can now obtain. One is lost in admiration at the solidity of one's grandparents' taste, when one attempts to read the tragedies they delighted in, and yet "Rienzi" sold four thousand copies and was acted forty-five times; and at one time Miss Mitford had two tragedies rehearsed upon the boards together; one at Covent Garden and one at Drury Lane, with Charles Kemble and Macready disputing for her work. Has not one also read similar descriptions of the triumphs of Hannah More, or of Joanna Baillie; cheered by enthusiastic audiences, while men shed tears. [1]

"Julian" was the first of Miss Mitford's acted plays. It was brought out at Covent Garden in 1823, when she was thirty-

[1] Mem. Hannah More, v.i. p.124.

six years old; Macready played the principal part. "If the play do reach the ninth night," Miss Mitford writes to Macready, "it will be a very complete refutation of Mr. Kemble's axiom that no single performer can fill the theatre; for except our pretty Alfonso (Miss Foote) there is only Julian, one and only one. Let him imagine how deeply we feel his exertions and his kindness. [1]..."

"Julian" was stopped on the eighth night, to her great disappointment, but she is already engaged on another—on several more—tragedies; she wants the money badly; for the editor of her magazine has absconded, owing her 50 pounds. Some trying and bewildering quarrel then ensues between Charles Kemble and Macready, which puts off her tragedies, and sadly affects poor Miss Mitford's nerves and profits. She has one solace. Her father, partly instigated, she says, by the effect which the terrible feeling of responsibility and want of power has had upon her health and spirits, at last resolves to try if he can HIMSELF obtain any employment that may lighten the burthen of the home. It is a good thing that Dr. Mitford has braced himself to this heroic determination. "The addition of two or even one hundred a year to our little income, joined to

---

[1] In Macready's diary we find an entry which is not over gracious. " 'Julian' acted March the 15th. Had but moderate success. The C. G. company was no longer equal to the support of plays containing moral characters. The authoress in her dedication to me was profuse in her acknowledgments and compliments, but the performance made little impression, and was soon forgotten."

what I am, in a manner, sure of gaining by mere industry, would take a load from my heart of which I can scarcely give you an idea... even 'Julian' was written under a pressure of anxiety which left me not a moment's rest...." So she fondly dwells upon the delightful prospects. Then comes the next letter to Sir William Elford, and we read that her dear father, "relying with a blessed sanguineness on my poor endeavours, has not, I believe, even inquired for a situation, and I do not press the matter, though I anxiously wish it; being willing to give one more trial to the theatre."

On one of the many occasions when Miss Mitford writes to her trustee imploring him to sell out the small remaining fragment of her fortune, she says, "My dear father has, years ago, been improvident, is still irritable and difficult to live with, but he is a person of a thousand virtues...there are very few half so good in this mixed world; it is my fault that this money is needed, entirely my fault, and if it be withheld, my dear father will be overthrown, mind and body, and I shall never know another happy hour."

No wonder Mr. Harness, who was behind the scenes, remonstrated against the filial infatuation which sacrificed health, sleep, peace of mind, to gratify every passing whim of the Doctor's. At a time when she was sitting up at night and slaving, hour after hour, to earn the necessary means of living, Dr. Mitford must needs have a cow, a stable, and dairy implements procured for his amusement, and when he died he left 1,000 pounds of debts for the scrupulous woman to pay off. She is determined to pay, if she sells her clothes to do so. Meanwhile, the Doctor is still alive, and Miss Mitford is straining every nerve to keep him so. She is engaged (in strict confidence) on a grand historical subject, Charles and Cromwell, the finest episode in English history, she says. Here, too, fresh obstacles arise. This time it is the theatrical censor who interferes. It would be dangerous for the country to touch upon such topics; Mr. George Colman dwells upon this theme, although he gives the lady full credit for no evil intentions; but for the present all her work is again thrown away. While Miss Mitford is struggling on as best she can against this confusion of worries and difficulty (she eventually received 200 pounds for "Julian" from a Surrey theatre), a new firm "Whittaker" undertakes to republish the "village sketches" which had been written for the absconding editor. The book is to be published under the title of "Our Village."

IV.

"Are your characters and descriptions true?" somebody once asked our authoress. "Yes, yes, yes, as true, as true as is well possible," she answers. "You, as a great landscape painter, know that in painting a favourite scene you do a little embellish and can't help it; you avail yourself of happy accidents of atmosphere; if anything be ugly you strike it out, or if anything be wanting, you put it in. But still the picture is a likeness."

So wrote Miss Mitford, but with all due respect for her and for Sir William Elford, the great landscape painter, I cannot help thinking that what is admirable in her book, are not her actual descriptions and pictures of intelligent villagers and greyhounds, but the more imaginative things; the sense of space and nature and progress which she knows how to convey; the sweet and emotional chord she strikes with so true a touch. Take at hazard her description of the sunset. How simple and yet how finely felt it is. Her genuine delight reaches us and carries us along; it is not any embellishing of effects, or exaggeration of facts, but the reality of a true and very present feeling... "The narrow line of clouds which a few minutes ago lay like long vapouring streaks along the horizon, now lighted with a golden splendour, that the eye can scarcely endure; those still softer clouds which floated above, wreathing and curling into a thousand fantastic forms as thin and changeful as summer smoke, defined and deepened into grandeur, and hedged with ineffable, insufferable light. Another minute and the brilliant orb totally disappears and the sky above grows, every moment, more varied and more beautiful, as the dazzling golden lines are mixed with glowing red and gorgeous purple, dappled with small dark specks, and mingled with such a blue as the egg of the hedge-sparrow.... To look up at that glorious sky, and then to see that magnificent picture reflected in the clear and lovely Loddon water, is a pleasure never to be described, and never to be forgotten. My heart swells, and my eyes fill as I write of it, and think of the immeasurable majesty of nature and the unspeakable goodness of God, who has spread an enjoyment so pure, so peaceful, and so intense before the meanest and lowliest of His creatures."

But it is needless now to go on praising "Our Village," or to recount what a success was in store for the little book. Certain books hold their own by individual right and might; they are part of everybody's life as a matter of course. They are not always read, but they tacitly take their place among us. The editions succeeded editions here and in America; artists came down to illustrate the scenes. Miss Mitford, who was so delighted with the drawings by Mr. Baxter, should have lived to see the charming glimpses of rural life we owe to Mr. Thomson. "I don't mind 'em," says Lizzy to the cows, as they stand with spirited bovine grace behind the stable door. "Don't mind them indeed!"

I think the author would assuredly have enjoyed the picture of the baker, the wheelwright and the shoemaker, each following his special Alderney along the road to the village, or of the farmer driving his old wife in the gig.... One design, that of the lady in her pattens, comes home to the writer of these notes, who has perhaps the distinction of being the only authoress now alive who has ever walked out in pattens. At the age of seven years she was provided with a pair by a great-great-aunt, a kind old lady living at Fareham, in Hampshire, where they were still in use. How interesting the little circles looked stamped upon the muddy road, and how nearly down upon one's nose one was at every other step!

But even with all her success, Miss Mitford was not out of her troubles. She writes to Mr. Harness saying: "You cannot imagine how perplexed I am. There are points in my domestic situation too long and too painful to write about; the terrible improvidence of one dear parent, the failure of memory and decay of faculty in that other who is still dearer, cast on me a weight of care and fear that I can hardly bear up against." Her difficulties were unending. The new publisher now stopped payment, so that even "Our Village" brought in no return for the moment; Charles Kemble was unable to make any offer for "Foscari." She went up to town in the greatest hurry to try and collect some of the money owing to her from her various publishers, but, as Mr. Harness says, received little from her debtors beyond invitations and compliments. She meditates a novel, she plans an opera, "Cupid and Psyche."

At last, better times began to dawn, and she receives 150 pounds down for a new novel and ten guineas from Blackwood as a retaining fee. Then comes a letter from Charles Kemble giving her new hope, for her tragedy, which was soon afterwards produced at Covent Garden.

The tragedies are in tragic English, of course that language of the boards, but not without a simplicity and music of their own. In the introduction to them, in some volumes published by Hurst and Blacket in 1854, Miss Mitford describes "the scene of indescribable chaos preceding the performance, the vague sense of obscurity and confusion; tragedians, hatted and coated, skipping about, chatting and joking; the only very grave person being Liston himself. Ballet-girls walking through their quadrilles to the sound of a solitary fiddle, striking up as if of its own accord, from amid the tall stools and music-desks of the orchestra, and piercing, one hardly knew how, through the din that was going on incessantly. Oh, that din! Voices from every part; above, below, around, and in every key. Heavy weights rolling here and falling there. Bells ringing, one could not tell why, and the ubiquitous call-boy everywhere."

She describes her astonishment when the play succeeds. "Not that I had nerve enough to attend the first representation of my tragedies. I sat still and trembling in some quiet apartment near, and thither some friend flew to set my heart at ease. Generally the messenger of good tidings was poor Haydon, whose quick and ardent spirit lent him wings on such an occasion."

We have the letter to her mother about "Foscari," from which I have quoted; and on the occasion of the production of "Rienzi" at Drury Lane (two years later in October 1828), the letter to Sir William Elford when the poor old mother was no longer here to rejoice in her daughter's success.

Miss Mitford gratefully records the sympathy of her friends, the warm-hearted muses of the day. Mrs. Trollope, Miss Landon, Miss Edgeworth, Miss Porden, Mrs. Hofland, Mrs.

Opie, who all appear with their congratulations.

Miss Mitford says that Haydon, above all, sympathised with her love for a large canvas. The Classics, Spain, Italy, Mediaeval Rome, these are her favourite scenes and periods. Dukes and tribunes were her heroes; daggers, dungeons, and executioners her means of effects.

She moralises very sensibly upon Dramatic success. "It is not," she says, "so delicious, so glorious, so complete a gratification as, in our secret longings, we all expect. It does not fill the heart, —it is an intoxication followed by a dismal reaction." She tells a friend that never in all her life was she so depressed and out of spirits as after "Rienzi," her first really successful venture. But there is also a passing allusion to her father's state of mind, to his mingled irritation and sulkiness, which partly explains things. Could it be that the Doctor added petty jealousy and envy to his other inconvenient qualities? His intolerance for any author or actor, in short, for any one not belonging to a county family, his violent annoyance at any acquaintances such as those which she now necessarily made, would naturally account for some want of spirits on the daughter's part; overwrought, over-taxed, for ever on the strain, her work was exhausting indeed. The small pension she afterwards obtained from the Civil List must have been an unspeakable boon to the poor harassed woman.

Tragedy seems to have resulted in a substantial pony and a basket carriage for Miss Mitford, and in various invitations (from the Talfourds, among the rest) during which she is lionised right and left. It must have been on this occasion that Serjeant Talfourd complained so bitterly of a review of "Ion" which appeared about that time. His guest, to soothe him, unwarily said, "she should not have minded such a review of HER Tragedy."

"YOUR 'Rienzi,' indeed! I should think not," says the serjeant. " 'Ion' is very different." The Talfourd household, as it is described by Mr. Lestrange, is a droll mixture of poetry and prose, of hospitality, of untidiness, of petulance, of most genuine kindness and most genuine human nature.

There are also many mentions of Miss Mitford in the "Life of Macready" by Sir F. Pollock. The great tragedian seems not to have liked her with any cordiality; but he gives a pleasant account of a certain supper-party in honour of "Ion" at which she is present, and during which she asks Macready if he will not now bring out her tragedy. The tragedian does not answer, but Wordsworth, sitting by, says, "Ay, keep him to it."

V.

Besides the "Life of Miss Mitford" by Messrs. Harness and Lestrange, there is also a book of the "Friendships of Mary Russell Mitford," consisting of the letters she received rather than of those which she wrote. It certainly occurs to one, as one looks through the printed correspondence of celebrated people, how different are written from printed letters. Your friend's voice sounds, your friend's eyes look out, of the written page, even its blots and erasures remind you of your human being. But the magnetism is gone out of these printer's lines with their even margins; in which everybody's handwriting is exactly alike; in which everybody uses the same type, the same expressions; in which the eye roams from page to page untouched, unconvinced. I can imagine the pleasure each one of these letters may have given to Miss Mitford to receive in turn. They come from well-known ladies, accustomed to be considered. Mrs. Trollope, Mrs. Hofland, Mrs. Howitt, Mrs. S. C. Hall, Miss Strickland, Mrs. Opie; there, too, are Miss Barrett and Mrs. Jamieson and Miss Sedgwick who writes from America; they are all interesting people, but it must be confessed that the correspondence is not very enlivening. Miss Barrett's is an exception, that is almost as good as handwriting to read. But there is no doubt that compliments to OTHER authoresses are much less amusing, than those one writes or receives oneself; apologies also for not writing sooner, CAN pall upon one in print, however soothing they may be to the justly offended recipient, or to the conscience-stricken correspondent.

"I must have seemed a thankless wretch, my dear Miss Mitford," etc. etc. "You, my dear friend, know too well what it is to have to finish a book, to blame my not attempting," etc. etc. "This is the thirty-ninth letter I have written since yesterday morning," says Harriet Martineau. "Oh, I can scarcely hold the pen! I will not allow my shame for not having written, to prevent me from writing now." All these people seem to have been just as busy as people are now, as amusing, as tiresome. They had the additional difficulty of having to procure franks, and of having to cover four pages instead of a post-card. OUR letters may be dull, but at all events they are not nearly so long. We come sooner to the point and avoid elegant circumlocutions. But one is struck, among other things, by the keener literary zest of those days, and by the immense numbers of MSS. and tragedies in circulation, all of which their authors confidingly send from one to another. There are also whole flights of travelling poems flapping their wings and uttering their cries as they go.

An enthusiastic American critic who comes over to England emphasises the situation. Mr. Willis's "superlative admiration" seems to give point to everything, and to all the enthusiasm. Miss Austen's Collins himself could not have been more appreciative, not even if Miss de Burgh had tried her hand at a MS.... Could he—Mr. Willis—choose, he would have tragedy once a year from Miss Mitford's pen. "WHAT an intoxicating life it is," he cries; "I met Jane Porter and Miss Aikin and Tom Moore and a troop more beaux esprits at dinner yesterday! I never shall be content elsewhere."

Miss Mitford's own letters speak in a much more natural voice.

"I never could understand what people could find to like

in my letters," Miss Mitford writes, "unless it be that they have a ROOT to them." The root was in her own kind heart. Miss Mitford may have been wanting a little in discrimination, but she was never wanting in sympathy. She seems to have loved people for kindness's sake indiscriminately as if they were creations of her own brain: but to friendliness or to trouble of any sort she responds with fullest measure. Who shall complain if some rosy veil coloured the aspects of life for her?

"Among the many blessings I enjoy, —my dear father, my admirable mother, my tried and excellent friends, —there is nothing for which I ought to thank God so earnestly as for the constitutional buoyancy of spirits, the aptness to hope, the will to be happy WHICH I INHERIT FROM MY FATHER," she writes. Was ever filial piety so irritating as hers? It is difficult to bear, with any patience, her praises of Dr. Mitford. His illusions were no less a part of his nature than his daughter's, the one a self-centred absolutely selfish existence, the other generous, humble, beautiful. She is hardly ever really angry except when some reports get about concerning her marriage. There was an announcement that she was engaged to one of her own clan, and the news spread among her friends. The romantic Mrs. Hofland had conjured up the suggestion, to Miss Mitford's extreme annoyance. It is said Mrs. Hofland also married off Miss Edgeworth in the same manner.

Mary Mitford found her true romance in friendship, not in

love. One day Mr. Kenyon came to see her while she was staying in London, and offered to show her the Zoological Gardens, and on the way he proposed calling in Gloucester Place to take up a young lady, a connection of his own, Miss Barrett by name. It was thus that Miss Mitford first made the acquaintance of Mrs. Browning, whose friendship was one of the happiest events of her whole life. A happy romance indeed, with that added reality which must have given it endurance. And indeed to make a new friend is like learning a new language. I myself have a friend who says that we have each one of us a chosen audience of our own to whom we turn instinctively, and before whom we rehearse that which is in our minds; whose opinion influences us, whose approval is our secret aim. All this Mrs. Browning seems to have been to Miss Mitford.

"I sit and think of you and of the poems that you will write, and of that strange rainbow crown called fame, until the vision is before me.... My pride and my hopes seem altogether merged in you. At my time of life and with so few to love, and with a tendency to body forth images of gladness, you cannot think what joy it is to anticipate...." So wrote the elder woman to the younger with romantic devotion. What Miss Mitford once said of herself was true, hers was the instinct of the bee sucking honey from the hedge flower. Whatever sweetness and happiness there was to find she turned to with unerring directness.

It is to Miss Barrett that she sometimes complains. "It

will help you to understand how impossible it is for me to earn money as I ought to do, when I tell you that this very day I received your dear letter and sixteen others; then my father brought into my room the newspaper to hear the ten or twelve columns of news from India; then I dined and breakfasted in one; then I got up, and by that time there were three parties of people in the garden; eight others arrived soon after.... I was forced to leave, being engaged to call on Lady Madeline Palmer. She took me some six miles on foot in Mr. Palmer's beautiful plantations, in search of that exquisite wild-flower the bog-bean, do you know it? most beautiful of flowers, either wild—or, as K. puts it, —'tame.' After long search we found the plant not yet in bloom."

Dr. Mitford weeps over his daughter's exhaustion, telling everybody that she is killing herself by her walks and drives. He would like her never to go beyond the garden and beyond reach of the columns of his newspaper. She declares that it is only by getting out and afield that she can bear the strain and the constant alternation of enforced work and anxiety. Nature was, indeed, a second nature to her. Charles Kingsley himself could scarcely write better of the East wind....

"We have had nine weeks of drought and east wind, scarcely a flower to be seen, no verdure in the meadows, no leaves in the hedgerows; if a poor violet or primrose did make its appearance it was scentless. I have not once heard my aversion the cuckoo... and in this place, so evidently the rendezvous of swallows, that it takes its name from them, not a swallow has yet appeared. The only time that I have heard the nightingale, I drove, the one mild day we have had, to a wood where I used to find the wood sorrel in beds; only two blossoms of that could be found, but a whole chorus of nightingales saluted me the moment I drove into the wood."

There is something of Madame de Sévigné in her vivid realisation of natural things.

She nursed her father through a long and trying illness, and when he died found herself alone in the world with impaired health and very little besides her pension from the Civil List to live upon. Dr. Mitford left 1000 pounds worth of debts, which this honourable woman then and there set to work to try and pay. So much courage and devotion touched the hearts of her many friends and readers, and this sum was actually subscribed by them. Queens, archbishops, dukes, and marquises subscribe to the testimonial, so do the literary ladies, Mesdames Bailey, Edgeworth, Trollope; Mrs. Opie is determined to collect twenty pounds at least, although she justly says she wishes it were for anything but to pay the Doctor's debts.

In 1844 it is delightful to read of a little ease at last in this harassed life; of a school-feast with buns and flags organised by the kind lady, the children riding in waggons decked with laurel, Miss Mitford leading the way, followed by eight or ten neighbouring carriages, and the whole party waiting in

Swallowfield Lane to see the Queen and Prince Albert returning from their visit to the Duke of Wellington. "Our Duke went to no great expense," says Miss Mitford. (Dr. Mitford would have certainly disapproved had he been still alive.) One strip of carpet the Duke did buy, the rest of the furniture he hired in Reading for the week. The ringers, after being hard at work for four hours, sent a can to the house to ask for some beer, and the can was sent back empty.

It was towards the end of her life that Miss Mitford left Three Mile Cross and came to Swallowfield to stay altogether. "The poor cottage was tumbling around us, and if we had stayed much longer we should have been buried in the ruins," she says; "there I had toiled and striven and tasted as bitterly of bitter anxiety, of fear and hope, as often falls to the lot of women." Then comes a charming description of the three miles of straight and dusty road. "I walked from one cottage to the other on an autumn evening when the vagrant birds, whose habit of assembling there for their annual departure, gives, I suppose, its name of Swallowfield to the village, were circling over my head, and I repeated to myself the pathetic lines of Hayley as he saw those same birds gathering upon his roof during his last illness: —

> 'Ye gentle birds, that perch aloof,
> And smooth your pinions on my roof...

Prepare for your departure hence
Ere winter's angry threats commence;
Like you my soul would smooth her plume
For longer flights beyond the tomb.

May God by whom is seen and heard
Departing men and wandering bird,
In mercy mark us for His own
And guide us to the land unknown!' "

Thoughts soothing and tender came with those touching lines, and gayer images followed....

It is from Swallowfield that she writes: "I have fell this blessing of being able to respond to new friendships very strongly lately, for I have lost many old and valued connections during this trying spring. I thank God far more earnestly for such blessings than for my daily bread, for friendship is the bread of the heart."

It was late in life to make such warm new ties as those which followed her removal from Three Mile Cross; but some of the most cordial friendships of her life date from this time. Mr. James Payn and Mr. Fields she loved with some real motherly feeling, and Lady Russell who lived at the Hall became her tender and devoted friend.

VI.

We went down to Reading the other day, as so many of Miss Mitford's friends have done before, to look at "our village" with our own eyes, and at the cottage in which she lived for so long. A phaeton with a fast-stepping horse met us at the station and whirled us through the busy town and along the straight dusty road beyond it. As we drove along in the soft clouded sunshine I looked over the hedges on either side, and I could see fields and hedgerows and red roofs clustering here and there, while the low background of blue hills spread towards the horizon. It was an unpretentious homely prospect intercepted each minute by the detestable advertisement hoardings recommending this or that rival pill. "Tongues in trees" indeed, in a very different sense from the exiled duke's experience! Then we come within sight of the running brook, uncontaminated as yet; the river flowing cool and swift, without quack medicines stamped upon its waters: we reach Whitley presently, with its pretty gabled hostel (Mrs. Mitford used to drive to Whitley and back for her airing), the dust rises on the fresh keen wind, the scent of the ripe corn is in the air, the cows stoop under the elm trees, looking exactly as they do in Mr. Thomson's pretty pictures, dappled and brown, with delicate legs and horns. We pass very few people, a baby lugged along in its cart, and accompanied by its brothers and sisters; a fox-terrier comes barking at our wheels; at last the phaeton stops abruptly between two or three roadside houses, and the coachman, pointing with his whip, says, "That is 'The Mitford,' ma'am. —That's where Miss Mitford used to live!"

Was that all? I saw two or three commonplace houses skirting the dusty road, I saw a comfortable public-house with an elm tree, and beside it another grey unpretentious little house, with a slate roof and square walls, and an inscription, "The Mitford," painted over the doorway....

I had been expecting I knew not what; a spire, a pump, a green, a winding street: my preconceived village in the air had immediately to be swept into space, and in its stead, behold the inn with its sign-post, and these half-dozen brick tenements, more or less cut to one square pattern! So this was all! This was "our village" of which the author had written so charmingly! These were the sights the kind eyes had dwelt upon, seeing in them all, the soul of hidden things, rather than dull bricks and slates. Except for one memory, Three Mile Cross would seem to be one of the dullest and most uninteresting of country places....

But we have Miss Mitford's own description. "The Cross is not a borough, thank Heaven, either rotten or independent. The inhabitants are quiet, peaceable people who would not think of visiting us, even if we had a knocker to knock at. Our residence is a cottage" (she is writing to her correspondent, Sir William Elford), "no, not a cottage, it does not deserve the name— a messuage or tenement such as a little farmer who had made 1400 pounds might retire to when he left off business to live on his means. It consists of a series of closets, the largest of which may be about eight feet square, which they call parlours and kitchens and pantries, some of them minus a corner, which has been unnaturally filched for a chimney, others deficient in half a side, which has been truncated by a shelving roof. Behind is a garden about the size of a good drawing-room, with an arbour, which is a complete sentry-box of privet. On one side a public-house, on the other a village shop, and right opposite a cobbler's stall. Notwithstanding all this 'the cabin,' as Boabdil says, 'is convenient.' It is within reach of my dear old walks, the banks where I find my violets, the meadows full of cowslips, and the woods where the wood sorrel blows.... Papa has already had the satisfaction of setting the neighbourhood to rights and committing a disorderly person who was the pest of 'The Cross' to Bridewell.... Mamma has furbished up an old dairy; I have lost my only key and stuffed the garden with flowers...." So writes the contented young woman.

How much more delightful is all this than any common-place stagey effect of lattice and gable; and with what pleasant unconscious art the writer of this letter describes what is NOT there and brings in her banks of violets to perfume the dull rooms. The postscript to this letter is Miss Mitford all over. "Pray excuse my blots and interlineations. They have been caused by my attention being distracted by a nightingale in full song who is pouring a world of music through my window."

"Do you not like to meet with good company in your

friends' hearts?" Miss Mitford says somewhere, —to no one better than to herself does this apply. Her heart was full of gracious things, and the best of company was ever hers, "La fleur de la hotte," as Madame de Sévigné says.

We walked into the small square hall where Dr. Mitford's bed was established after his illness, whilst visitors and all the rest of the household came and went through the kitchen door. In the parlour, once kept for his private use, now sat a party of homely friends from Reading, resting and drinking tea: we too were served with smoking cups, and poured our libation to her who once presided in the quiet place; and then the landlady took us round and about, showed us the kitchen with its comfortable corners and low window-frames—"I suppose this is scarcely changed at all?" said one of us.

"Oh yes, ma'am," says the housekeeper—"WE uses a Kitchener, Miss Mitford always kept an open range."

The garden, with its sentry-box of privet, exists no longer; an iron mission-room stands in its place, with the harmonium, the rows of straw chairs, the table and the candlesticks de circonstance. Miss Mitford's picture hangs on the wall, a hand-coloured copy of one of her portraits. The kindly homely features smile from the oils, in good humour and attentive intelligence. The sentiment of to-day is assuredly to be found in the spirit of things rather than in their outward signs.... Any one of us can feel the romance of a wayside shrine put up to the memory of some mediaeval well-dressed saint with a nimbus at the back of her head, and a trailing cloak and veil.... Here, after all, is the same sentiment, only translated into nineteenth-century language; uses corrogated iron sheds, and cups of tea, and oakum matting. "Mr. Palmer, he bought the place," says the landlady, "he made it into a Temperance Hotel, and built the Temperance Hall in the garden."....

No romantic marble shrine, but a square meeting-house of good intent, a tribute not less sincere because it is square, than if it were drawn into Gothic arch and curve. It speaks, not of a holy and mythical saint, but of a good and warm-hearted woman; of a life-long penance borne with charity and cheerfulness; of sweet fancies and blessings which have given innocent pleasure to many generations!

VII.

There is a note, written in a close and pretty writing, something between Sir Walter Scott's and Mrs. Browning's, which the present writer has possessed for years, fastened in a book among other early treasures: —

Thank you, dearest Miss Priscilla, for your great kindness. I return the ninth volume of [illegible], with the four succeeding ones, all that I have; probably all that are yet published. You shall have the rest when I get them. Tell dear Mr. George (I must not call him Vert-Vert) that I have recollected the name of the author of the clever novel "Le Rouge et le Noir" (that is the right title of the book, which has nothing to do with the name); the author's name is Stendhal, or so he calls himself. I think that he was either a musician or a musical critic, and that he is dead.... My visitor has not yet arrived (6 o'clock, p.m.), frightened no doubt by the abruptness of the two notes which I wrote in reply to hers yesterday morning; and indeed nobody could fancy the hurry in which one is forced to write by this walking post....

Tell my visitors of yesterday with my kind love that they did me all the good in the world, as indeed everybody of your house does.

—Ever, dear Miss Priscilla, very affectionately yours,

M. R. MITFORD.

In the present writer's own early days, when the now owner of Swallowfield was a very young, younger son, she used to hear him and his sister, Mrs. Brackenbury (the Miss Priscilla of the note), speaking with affectionate remembrance of the old friend lately gone, who had dwelt at their very gates; through which friendly gates one is glad, indeed, to realise what delightful companionship and loving help came to cheer the end of that long and toilsome life; and when Messrs. Macmillan suggested this preface the writer looked for her old autograph-book, and at its suggestion wrote (wondering whether any links existed still) to ask for information concerning Miss Mitford, and so it happened that she found herself also kindly entertained at Swallowfield, and invited to visit the scenes of which the author of "Our Village" had written with so much delight.

I think I should like to reverse the old proverb about letting those who run read, my own particular fancy being for reading first and running afterwards. There are few greater pleasures than to meet with an Individuality, to listen to it speaking from a printed page, recounting, suggesting, growing upon you every hour, gaining in life and presence, and then, while still under its influence, to find oneself suddenly transported into the very scene of that life, to stand among its familiar impressions and experiences, realising another distinct existence by some odd metempsychosis, and what may—or rather, what MUST have been. It is existing a book rather than reading it when this happens to one.

The house in Swallowfield Park is an old English country home, a fastness still piled up against time; whose stately walls and halls within, and beautiful century-old trees in the park without, record great times and striking figures. The manor was a part of the dowry of Henry the VIII.'s luckless queens. The modern house was built by Clarendon, and the old church among the elms dates from 1200, with carved signs and symbols and brasses of knights and burgesses, and names of strange sound and bygone fashion.

Lady Russell, who had sent the phaeton with the fast-stepping horse to meet us, was walking in the park as we drove up, and instead of taking us back to the house, she first led the way across the grass and by the stream to the old church, standing in its trim sweet garden, where Death itself seems smiling and fearless; where kind Mary Mitford's warm heart rests quiet, and "her busy hand," as she says herself, "is lying in peace there, where the sun glances through the great elm trees in the beautiful churchyard of Swallowfield."

The last baronet, Sir Charles, who fought in the Crimea, and who succeeded his father, Sir Henry, moved the dividing rail so that his old friend should be well within the shadow of these elm trees. Lady Russell showed us the tranquil green place, and told us its story, and how the old church had once been doomed to destruction when Kingsley came over by chance, and pleaded that it should be spared; and how, when rubbish and outward signs of decay had been cleared away, the restorers were rewarded for their piety, by coming upon noble beams of oak, untouched by time, upon some fine old buried monuments and brasses and inscriptions, among which the people still say their prayers in the shrine where their fathers knelt, and of which the tradition is not yet swept away. The present Lady of the Manor, who loves old traditions, has done her part to preserve the records for her children.

So Miss Mitford walked from Three Mile Cross to Swallowfield to end her days, with these kind friends to cheer and to comfort her. Sir Henry Russell was alive when she first established herself, but he was already suffering from some sudden seizure, which she, with her usual impetuosity, describes in her letters as a chronic state of things. After his death, his widow, the Lady Russell of those days, was her kindest friend and comforter.

The little Swallowfield cottage at the meeting of the three roads, to which Mary Mitford came when she left Three Mile Cross, has thrown out a room or two, as cottages do, but otherwise I think it can be little changed. It was here Miss Mitford was visited by so many interesting people, here she used to sit writing at her big table under the "tassels of her acacia tree." When the present Lady of the Manor brought us to the gate, the acacia flowers were over, but a balmy breath of summer was everywhere; a beautiful rose was hanging upon the wall beneath the window (it must have taken many years to grow to such a height), and beyond the palings of the garden spread the fields, ripening in the late July, and turning to gold. The farmer and his son were at work with their scythes; the birds were still flying, the sweet scents were in the air.

From a lady who had known her, "my own Miss Anne" of the letters, we heard something more that day of the author of "Our Village"; of her charming intellect, her gift of talk, her impulsiveness, her essential sociability, and rapid grace of mind. She had the faults of her qualities; she jumped too easily to conclusions; she was too much under the influence

of those with whom she lived. She was born to be a victim, —
even after her old tyrant father's death, she was more or less
over-ridden by her servants. Neighbours looked somewhat
doubtfully on K. and Ben, but they were good to her, on the
whole, and tended her carefully. Miss Russell said that when
she and her brother took refuge in the cottage, one morning
from a storm, while they dried themselves by the fire, they saw
the careful meal carried up to the old lady, the kidneys, the
custard, for her *déjeuner à la fourchette*.

When Miss Mitford died, she left everything she had to
her beloved K. and to Ben, except that she said she wished that
one book from her well-stocked library should be given to each
of her friends. The old Doctor, with all his faults, had loved
books, and bought handsome and valuable first editions of
good authors. K. and Ben also seem to have loved books and
first editions. To the Russells, who had nursed Miss Mitford,
comforted her, by whose gates she dwelt, in whose arms she
died, Ben brought, as a token of remembrance, an old shilling
volume of one of G. P. R. James's novels, which was all he
could bear to part with. A prettier incident was told me by Miss
Russell, who once went to visit Miss Mitford's grave. She found
a young man standing there whom she did not know. "Don't
you know me?" said he; "I am Henry, ma'am. I have just come
back from Australia." He was one of the children of the couple
who had lived in the cottage, and his first visit on his return
from abroad had been to the tomb of his old protectress.

I also heard a friend who knew Miss Mitford in her latest days, describe going to see her within a very few months of her death; she was still bright and responding as ever, though very ill. The young visitor had herself been laid up and absent from the invalid's bedside for some time. They talked over many things, —an authoress among the rest, concerning whose power of writing a book Miss Mitford seems to have been very doubtful. After her visitor was gone, the sick woman wrote one of her delicate pretty little notes and despatched it with its tiny seal (there it is still unbroken, with its M. R. M. just as she stamped it), and this is the little letter: —

Thank you, dearest Miss...for once again showing me your fair face by the side of the dear, dear friend [Lady Russell] for whose goodness I have neither thanks nor words. To the end of my life I shall go on sinning and repenting. Heartily sorry have I been ever since you went away to have spoken so unkindly to Mrs.... Heaven forgive me for it, and send her a happier conclusion to her life than the beginning might warrant. If you have an idle lover, my dear, present over to him my sermon, for those were words of worth.

God bless you all! Ever, most faithfully and affectionately yours,

M. R. MITFORD.

Sunday Evening.

VIII.

When one turns from Miss Mitford's works to the notices in the biographical dictionary (in which Miss Mitford and Mithridates occupy the same page), one finds how firmly her reputation is established. "*Dame auteur*," says my faithful mentor, the Biographic Generale, "*considerée comme le peintre le plus fidéle de la vie rurale en Angleterre.*" "Author of a remarkable tragedy, 'Julian,' in which Macready played a principal part, followed by 'Foscari,' 'Rienzi,' and others," says the English Biographical Dictionary.

"I am charmed with my new cottage," she writes soon after her last installation; "the neighbours are most kind." Kingsley was one of the first to call upon her. "He took me quite by surprise in his extraordinary fascination," says the old lady.

Mr. Fields, the American publisher, also went to see Miss Mitford at Swallowfield, and immediately became a very great ally of hers. It was to him that she gave her own portrait, by Lucas. Mr. Fields has left an interesting account of her in his "Yesterdays with Authors"—"Her dogs and her geraniums," he says, "were her great glories! She used to write me long letters about Fanchon, a dog whose personal acquaintance I had made some time before, while on a visit to her cottage. Every virtue under heaven she attributed to that canine individual; and I was obliged to allow in my return letters that since our planet began to spin, nothing comparable to Fanchon had ever run on four legs. I had also known Flush, the ancestor of Fanchon, intimately, and had been accustomed to hear wonderful things of that dog, but Fanchon had graces and genius unique. Miss Mitford would have joined with Hamerton, when he says, 'I humbly thank Divine Providence for having invented dogs, and I regard that man with wondering pity who can lead a dogless life.' "

Another of Miss Mitford's great friends was John Ruskin[1], and one can well imagine how much they must have had in common. Of Miss Mitford's writings Ruskin says, "They have the playfulness and purity of *The Vicar of Wakefield* without the naughtiness of its occasional wit, or the dust of the world's great road on the other side of the hedge...."

Neither the dust nor the ethics of the world of men quite belonged to Miss Mitford's genius. It is always a sort of relief to turn from her criticism of people, her praise of Louis Napoleon, her facts about Mr. Dickens, whom she describes as a dull companion, or about my father, whom she looked upon as an utter heartless worldling, to the natural spontaneous sweet flow of nature in which she lived and moved instinctively.

Mr. James Payn gives, perhaps, the most charming of all the descriptions of the author of "Our Village." He has many

---

[1]   It is Mr. Harness who says, writing of Ruskin and Miss Mitford, "His kindness cheered her closing days. He sent her every book that would interest, every delicacy that would strengthen her."

letters from her to quote from. "The paper is all odds and ends," he says, "and not a scrap of it but is covered and crossed. The very flaps of the envelopes and the outsides of them have their message."

Mr. Payn went to see her at Swallowfield, and describes the small apartment lined with books from floor to ceiling and fragrant with flowers. "Its tenant rose from her arm-chair with difficulty, but with a sunny smile and a charming manner bade me welcome. My father had been an old friend of hers, and she spoke of my home and belongings as only a woman can speak of such things, then we plunged into *medea res*, into men and books. She seemed to me to have known everybody worth knowing from the Duke of Wellington to the last new verse-maker. And she talked like an angel, but her views upon poetry as a calling in life, shocked me not a little. She said she preferred a *mariage de convenance* to a love match, because it generally turned out better. 'This surprises you,' she said, smiling, 'but then I suppose I am the least romantic person that ever wrote plays.' She was much more proud of her plays, even then well-nigh forgotten, than of the works by which she was well known, and which at that time brought people from the ends of the earth to see her....

"Nothing ever destroyed her faith in those she loved. If I had not known all about him from my own folk I should have thought her father had been a patriot and a martyr. She spoke of him as if there had never been such a father—which in a sense was true."

Mr. Payn quotes Miss Mitford's charming description of K., "for whom she had the highest admiration." "K. is a great curiosity, by far the cleverest woman in these parts, not in a literary way [this was not to disappoint me], but in everything that is useful. She could make a Court dress for a duchess or cook a dinner for a Lord Mayor, but her principal talent is shown in managing everybody whom she comes near. Especially her husband and myself; she keeps the money of both and never allows either of us to spend sixpence without her knowledge.... You should see the manner in which she makes Ben reckon with her, and her contempt for all women who do not manage their husbands."

Another delightful quotation is from one of Charles Kingsley's letters to Mr. Payn. It brings the past before us from another point of view.

"I can never forget the little figure rolled up in two chairs in the little Swallowfield room, packed round with books up to the ceiling—the little figure with clothes on of no recognised or recognisable pattern; and somewhere, out of the upper end of the heap, gleaming under a great deep globular brow, two such eyes as I never perhaps saw in any other Englishwoman— though I believe she must have had French blood in her veins to breed such eyes and such a tongue, the beautiful speech which came out of that ugly (it was that) face, and the glitter and depth too of the eyes, like live coals—perfectly honest the while...."

One would like to go on quoting and copying, but here my preface must cease, for it is but a preface after all, one of those many prefaces written out of the past and when everything is over.

COUNTRY PICTURES

Of all situations for a constant residence, that which appears to me most delightful is a little village far in the country; a small neighbourhood, not of fine mansions finely peopled, but of cottages and cottage-like houses, "messuages or tenements," as a friend of mine calls such ignoble and nondescript dwellings, with inhabitants whose faces are as familiar to us as the flowers in our garden; a little world of our own, close-packed and insulated like ants in an ant-hill, or bees in a hive, or sheep in a fold, or nuns in a convent, or sailors in a ship; where we know every one, are known to every one, interested in every one, and authorised to hope that every one feels an interest in us. How pleasant it is to slide into these true-hearted feelings from the kindly and unconscious influence of habit, and to learn to know and to love the people about us, with all their peculiarities, just as we learn to know and to love the nooks and turns of the shady lanes and sunny commons that we pass every day. Even in books I like a confined locality, and so do the critics when they talk of the unities. Nothing is so tiresome as to be whirled half over Europe at the chariot-wheels of a hero, to go to sleep at Vienna, and awaken at Madrid; it produces a real fatigue, a weariness of spirit. On the other hand, nothing is so delightful as to sit down in a country village in one of Miss Austen's delicious novels, quite sure before we leave it to become intimate with every spot and every person it contains; or to ramble with Mr. White [①] over his own parish of Selborne, and form a friendship with the fields and coppices, as well as with the birds, mice, and squirrels, who inhabit them; or to sail with Robinson Crusoe to his island, and live there with him and his goats and his man Friday; —how much we dread any new comers, any fresh importation of savage or sailor! we never sympathise for a moment in our hero's want of company, and are quite grieved when he gets away; —or to be shipwrecked with Ferdinand on that other lovelier island—the island of Prospero, and Miranda, and Caliban, and Ariel, and nobody else, none of Dryden's exotic inventions: —that is best of all. And a small neighbourhood is as good in sober waking reality as in poetry or prose; a village neighbourhood, such as this Berkshire hamlet in which I write, a long, straggling, winding street at the bottom of a fine eminence, with a road through it,

---

① White's "Natural History and Antiquities of Selborne;" one of the most fascinating books ever written. I wonder that no naturalist has adopted the same plan.

always abounding in carts, horsemen, and carriages, and lately enlivened by a stage-coach from B—— to S——, which passed through about ten days ago, and will I suppose return some time or other. There are coaches of all varieties nowadays; perhaps this may be intended for a monthly diligence, or a fortnight fly. Will you walk with me through our village, courteous reader? The journey is not long. We will begin at the lower end, and proceed up the hill.

The tidy, square, red cottage on the right hand, with the long well-stocked garden by the side of the road, belongs to a retired publican from a neighbouring town; a substantial person with a comely wife; one who piques himself on independence and idleness, talks politics, reads newspapers, hates the minister, and cries out for reform. He introduced into our peaceful vicinage the rebellious innovation of an illumination on the Queen's acquittal. Remonstrance and persuasion were in vain; he talked of liberty and broken windows—so we all lighted up. Oh! how he shone that night with candles, and laurel, and white bows, and gold paper, and a transparency (originally designed for a pocket-handkerchief) with a flaming portrait of her Majesty, hatted and feathered, in red ochre. He had no rival in the village, that we all acknowledged; the very bonfire was less splendid; the little boys reserved their best crackers to be expended in his honour, and he gave them full sixpence more than any one else. He would like an illumination once a month; for it must not be concealed that, in spite of gardening, of newspaper reading, of jaunting about in his little cart, and frequenting both church and meeting, our worthy neighbour begins to feel the weariness of idleness. He hangs over his gate, and tries to entice passengers to stop and chat; he volunteers little jobs all round, smokes cherry trees to cure the blight, and traces and blows up all the wasps'-nests in the parish. I have seen a great many wasps in our garden to-day, and shall enchant him with the intelligence. He even assists his wife in her sweepings and dustings. Poor man! he is a very respectable person, and would be a very happy one, if he would add a little employment to his dignity. It would be the salt of life to him.

Next to his house, though parted from it by another long garden with a yew arbour at the end, is the pretty dwelling of the shoemaker, a pale, sickly-looking, black-haired man, the very model of sober industry. There he sits in his little shop from early morning till late at night. An earthquake would hardly stir him: the illumination did not. He stuck immovably to his last, from the first lighting up, through the long blaze and the slow decay, till his large solitary candle was the only light in the place. One cannot conceive anything more perfect than the contempt which the man of transparencies and the man of shoes must have felt for each other on that evening. There was at least as much vanity in the sturdy industry as in the strenuous idleness, for our shoemaker is a man of substance; he employs three journeymen, two lame, and one a dwarf, so that his shop looks like an hospital; he has purchased the lease of his commodious dwelling, some even say that he has bought it out and out; and he has only one pretty daughter, a light, delicate, fair-haired girl of fourteen, the champion, protectress, and playfellow of every brat under three years old, whom she jumps, dances, dandles, and feeds all day long. A very attractive person is that child-loving girl. I have never seen any one in her station who possessed so thoroughly that undefinable charm, the lady-look. See her on a Sunday in her simplicity and her white frock, and she might pass for an earl's daughter. She likes flowers too, and has a profusion of white stocks under her window, as pure and delicate as herself.

The first house on the opposite side of the way is the blacksmith's; a gloomy dwelling, where the sun never seems to shine; dark and smoky within and without, like a forge. The blacksmith is a high officer in our little state, nothing less than a constable; but, alas! alas! when tumults arise, and the constable is called for, he will commonly be found in the thickest of the fray. Lucky would it be for his wife and her eight children if there were no public-house in the land: an inveterate inclination to enter those bewitching doors is Mr. Constable's only fault.

Next to this official dwelling is a spruce brick tenement, red, high, and narrow, boasting, one above another, three sash-windows, the only sash-windows in the village, with a clematis on one side and a rose on the other, tall and narrow like itself. That slender mansion has a fine, genteel look. The little parlour seems made for Hogarth's old maid and her stunted footboy;

for tea and card parties, —it would just hold one table; for the rustle of faded silks, and the splendour of old china; for the delight of four by honours, and a little snug, quiet scandal between the deals; for affected gentility and real starvation. This should have been its destiny; but fate has been unpropitious: it belongs to a plump, merry, bustling dame, with four fat, rosy, noisy children, the very essence of vulgarity and plenty.

Then comes the village shop, like other village shops, multifarious as a bazaar; a repository for bread, shoes, tea, cheese, tape, ribands, and bacon; for everything, in short, except the one particular thing which you happen to want at the moment, and will be sure not to find. The people are civil and thriving, and frugal withal; they have let the upper part of their house to two young women (one of them is a pretty blue-eyed girl) who teach little children their A B C, and make caps and gowns for their mammas, —parcel schoolmistress, parcel mantua-maker. I believe they find adorning the body a more profitable vocation than adorning the mind.

Divided from the shop by a narrow yard, and opposite the shoemaker's, is a habitation of whose inmates I shall say nothing. A cottage—no—a miniature house, with many additions, little odds and ends of places, pantries, and what not; all angles, and of a charming in-and-outness; a little bricked court before one half, and a little flower-yard before the other; the walls, old and weather-stained, covered with hollyhocks, roses, honeysuckles, and a great apricot-tree; the casements full of geraniums (ah!

there is our superb white cat peeping out from among them); the closets (our landlord has the assurance to call them rooms) full of contrivances and corner-cupboards; and the little garden behind full of common flowers, tulips, pinks, larkspurs, peonies, stocks, and carnations, with an arbour of privet, not unlike a sentry-box, where one lives in a delicious green light, and looks out on the gayest of all gay flower-beds. That house was built on purpose to show in what an exceeding small compass comfort may be packed. Well, I will loiter there no longer.

The next tenement is a place of importance, the Rose Inn: a white-washed building, retired from the road behind its fine swinging sign, with a little bow-window room coming out on one side, and forming, with our stable on the other, a sort of open square, which is the constant resort of carts, waggons, and return chaises. There are two carts there now, and mine host is serving them with beer in his eternal red waistcoat. He is a thriving man and a portly, as his waistcoat attests, which has been twice let out within this twelvemonth. Our landlord has a stirring wife, a hopeful son, and a daughter, the belle of the village; not so pretty as the fair nymph of the shoe-shop, and far less elegant, but ten times as fine; all curl-papers in the morning, like a porcupine, all curls in the afternoon, like a poodle, with more flounces than curl-papers, and more lovers than curls. Miss Phoebe is fitter for town than country; and to do her justice, she has a consciousness of that fitness, and turns her steps townward as often as she can. She is gone to B——

to-day with her last and principal lover, a recruiting sergeant— a man as tall as Sergeant Kite, and as impudent. Some day or other he will carry off Miss Phoebe.

In a line with the bow-window room is a low garden-wall, belonging to a house under repair: —the white house opposite the collarmaker's shop, with four lime-trees before it, and a waggon-load of bricks at the door. That house is the plaything of a wealthy, well-meaning, whimsical person who lives about a mile off. He has a passion for brick and mortar, and, being too wise to meddle with his own residence, diverts himself with altering and re-altering, improving and re-improving, doing and undoing here. It is a perfect Penelope's web. Carpenters and bricklayers have been at work for these eighteen months, and yet I sometimes stand and wonder whether anything has really been done. One exploit in last June was, however, by no means equivocal. Our good neighbour fancied that the limes shaded the rooms, and made them dark (there was not a creature in the house but the workmen), so he had all the leaves stripped from every tree. There they stood, poor miserable skeletons, as bare as Christmas under the glowing midsummer sun. Nature revenged herself, in her own sweet and gracious manner; fresh leaves sprang out, and at nearly Christmas the foliage was as brilliant as when the outrage was committed.

Next door lives a carpenter, "famed ten miles round, and worthy all his fame," —few cabinet-makers surpass him, with his excellent wife, and their little daughter Lizzy, the plaything and queen of the village, a child three years old according to the register, but six in size and strength and intellect, in power and in self-will. She manages everybody in the place, her schoolmistress included; turns the wheeler's children out of their own little cart, and makes them draw her; seduces cakes and lollypops from the very shop window; makes the lazy carry her, the silent talk to her, the grave romp with her; does anything she pleases; is absolutely irresistible. Her chief attraction lies in her exceeding power of loving, and her firm reliance on the love and indulgence of others. How impossible it would be to disappoint the dear little girl when she runs to meet you, slides her pretty hand into yours, looks up gladly in your face, and says "Come!" You must go: you cannot help it. Another part of her charm is her singular beauty. Together with a good deal of the character of Napoleon, she has something of his square, sturdy, upright form, with the finest limbs in the world, a complexion purely English, a round laughing face, sunburnt and rosy, large merry blue eyes, curling brown hair, and a wonderful play of countenance. She has the imperial attitudes too, and loves to stand with her hands behind her, or folded over her bosom; and sometimes, when she has a little touch of shyness, she clasps them together on the top of her head, pressing down her shining curls, and looking so exquisitely pretty! Yes, Lizzy is queen of the village! She has but one rival in her dominions, a certain white greyhound called Mayflower, much her friend, who resembles her in beauty and strength, in playfulness, and almost in sagacity, and reigns over the animal world as she over the human. They are both coming with me, Lizzy and Lizzy's "pretty May." We are now at the end of the street; a cross-lane, a rope-walk shaded with limes and oaks, and a cool clear pond overhung with elms, lead us to the bottom of the hill. There is still one house round the corner, ending in a picturesque wheeler's shop. The dwelling-house is more ambitious. Look at the fine flowered window-blinds, the green door with the brass knocker, and the somewhat prim but very civil person, who is sending off a labouring man with sirs and curtsies enough for a prince of the blood. Those are the curate's lodgings— apartments his landlady would call them; he lives with his own family four miles off, but once or twice a week he comes to his neat little parlour to write sermons, to marry, or to bury, as the case may require. Never were better or kinder people than his host and hostess; and there is a reflection of clerical importance about them since their connection with the Church, which is quite edifying—a decorum, a gravity, a solemn politeness. Oh, to see the worthy wheeler carry the gown after his lodger on a Sunday, nicely pinned up in his wife's best handkerchief! —or to hear him rebuke a squalling child or a squabbling woman! The curate is nothing to him. He is fit to be perpetual churchwarden.

We must now cross the lane into the shady rope-walk. That pretty white cottage opposite, which stands straggling at the end of the village in a garden full of flowers, belongs to our mason, the shortest of men, and his handsome, tall wife: he, a dwarf, with the voice of a giant; one starts when he begins to talk as if he were shouting through a speaking trumpet; she, the sister, daughter, and grand-daughter, of a long line of gardeners, and no contemptible one herself. It is very magnanimous in me not to hate her; for she beats me in my own way, in chrysanthemums, and dahlias, and the like gauds. Her plants are sure to live; mine have a sad trick of dying, perhaps because I love them, "not wisely, but too well," and kill them with over-kindness. Half-way up the hill is another detached cottage, the residence of an officer, and his beautiful family. That eldest boy, who is hanging over the gate, and looking with such intense childish admiration at my Lizzy, might be a model for a Cupid.

How pleasantly the road winds up the hill, with its broad green borders and hedgerows so thickly timbered! How finely the evening sun falls on that sandy excavated bank, and touches the farmhouse on the top of the eminence! and how clearly defined and relieved is the figure of the man who is just coming down! It is poor John Evans, the gardener—an excellent gardener till about ten years ago, when he lost his wife, and became insane. He was sent to St. Luke's, and dismissed as cured; but his power was gone and his strength; he could no longer manage a garden, nor submit to the restraint, nor encounter the fatigue of regular employment: so he retreated to the workhouse, the pensioner and factotum of the village, amongst whom he divides his services. His mind often wanders, intent on some fantastic and impracticable plan, and lost to present objects; but he is perfectly harmless, and full of a childlike simplicity, a smiling contentedness, a most touching gratitude. Every one is kind to John Evans, for there is that about him which must be loved; and his unprotectedness, his utter defencelessness, have an irresistible claim on every better feeling. I know nobody who inspires so deep and tender a pity; he improves all around him. He is useful, too, to the extent of his little power; will do anything, but loves gardening best, and still piques himself on his old arts of pruning fruit-trees, and raising cucumbers. He is the happiest of men just now, for he has the management of a melon bed—a melon bed! —fie! What a grand pompous name was that for three melon plants under a hand-light! John Evans is sure that they will succeed. We shall see: as the chancellor said, "I doubt."

We are now on the very brow of the eminence, close to the Hill-house and its beautiful garden. On the outer edge of the paling, hanging over the bank that skirts the road, is an old thorn—such a thorn! The long sprays covered with snowy blossoms, so graceful, so elegant, so lightsome, and yet so rich! There only wants a pool under the thorn to give a still lovelier reflection, quivering and trembling, like a tuft of feathers, whiter and greener than the life, and more prettily mixed with the bright blue sky. There should indeed be a pool; but on the dark grass-plat, under the high bank, which is crowned by that magnificent plume, there is something that does almost as well, —Lizzy and Mayflower in the midst of a game at romps, "making a sunshine in the shady place;" Lizzy rolling, laughing, clapping her hands, and glowing like a rose; Mayflower playing about her like summer lightning, dazzling the eyes with her sudden turns, her leaps, her bounds, her attacks, and her escapes. She darts round the lovely little girl, with the same momentary touch that the swallow skims over the water, and has exactly the same power of flight, the same matchless ease and strength and grace. What a pretty picture they would make; what a pretty foreground they do make to the real landscape! The road winding down the hill with a slight bend, like that in the High Street at Oxford; a waggon slowly ascending, and a horseman passing it at a full trot—(ah! Lizzy, Mayflower will certainly desert you to have a gambol with that blood-horse!) half-way down, just at the turn, the red cottage of the lieutenant, covered with vines, the very image of comfort and content; farther down, on the opposite side, the small white dwelling of the little mason; then the limes and the rope-walk; then the village street, peeping through the trees, whose clustering tops hide all but the chimneys, and various roofs of the houses, and here and there some angle of a wall; farther on, the elegant town of B——, with its fine old church-towers and spires; the whole view shut in by a range of chalky hills and over every part of the picture, trees so profusely scattered, that it appears like a woodland scene, with glades and villages intermixed. The trees are of all kinds and all hues, chiefly the finely-shaped elm, of so bright and deep a green, the tips of whose high outer branches drop down with such a crisp and garland-like richness, and the oak, whose stately form is just now so splendidly adorned by the sunny colouring of the young leaves.

Turning again up the hill, we find ourselves on that peculiar charm of English scenery, a green common, divided by the road; the right side fringed by hedgerows and trees, with cottages and farmhouses irregularly placed, and terminated by a double avenue of noble oaks; the left, prettier still, dappled by bright pools of water, and islands of cottages and cottage-gardens, and sinking gradually down to cornfields and meadows, and an old farmhouse, with pointed roofs and clustered chimneys, looking out from its blooming orchard, and backed by woody hills. The common is itself the prettiest part of the prospect; half covered with low furze, whose golden blossoms reflect so intensely the last beams of the setting sun, and alive with cows and sheep, and two sets of cricketers; one of young men, surrounded by spectators, some standing, some sitting, some stretched on the grass, all taking a delighted interest in the game; the other, a merry group of little boys, at a humble distance, for whom even cricket is scarcely lively enough, shouting, leaping, and enjoying themselves to their hearts' content. But cricketers and country boys are too important persons in our village to be talked of merely as figures in the landscape. They deserve an individual introduction—an essay to themselves—and they shall have it. No fear of forgetting the good-humoured faces that meet us in our walks every day.

WALKS IN THE COUNTRY

Frost.

January 23rd. —At noon to-day I and my white greyhound, Mayflower, set out for a walk into a very beautiful world, —a sort of silent fairyland, —a creation of that matchless magician the hoar-frost. There had been just snow enough to cover the earth and all its covers with one sheet of pure and uniform white, and just time enough since the snow had fallen to allow the hedges to be freed of their fleecy load, and clothed with a delicate coating of rime. The atmosphere was deliciously calm; soft, even mild, in spite of the thermometer; no perceptible air, but a stillness that might almost be felt, the sky, rather grey than blue, throwing out in bold relief the snow-covered roofs of our village, and the rimy trees that rise above them, and the sun shining dimly as through a veil, giving a pale fair light, like the moon, only brighter. There was a silence, too, that might become the moon, as we stood at our little gate looking up the quiet street; a Sabbath-like pause of work and play, rare on a work-day; nothing was audible but the pleasant hum of frost, that low monotonous sound, which is perhaps the nearest approach that life and nature can make to absolute silence. The very waggons as they come down the hill along the beaten track of crisp yellowish frost-dust, glide along like shadows; even May's bounding footsteps, at her height of glee and of speed, fall like snow upon snow.

But we shall have noise enough presently: May has stopped at Lizzy's door; and Lizzy, as she sat on the window-sill with her bright rosy face laughing through the casement, has seen her and disappeared. She is coming. No! The key is turning in the door, and sounds of evil omen issue through the keyhole— sturdy "let me outs," and "I will goes," mixed with shrill cries on May and on me from Lizzy, piercing through a low continuous harangue, of which the prominent parts are apologies, chilblains, sliding, broken bones, lollypops, rods, and gingerbread, from Lizzy's careful mother. "Don't scratch the door, May! Don't roar so, my Lizzy! We'll call for you as we come back." "I'll go now! Let me out! I will go!" are the last words of Miss Lizzy. Mem. Not to spoil that child—if I can help it. But I do think her mother might have let the poor little soul walk with us to-day. Nothing worse for children than coddling. Nothing better for chilblains than exercise. Besides, I don't believe she has any— and as to breaking her bones in sliding, I don't suppose there's a slide on the common. These murmuring cogitations have brought us up the hill, and half-way across the light and airy common, with its bright expanse of snow and its clusters of cottages, whose turf fires send such wreaths of smoke sailing up the air, and diffuse such aromatic fragrance around. And now comes the delightful sound of childish voices, ringing with glee and merriment almost from beneath our feet. Ah, Lizzy, your mother was right! They are shouting from that deep irregular pool, all glass now, where, on two long, smooth, liny slides, half a dozen ragged urchins are slipping along in tottering triumph. Half a dozen steps bring us to the bank right above them. May can hardly resist the temptation of joining her friends, for most of the varlets are of her acquaintance, especially the rogue who leads the slide, —he with the brimless hat, whose bronzed complexion and white flaxen hair, reversing the usual lights and shadows of the human countenance, give so strange and foreign a look to his flat and comic features. This hobgoblin, Jack Rapley by name, is May's great crony; and she stands on the brink of the steep, irregular descent, her black eyes fixed full upon him, as if she intended him the favour of jumping on his head. She does: she is down, and upon him; but Jack Rapley is not easily to be knocked off his feet. He saw her coming, and in the moment of her leap sprung dexterously off the slide on the rough ice, steadying himself by the shoulder of the next in the file, which unlucky follower, thus unexpectedly checked in his career, fell plump backwards, knocking down the rest of the line like a nest of card-houses. There is no harm done; but there they lie, roaring, kicking, sprawling, in every attitude of comic distress, whilst Jack Rapley and Mayflower, sole authors of this calamity, stand apart from the throng, fondling, and coquetting, and complimenting each other, and very visibly laughing, May in her black eyes, Jack in his wide, close-shut mouth, and his whole monkey-face, at their comrades' mischances. I think, Miss May, you may as well come up again, and leave Master Rapley to fight your battles. He'll get out of the scrape. He is a rustic wit— a sort of Robin Goodfellow—the sauciest, idlest, cleverest, best-natured boy in the parish; always foremost in mischief, and always ready to do a good turn. The sages of our village predict sad things of Jack Rapley, so that I am sometimes a little ashamed to confess, before wise people, that I have a lurking predilection for him (in common with other naughty ones), and that I like to hear him talk to May almost as well as she does. "Come, May!" and up she springs, as light as a bird. The road is gay now; carts and post-chaises, and girls in red cloaks, and, afar off, looking almost like a toy, the coach. It meets us fast and soon. How much happier the walkers look than the riders— especially the frost-bitten gentleman, and the shivering lady with the invisible face, sole passengers of that commodious machine! Hooded, veiled, and bonneted, as she is, one sees from her attitude how miserable she would look uncovered.

Another pond, and another noise of children. More sliding? Oh no! This is a sport of higher pretension. Our good neighbour, the lieutenant, skating, and his own pretty little boys, and two or three other four-year-old elves, standing on the brink in an ecstasy of joy and wonder! Oh what happy spectators! And what a happy performer! They admiring, he admired, with an ardour and sincerity never excited by all the quadrilles and the spread-eagles of the Seine and the Serpentine. He really skates well though, and I am glad I came this way; for, with all the father's feelings sitting gaily at his heart, it must still gratify the pride of skill to have one spectator at that solitary pond who has seen skating before.

Now we have reached the trees, —the beautiful trees! never so beautiful as to-day. Imagine the effect of a straight and regular double avenue of oaks, nearly a mile long, arching overhead, and closing into perspective like the roof and columns of a cathedral, every tree and branch incrusted with the bright and delicate congelation of hoar-frost, white and pure as snow, delicate and defined as carved ivory. How beautiful it is, how uniform, how various, how filling, how satiating to the eye and to the mind—above all, how melancholy! There is a thrilling awfulness, an intense feeling of simple power in that naked and colourless beauty, which falls on the earth like the thoughts of death—death pure, and glorious, and smiling, —but still death. Sculpture has always the same effect on my imagination, and painting never. Colour is life. —We are now at the end of this magnificent avenue, and at the top of a steep eminence commanding a wide view over four counties—

a landscape of snow. A deep lane leads abruptly down the hill; a mere narrow cart-track, sinking between high banks clothed with fern and furze and low broom, crowned with luxuriant hedgerows, and famous for their summer smell of thyme. How lovely these banks are now—the tall weeds and the gorse fixed and stiffened in the hoar-frost, which fringes round the bright prickly holly, the pendent foliage of the bramble, and the deep orange leaves of the pollard oaks! Oh, this is rime in its loveliest form! And there is still a berry here and there on the holly, "blushing in its natural coral" through the delicate tracery, still a stray hip or haw for the birds, who abound here always. The poor birds, how tame they are, how sadly tame! There is the beautiful and rare crested wren, "that shadow of a bird," as White of Selborne calls it, perched in the middle of the hedge, nestling as it were amongst the cold bare boughs, seeking, poor pretty thing, for the warmth it will not find. And there, farther on, just under the bank, by the slender runlet, which still trickles between its transparent fantastic margin of thin ice, as if it were a thing of life, —there, with a swift, scudding motion, flits, in short low flights, the gorgeous kingfisher, its magnificent plumage of scarlet and blue flashing in the sun, like the glories of some tropical bird. He is come for water to this little spring by the hillside, —water which even his long bill and slender head can hardly reach, so nearly do the fantastic forms of those garland-like icy margins meet over the tiny stream beneath. It is rarely that one sees the shy beauty so close or so long; and it is pleasant to see him in the grace and beauty of his natural liberty, the only way to look at a bird. We used, before we lived in a street, to fix a little board outside the parlour window, and cover it with bread crumbs in the hard weather. It was quite delightful to see the pretty things come and feed, to conquer their shyness, and do away their mistrust. First came the more social tribes, "the robin redbreast and the wren," cautiously, suspiciously, picking up a crumb on the wing, with the little keen bright eye fixed on the window; then they would stop for two pecks; then stay till they were satisfied. The shyer birds, tamed by their example, came next; and at last one saucy fellow of a blackbird—a sad glutton, he would clear the board in two minutes, —used to tap his yellow bill against the window for more. How we loved the fearless confidence of that fine, frank-hearted creature! And surely he loved us. I wonder the practice is not more general. "May! May! naughty May!" She has frightened away the kingfisher; and now, in her coaxing penitence, she is covering me with snow. "Come, pretty May! it is time to go home."

Thaw.

January 28th. —We have had rain, and snow, and frost, and rain again four days of absolute confinement. Now it is a thaw and a flood; but our light gravelly soil, and country boots, and country hardihood, will carry us through. What a dripping, comfortless day it is! just like the last days of November: no sun, no sky, grey or blue; one low, overhanging, dark, dismal cloud, like London smoke; Mayflower is out coursing too, and Lizzy gone to school. Never mind. Up the hill again! Walk we must. Oh what a watery world to look back upon! Thames, Kennet, Loddon—all overflowed; our famous town, inland once, turned into a sort of Venice; C. park converted into an island; and the long range of meadows from B. to W. one huge unnatural lake, with trees growing out of it. Oh what a watery world! —I will look at it no longer. I will walk on. The road is alive again. Noise is reborn. Waggons creak, horses splash, carts rattle, and pattens paddle through the dirt with more than their usual clink. The common has its old fine tints of green and brown, and its old variety of inhabitants, horses, cows, sheep, pigs, and donkeys. The ponds are unfrozen, except where some melancholy piece of melting ice floats sullenly on the water; and cackling geese and gabbling ducks have replaced the lieutenant and Jack Rapley. The avenue is chill and dark, the hedges are dripping, the lanes knee-deep, and all nature is in a state of "dissolution and thaw."

THE FIRST PRIMROSE

March 6th. —Fine March weather: boisterous, blustering, much wind and squalls of rain; and yet the sky, where the clouds are swept away, deliciously blue, with snatches of sunshine, bright, and clear, and healthful, and the roads, in spite of the slight glittering showers, crisply dry. Altogether the day is tempting, very tempting. It will not do for the dear common, that windmill of a walk; but the close sheltered lanes at the bottom of the hill, which keep out just enough of the stormy air, and let in all the sun, will be delightful. Past our old house, and round by the winding lanes, and the workhouse, and across the lea, and so into the turnpike-road again, —that is our route for to-day. Forth we set, Mayflower and I, rejoicing in the sunshine, and still more in the wind, which gives such an intense feeling of existence, and, co-operating with brisk motion, sets our blood and our spirits in a glow. For mere physical pleasure, there is nothing perhaps equal to the enjoyment of being drawn, in a light carriage, against such a wind as this, by a blood-horse at his height of speed. Walking comes next to it; but walking is not quite so luxurious or so spiritual, not quite so much what one fancies of flying, or being carried above the clouds in a balloon.

Nevertheless, a walk is a good thing; especially under this southern hedgerow, where nature is just beginning to live again; the periwinkles, with their starry blue flowers, and their shining myrtle-like leaves, garlanding the bushes; woodbines and elder-trees pushing out their small swelling buds; and grasses and mosses springing forth in every variety of brown and green. Here we are at the corner where four lanes meet, or rather where a passable road of stones and gravel crosses an impassable one of beautiful but treacherous turf, and where the small white farmhouse, scarcely larger than a cottage, and the well-stocked rick-yard behind, tell of comfort and order, but leave all unguessed the great riches of the master. How he became so rich is almost a puzzle; for, though the farm be his own, it is not large; and though prudent and frugal on ordinary occasions, Farmer Barnard is no miser. His horses, dogs, and pigs are the best kept in the parish, —May herself, although her beauty be injured by her fatness, half envies the plight of his bitch Fly: his wife's gowns and shawls cost as much again as any shawls or gowns in the village; his dinner parties (to be sure they are not frequent) display twice the ordinary quantity of good things—two couples of ducks, two dishes of green peas, two turkey poults, two gammons of bacon, two plum-puddings; moreover, he keeps a single-horse chaise, and has built and endowed a Methodist chapel. Yet is he the richest man in these parts. Everything prospers with him. Money drifts about him like snow. He looks like a rich man. There is a sturdy squareness of face and figure; a good-humoured obstinacy; a civil importance. He never boasts of his wealth, or gives himself undue airs; but nobody can meet him at market or vestry without finding out immediately that he is the richest man there. They have no child to all this money; but there is an adopted nephew, a fine spirited lad, who may, perhaps, some day or other, play the part of a fountain to the reservoir.

Now turn up the wide road till we come to the open common, with its park-like trees, its beautiful stream, wandering and twisting along, and its rural bridge. Here we turn again, past that other white farmhouse, half hidden by the magnificent elms which stand before it. Ah! riches dwell not there, but there is found the next best thing—an industrious and light-hearted poverty. Twenty years ago Rachel Hilton was the prettiest and merriest lass in the country. Her father, an old gamekeeper, had retired to a village alehouse, where his good beer, his social humour, and his black-eyed daughter, brought much custom. She had lovers by the score; but Joseph White, the dashing and lively son of an opulent farmer, carried off the fair Rachel. They married and settled here, and here they live still, as merrily as ever, with fourteen children of all ages and sizes, from nineteen years to nineteen months, working harder than any people in the parish, and enjoying themselves more. I would match them for labour and laughter against any family in England. She is a blithe, jolly dame, whose beauty has amplified into comeliness; he is tall, and thin, and bony, with sinews like whipcord, a strong lively voice, a sharp weather-beaten face, and eyes and lips that smile and brighten when he speaks into a most contagious hilarity. They are very poor, and I often wish them richer; but I don't know—perhaps it might put them out.

Quite close to Farmer White's is a little ruinous cottage, white-washed once, and now in a sad state of betweenity, where dangling stockings and shirts, swelled by the wind, drying in a neglected garden, give signal of a washerwoman. There dwells, at present in single blessedness, Betty Adams, the wife of our sometimes gardener. I never saw any one who so much reminded me in person of that lady whom everybody knows, Mistress Meg Merrilies; —as tall, as grizzled, as stately, as dark, as gipsy-looking, bonneted and gowned like her prototype, and almost as oracular. Here the resemblance ceases. Mrs. Adams is a perfectly honest, industrious, painstaking person, who earns a good deal of money by washing and charing, and spends it in other luxuries than tidiness, —in green tea, and gin, and snuff. Her husband lives in a great family, ten miles off. He is a capital gardener—or rather he would be so, if he were not too ambitious. He undertakes all things, and finishes none. But a smooth tongue, a knowing look, and a great capacity of labour, carry him through. Let him but like his ale and his master and he will do work enough for four. Give him his own way, and his full quantum, and nothing comes amiss to him.

Ah, May is bounding forward! Her silly heart leaps at the sight of the old place—and so in good truth does mine. What a pretty place it was—or rather, how pretty I thought it! I suppose I should have thought any place so where I had spent eighteen happy years. But it was really pretty. A large, heavy, white house, in the simplest style, surrounded by fine oaks and elms, and tall massy plantations shaded down into a beautiful lawn by wild overgrown shrubs, bowery acacias, ragged sweet-briers, promontories of dogwood, and Portugal laurel, and bays, overhung by laburnum and bird-cherry; a long piece of water letting light into the picture, and looking just like a natural stream, the banks as rude and wild as the shrubbery, interspersed with broom, and furze, and bramble, and pollard oaks covered with ivy and honeysuckle; the whole enclosed by an old mossy park paling, and terminating in a series of rich meadows, richly planted. This is an exact description of the home which, three years ago, it nearly broke my heart to leave. What a tearing up by the root it was! I have pitied cabbage-plants and celery, and all transplantable things, ever since; though, in common with them, and with other vegetables, the first agony of the transportation being over, I have taken such firm and tenacious hold of my new soil, that I would not for the world be pulled up again, even to be restored to the old beloved ground; —not even if its beauty were undiminished, which is by no means the case; for in those three years it has thrice changed masters, and every successive possessor has brought the curse of improvement upon the place; so that between filling up the water to cure dampness, cutting down trees to let in prospects, planting to keep them out, shutting up windows to darken the inside of the house (by which means one end looks precisely as an eight of spades would do that should have the misfortune to lose one of his corner pips), and building colonnades to lighten the out, added to a general clearance of pollards, and brambles, and ivy, and honeysuckles, and park palings, and irregular shrubs, the poor place is so transmogrified, that if it had its old looking-glass, the water, back again, it would not know its own face. And yet I love to haunt round about it: so does May. Her particular attraction is a certain broken bank full of rabbit burrows, into which she insinuates her long pliant head and neck, and tears her pretty feet by vain scratchings: mine is a warm sunny hedgerow, in the same remote field, famous for early flowers. Never was a spot more variously flowery: primroses yellow, lilac white, violets of either hue, cowslips, oxslips, arums, orchises, wild hyacinths, ground ivy, pansies, strawberries, heart's-ease, formed a small part of the Flora of that wild hedgerow. How profusely they covered the sunny open slope under the weeping birch, "the lady of the woods"—and how often have I started to see the early innocent brown snake, who loved the spot as well as I did, winding along the young blossoms, or rustling amongst the fallen leaves! There are primrose leaves already, and short green buds, but no flowers; not even in that furze cradle so full of roots, where they used to blow as in a basket. No, my May, no rabbits! no primroses! We may as well get over the gate into the woody winding lane, which will bring us home again.

Here we are making the best of our way between the old elms that arch so solemnly over head, dark and sheltered even now. They say that a spirit haunts this deep pool—a white lady without a head. I cannot say that I have seen her, often as I have paced this lane at deep midnight, to hear the nightingales, and look at the glow-worms; —but there, better and rarer than a thousand ghosts, dearer even than nightingales or glow-worms, there is a primrose, the first of the year; a tuft of primroses, springing in yonder sheltered nook, from the mossy roots of an old willow, and living again in the clear bright pool. Oh, how beautiful they are—three fully blown, and two bursting buds! How glad I am I came this way! They are not to be reached. Even Jack Rapley's love of the difficult and the unattainable would fail him here: May herself could not stand on that steep bank. So much the better. Who would wish to disturb them? There they live in their innocent and fragrant beauty, sheltered from the storms, and rejoicing in the sunshine, and looking as if they could feel their happiness. Who would disturb them? Oh, how glad I am I came this way home!

VIOLETING

March 27th. —It is a dull grey morning, with a dewy feeling in the air; fresh, but not windy; cool, but not cold; — the very day for a person newly arrived from the heat, the glare, the noise, and the fever of London, to plunge into the remotest labyrinths of the country, and regain the repose of mind, the calmness of heart, which has been lost in that great Babel. I must go violeting—it is a necessity—and I must go alone: the sound of a voice, even my Lizzy's, the touch of Mayflower's head, even the bounding of her elastic foot, would disturb the serenity of feeling which I am trying to recover. I shall go quite alone, with my little basket, twisted like a bee-hive, which I love so well, because SHE gave it to me, and kept sacred to violets and to those whom I love; and I shall get out of the high-road the moment I can. I would not meet any one just now, even of those whom I best like to meet.

Ha! —Is not that group—a gentleman on a blood-horse,

a lady keeping pace with him so gracefully and easily—see how prettily her veil waves in the wind created by her own rapid motion! —and that gay, gallant boy, on the gallant white Arabian, curveting at their side, but ready to spring before them every instant—is not that chivalrous-looking party Mr. and Mrs. M. and dear R.? No! the servant is in a different livery. It is some of the ducal family, and one of their young Etonians. I may go on. I shall meet no one now; for I have fairly left the road, and am crossing the lea by one of those wandering paths, amidst the gorse, and the heath, and the low broom, which the sheep and lambs have made—a path turfy, elastic, thymy, and sweet, even at this season.

We have the good fortune to live in an unenclosed parish, and may thank the wise obstinacy of two or three sturdy farmers, and the lucky unpopularity of a ranting madcap lord of the manor, for preserving the delicious green patches, the islets of wilderness amidst cultivation, which form, perhaps, the peculiar beauty of English scenery. The common that I am passing now—the lea, as it is called—is one of the loveliest of these favoured spots. It is a little sheltered scene, retiring, as it were, from the village; sunk amidst higher lands, hills would be almost too grand a word; edged on one side by one gay high-road, and intersected by another; and surrounded by a most picturesque confusion of meadows, cottages, farms, and orchards; with a great pond in one corner, unusually bright and clear, giving a delightful cheerfulness and daylight to the picture. The swallows haunt that pond; so do the children. There is a merry group round it now; I have seldom seen it without one. Children love water, clear, bright, sparkling water; it excites and feeds their curiosity; it is motion and life.

The path that I am treading leads to a less lively spot, to that large heavy building on one side of the common, whose solid wings, jutting out far beyond the main body, occupy three sides of a square, and give a cold, shadowy look to the court. On one side is a gloomy garden, with an old man digging in it, laid out in straight dark beds of vegetables, potatoes, cabbages, onions, beans; all earthy and mouldy as a newly-dug grave. Not a flower or flowering shrub! Not a rose-tree or currant-bush! Nothing but for sober, melancholy use. Oh, different from the long irregular slips of the cottage-gardens, with their gay bunches of polyanthuses and crocuses, their wallflowers sending sweet odours through the narrow casement, and their gooseberry-trees bursting into a brilliancy of leaf, whose vivid greenness has the effect of a blossom on the eye! Oh, how different! On the other side of this gloomy abode is a meadow of that deep, intense emerald hue, which denotes the presence of stagnant water, surrounded by willows at regular distances, and like the garden, separated from the common by a wide, moat-like ditch. That is the parish workhouse. All about it is solid, substantial, useful; —but so dreary! so cold! so dark! There are children in the court, and yet all is silent. I always hurry past that place as if it were a prison. Restraint, sickness, age, extreme poverty, misery, which I have no power to remove or alleviate, —these are the ideas, the feelings, which the sight of those walls excites; yet, perhaps, if not certainly, they contain less of that extreme desolation than the morbid fancy is apt to paint. There will be found order, cleanliness, food, clothing, warmth, refuge for the homeless, medicine and attendance for the sick, rest and sufficiency for old age, and sympathy, the true and active sympathy which the poor show to the poor, for the unhappy. There may be worse places than a parish workhouse— and yet I hurry past it. The feeling, the prejudice, will not be controlled.

The end of the dreary garden edges off into a close-sheltered lane, wandering and winding, like a rivulet, in gentle "sinuosities" (to use a word once applied by Mr. Wilberforce to the Thames at Henley), amidst green meadows, all alive with cattle, sheep, and beautiful lambs, in the very spring and pride of their tottering prettiness; or fields of arable land, more lively still with troops of stooping bean-setters, women and children, in all varieties of costume and colour; and ploughs and harrows, with their whistling boys and steady carters, going through, with a slow and plodding industry, the main business of this busy season. What work beansetting is! What a reverse of the position assigned to man to distinguish him from the beasts of the field! Only think of stooping for six, eight, ten hours a day, drilling holes in the earth with a little stick, and then dropping in the beans one by one. They are paid according to the quantity they plant; and some of the poor women used to be accused of clumping them—that is to say, of dropping more than one bean into a hole. It seems to me, considering the temptation, that not to clump is to be at the very pinnacle of human virtue.

Another turn in the lane, and we come to the old house standing amongst the high elms—the old farm-house, which always, I don't know why, carries back my imagination to Shakespeare's days. It is a long, low, irregular building, with one room, at an angle from the house, covered with ivy, fine white-veined ivy; the first floor of the main building projecting and supported by oaken beams, and one of the windows below, with its old casement and long narrow panes, forming the half of a shallow hexagon. A porch, with seats in it, surmounted by a pinnacle, pointed roofs, and clustered chimneys, complete the picture! Alas! it is little else but a picture! The very walls are crumbling to decay under a careless landlord and ruined tenant.

Now a few yards farther, and I reach the bank. Ah! I smell them already—their exquisite perfume steams and lingers in this moist, heavy air. Through this little gate, and along the green south bank of this green wheat-field, and they burst upon me, the lovely violets, in tenfold loveliness. The ground is covered with them, white and purple, enamelling the short dewy grass, looking but the more vividly coloured under the dull, leaden sky. There they lie by hundreds, by thousands. In former years I have been used to watch them from the tiny green bud, till one or two stole into bloom. They never came on me before in such a sudden and luxuriant glory of simple beauty, —and I do really owe one pure and genuine pleasure to feverish London! How beautifully they are placed too, on this sloping bank, with the palm branches waving over them, full of early bees, and mixing their honeyed scent with the more delicate violet odour! How transparent and smooth and lusty are the branches, full of sap and life! And there, just by the old mossy root, is a superb tuft of primroses, with a yellow butterfly hovering over them, like a flower floating on the air. What happiness to sit on this tufty knoll, and fill my basket with the blossoms! What a renewal of heart and mind! To inhabit such a scene of peace and sweetness is again to be fearless, gay, and gentle as a child. Then it is that thought becomes poetry, and feeling religion. Then it is that we are happy and good. Oh, that my whole life could pass so, floating on blissful and innocent sensation, enjoying in peace and gratitude the common blessings of Nature, thankful above all for the simple habits, the healthful temperament, which render them so dear! Alas! who may dare expect a life of such happiness? But I can at least snatch and prolong the fleeting pleasure, can fill my basket with pure flowers, and my heart with pure thoughts; can gladden my little home with their sweetness; can divide my treasures with one, a dear one, who cannot seek them; can see them when I shut my eyes and dream of them when I fall asleep.

THE COPSE

April 18th. —Sad wintry weather; a northeast wind; a sun that puts out one's eyes, without affording the slightest warmth; dryness that chaps lips and hands like a frost in December; rain that comes chilly and arrowy like hail in January; nature at a dead pause; no seeds up in the garden; no leaves out in the hedgerows; no cowslips swinging their pretty bells in the fields; no nightingales in the dingles; no swallows skimming round the great pond; no cuckoos (that ever I should miss that rascally sonneteer!) in any part. Nevertheless there is something of a charm in this wintry spring, this putting-back of the seasons. If the flower-clock must stand still for a month or two, could it choose a better time than that of the primroses and violets? I never remember (and for such gauds my memory, if not very good for aught of wise or useful, may be trusted) such an affluence of the one or such a duration of the other. Primrosy is the epithet which this year will retain in my recollection. Hedge, ditch, meadow, field, even the very paths and highways, are set with them; but their chief habitat is a certain copse, about a mile off, where they are spread like a carpet, and where I go to visit them rather oftener than quite comports with the dignity of a lady of mature age. I am going thither this very afternoon, and May and her company are going too.

This Mayflower of mine is a strange animal. Instinct and imitation make in her an approach to reason which is sometimes almost startling. She mimics all that she sees us do, with the dexterity of a monkey, and far more of gravity and apparent purpose; cracks nuts and eats them; gathers currants and severs them from the stalk with the most delicate nicety; filches and munches apples and pears; is as dangerous in an orchard as a schoolboy; smells to flowers; smiles at meeting; answers in a pretty lively voice when spoken to (sad pity that the language should be unknown!) and has greatly the advantage of us in a conversation, inasmuch as our meaning is certainly clear to her; —all this and a thousand amusing prettinesses (to say nothing of her canine feat of bringing her game straight to her master's feet, and refusing to resign it to any hand but his), does my beautiful greyhound perform untaught, by the mere effect of imitation and sagacity. Well, May, at the end of the coursing season, having lost Brush, our old spaniel, her great friend, and the blue greyhound, Mariette, her comrade and rival, both of which four-footed worthies were sent out to keep for the summer, began to find solitude a weary condition, and to look abroad for company. Now it so happened that the same suspension of sport which had reduced our little establishment from three dogs to one, had also dispersed the splendid kennel of a celebrated courser in our neighbourhood, three of whose finest young dogs came home to "their walk" (as the sporting phrase goes) at the collarmaker's in our village. May, accordingly, on the first morning of her solitude (she had never taken the slightest notice of her neighbours before, although they had sojourned in our street upwards of a fortnight), bethought herself of the timely resource offered to her by the vicinity of these canine beaux, and went up boldly and knocked at their stable door, which was already very commodiously on the half-latch. The three dogs came out with much alertness and gallantry, and May, declining apparently to enter their territories, brought them off to her own. This manoeuvre has been repeated every day, with one variation; of the three dogs, the first a brindle, the second a yellow, and the third a black, the two first only are now allowed to walk or consort with her, and the last, poor fellow, for no fault that I can discover except May's caprice, is driven away not only by the fair lady, but even by his old companions—is, so to say, sent to Coventry. Of her two permitted followers, the yellow gentleman, Saladin by name, is decidedly the favourite. He is, indeed, May's shadow, and will walk with me whether I choose or not. It is quite impossible to get rid of him unless by discarding Miss May also; —and to accomplish a walk in the country without her, would be like an adventure of Don Quixote without his faithful 'squire Sancho.

So forth we set, May and I, and Saladin and the brindle; May and myself walking with the sedateness and decorum befitting our sex and age (she is five years old this grass, rising six)—the young things, for the soldan and the brindle are (not meaning any disrespect) little better than puppies, frisking and frolicking as best pleased them.

Our route lay for the first part along the sheltered quiet lanes which lead to our old habitation; a way never trodden by me without peculiar and homelike feelings, full of the recollections, the pains and pleasures, of other days. But we are not to talk sentiment now; —even May would not understand that maudlin language. We must get on. What a wintry hedgerow this is for the eighteenth of April! Primrosy to be sure, abundantly spangled with those stars of the earth, — but so bare, so leafless, so cold! The wind whistles through the brown boughs as in winter. Even the early elder shoots, which do make an approach to springiness, look brown, and the small leaves of the woodbine, which have also ventured to peep forth, are of a sad purple, frost-bitten, like a dairymaid's elbows on a snowy morning. The very birds, in this season of pairing and building, look chilly and uncomfortable, and their nests! —"Oh, Saladin! come away from the hedge! Don't you see that what puzzles you and makes you leap up in the air is a redbreast's nest? Don't you see the pretty speckled eggs? Don't you hear the poor hen calling as it were for help? Come here this moment, sir!" And by good luck Saladin (who for a paynim has tolerable qualities) comes, before he has touched the nest, or before his playmate the brindle, the less manageable of the two, has espied it.

Now we go round the corner and cross the bridge, where the common, with its clear stream winding between clumps of elms, assumes so park-like an appearance. Who is this approaching so slowly and majestically, this square bundle of petticoat and cloak, this road-waggon of a woman? It is, it must be Mrs. Sally Mearing, the completest specimen within my knowledge of farmeresses (may I be allowed that innovation in language?) as they were. It can be nobody else.

Mrs. Sally Mearing, when I first became acquainted with her, occupied, together with her father (a superannuated man of ninety), a large farm very near our former habitation. It had been anciently a great manor-farm or court-house, and was still a stately, substantial building, whose lofty halls and spacious chambers gave an air of grandeur to the common offices to which they were applied. Traces of gilding might yet be seen on the panels which covered the walls, and on the huge carved chimney-pieces which rose almost to the ceilings; and the marble tables and the inlaid oak staircase still spoke of the former grandeur of the court. Mrs. Sally corresponded well with the date of her mansion, although she troubled herself little with its dignity. She was thoroughly of the old school, and had a most comfortable contempt for the new: rose at four in winter and summer, breakfasted at six, dined at eleven in the forenoon, supped at five, and was regularly in bed before eight, except when the hay-time or the harvest imperiously required her to sit up till sunset, a necessity to which she submitted with no very good grace. To a deviation from these hours, and to the modern iniquities of white aprons, cotton stockings, and muslin handkerchiefs (Mrs. Sally herself always wore check, black worsted, and a sort of yellow compound which she was wont to call "susy"), together with the invention of drill plough and thrashing-machines, and other agricultural novelties, she failed not to attribute all the mishaps or misdoings of the whole parish. The last-mentioned discovery especially aroused her indignation. Oh to hear her descant on the merits of the flail, wielded by a stout right arm, such as she had known in her youth (for by her account there was as great a deterioration in bones and sinews as in the other implements of husbandry), was enough to make the very inventor break his machine. She would even take up her favourite instrument, and thrash the air herself by way of illustrating her argument, and, to say truth, few men in these degenerate days could have matched the stout, brawny, muscular limb which Mrs. Sally displayed at sixty-five.

In spite of this contumacious rejection of agricultural improvements, the world went well with her at Court Farm. A good landlord, an easy rent, incessant labour, unremitting frugality, and excellent times, insured a regular though moderate profit; and she lived on, grumbling and prospering, flourishing

and complaining, till two misfortunes befell her at once—
her father died, and her lease expired. The loss of her father
although a bedridden man, turned of ninety, who could not
in the course of nature have been expected to live long, was
a terrible shock to a daughter, who was not so much younger
as to be without fears for her own life, and who had besides
been so used to nursing the good old man, and looking to his
little comforts, that she missed him as a mother would miss an
ailing child. The expiration of the lease was a grievance and a
puzzle of a different nature. Her landlord would have willingly
retained his excellent tenant, but not on the terms on which
she then held the land, which had not varied for fifty years; so
that poor Mrs. Sally had the misfortune to find rent rising and
prices sinking both at the same moment—a terrible solecism
in political economy. Even this, however, I believe she would
have endured, rather than have quitted the house where she was
born, and to which all her ways and notions were adapted, had
not a priggish steward, as much addicted to improvement and
reform as she was to precedent and established usages, insisted
on binding her by lease to spread a certain number of loads
of chalk on every field. This tremendous innovation, for never
had that novelty in manure whitened the crofts and pightles of
Court Farm, decided her at once. She threw the proposals into
the fire, and left the place in a week.

Her choice of a habitation occasioned some wonder, and
much amusement in our village world. To be sure, upon the

verge of seventy, an old maid may be permitted to dispense with the more rigid punctilio of her class, but Mrs. Sally had always been so tenacious on the score of character, so very a prude, so determined an avoider of the "men folk" (as she was wont contemptuously to call them), that we all were conscious of something like astonishment, on finding that she and her little handmaid had taken up their abode in one end of a spacious farmhouse belonging to the bluff old bachelor, George Robinson, of the Lea. Now Farmer Robinson was quite as notorious for his aversion to petticoated things, as Mrs. Sally for her hatred to the unfeathered bipeds who wear doublet and hose, so that there was a little astonishment in that quarter too, and plenty of jests, which the honest farmer speedily silenced, by telling all who joked on the subject that he had given his lodger fair warning, that, let people say what they would, he was quite determined not to marry her: so that if she had any views that way, it would be better for her to go elsewhere. This declaration, which must be admitted to have been more remarkable for frankness than civility, made, however, no ill impression on Mrs. Sally. To the farmer's she went, and at his house she lives still, with her little maid, her tabby cat, a decrepit sheep-dog, and much of the lumber of Court Farm, which she could not find in her heart to part from. There she follows her old ways and her old hours, untempted by matrimony, and unassailed (as far as I hear) by love or by scandal, with no other grievance than an occasional dearth of employment for herself and her young lass (even pewter dishes do not always want scouring), and now and then a twinge of the rheumatism.

Here she is, that good relique of the olden time—for, in spite of her whims and prejudices, a better and a kinder woman never lived—here she is, with the hood of her red cloak pulled over her close black bonnet, of that silk which once (it may be presumed) was fashionable, since it is still called mode, and her whole stout figure huddled up in a miscellaneous and most substantial covering of thick petticoats, gowns, aprons, shawls, and cloaks—a weight which it requires the strength of a thrasher to walk under—here she is, with her square honest visage, and her loud frank voice; —and we hold a pleasant disjointed chat of rheumatisms and early chickens, bad weather, and hats with feathers in them; —the last exceedingly sore subject being introduced by poor Jane Davis (a cousin of Mrs. Sally), who, passing us in a beaver bonnet, on her road from school, stopped to drop her little curtsy, and was soundly scolded for her civility. Jane, who is a gentle, humble, smiling lass, about twelve years old, receives so many rebukes from her worthy relative, and bears them so meekly, that I should not wonder if they were to be followed by a legacy: I sincerely wish they may. Well, at last we said good-bye; when, on inquiring my destination, and hearing that I was bent to the ten-acre copse (part of the farm which she ruled so long), she stopped me to tell a dismal story of two sheep-stealers who, sixty years ago, were found hidden in that copse, and only taken after great difficulty and resistance, and the maiming of a peace-officer. —"Pray don't go there, Miss! For mercy's sake don't be so venturesome! Think if they should kill you!" were the last words of Mrs. Sally.

Many thanks for her care and kindness! But, without being at all foolhardy in general, I have no great fear of the sheep-stealers of sixty years ago. Even if they escaped hanging for that exploit, I should greatly doubt their being in case to attempt another. So on we go: down the short shady lane, and out on the pretty retired green, shut in by fields and hedgerows, which we must cross to reach the copse. How lively this green nook is to-day, half covered with cows, and horses, and sheep! And how glad these frolicsome greyhounds are to exchange the hard gravel of the high-road for this pleasant short turf, which seems made for their gambols! How beautifully they are at play, chasing each other round and round in lessening circles, darting off at all kinds of angles, crossing and recrossing May, and trying to win her sedateness into a game at romps, turning round on each other with gay defiance, pursuing the cows and the colts, leaping up as if to catch the crows in their flight; —all in their harmless and innocent—"Ah, wretches! villains! rascals! four-footed mischiefs! canine plagues! Saladin! Brindle!"— They are after the sheep—"Saladin, I say!"—They have actually singled out that pretty spotted lamb—"Brutes, if I catch you! Saladin! Brindle!" We shall be taken up for sheep-stealing presently ourselves. They have chased the poor little lamb into a ditch, and are mounting guard over it, standing at bay. —"Ah, wretches, I have you now! for shame, Saladin! Get away, Brindle! See how good May is. Off with you, brutes! For shame! For shame!" and brandishing a handkerchief, which could hardly be an efficient instrument of correction, I succeeded in driving away the two puppies, who after all meant nothing more than play, although it was somewhat rough, and rather too much in the style of the old fable of the boys and the frogs. May is gone after them, perhaps to scold them: for she has been as grave as a judge during the whole proceeding, keeping ostentatiously close to me, and taking no part whatever in the mischief.

The poor little pretty lamb! here it lies on the bank quite motionless, frightened I believe to death, for certainly those villains never touched it. It does not stir. Does it breathe? Oh yes, it does! It is alive, safe enough. Look, it opens its eyes, and, finding the coast clear and its enemies far away, it springs up in a moment and gallops to its dam, who has stood bleating the whole time at a most respectful distance. Who would suspect a lamb of so much simple cunning? I really thought the pretty thing was dead—and now how glad the ewe is to recover her curling spotted little one! How fluttered they look! Well! this adventure has flurried me too; between fright and running, I warrant you my heart beats as fast as the lamb's.

Ah! here is the shameless villain Saladin, the cause of the commotion, thrusting his slender nose into my hand to beg pardon and make up! "Oh wickedest of soldans! Most iniquitous pagan! Soul of a Turk!"—but there is no resisting the good-humoured creature's penitence. I must pat him. "There! there! Now we will go to the copse; I am sure we shall find no worse malefactors than ourselves—shall we, May?—and the sooner we get out of sight of the sheep the better; for Brindle seems meditating another attack. *Allons, messieurs*, over this gate, across this meadow, and here is the copse."

How boldly that superb ash-tree with its fine silver bark rises from the bank, and what a fine entrance it makes with the holly beside it, which also deserves to be called a tree! But here we are in the copse. Ah! only one half of the underwood was cut last year, and the other is at its full growth: hazel, brier, woodbine, bramble, forming one impenetrable thicket, and almost uniting with the lower branches of the elms, and oaks, and beeches, which rise at regular distances overhead. No foot can penetrate that dense and thorny entanglement; but there is a walk all round by the side of the wide sloping bank, walk and bank and copse carpeted with primroses, whose fresh and balmy odour impregnates the very air. Oh how exquisitely beautiful! and it is not the primroses only, those gems of flowers, but the natural mosaic of which they form a part; that network of ground-ivy, with its lilac blossoms and the subdued tint of its purplish leaves, those rich mosses, those enamelled wild hyacinths, those spotted arums, and above all those wreaths of ivy linking all those flowers together with chains of leaves more beautiful than blossoms, whose white veins seem swelling amidst the deep green or splendid brown; —it is the whole earth that is so beautiful! Never surely were primroses so richly set, and never did primroses better deserve such a setting. There they are of their own lovely yellow, the hue to which they have given a name, the exact tint of the butterfly that overhangs them (the first I have seen this year! can spring really be coming at last?)—sprinkled here and there with tufts of a reddish purple, and others of the purest white, as some accident of soil affects that strange and inscrutable operation of nature, the colouring of flowers. Oh how fragrant they are, and how pleasant it is to sit in this sheltered copse, listening to the fine creaking of the wind amongst the branches, the most unearthly of sounds, with this gay tapestry under our feet, and the wood-pigeons flitting from tree to tree, and mixing the deep note of love with the elemental music.

Yes! spring is coming. Wood-pigeons, butterflies, and sweet flowers, all give token of the sweetest of the seasons. Spring is coming. The hazel stalks are swelling and putting forth their pale tassels, the satin palms with their honeyed odours are out on the willow, and the last lingering winter berries are dropping from the hawthorn, and making way for the bright and blossomy leaves.

THE WOOD

April 20th. —Spring is actually come now, with the fulness and almost the suddenness of a northern summer. To-day is completely April; —clouds and sunshine, wind and showers; blossoms on the trees, grass in the fields, swallows by the ponds, snakes in the hedgerows, nightingales in the thickets, and cuckoos everywhere. My young friend Ellen G. is going with me this evening to gather wood sorrel. She never saw that most elegant plant, and is so delicate an artist that the introduction will be a mutual benefit; Ellen will gain a subject worthy of her pencil, and the pretty weed will live; —no small favour to a flower almost as transitory as the gum cistus: duration is the only charm which it wants, and that Ellen will give it. The weather is, to be sure, a little threatening, but we are not people to mind the weather when we have an object in view; we shall certainly go in quest of the wood sorrel, and will take May, provided we can escape May's followers; for since the adventure of the lamb, Saladin has had an affair with a gander, furious in defence of his goslings, in which rencontre the gander came off conqueror; and as geese abound in the wood to which we are going (called by the country people the Pinge), and the victory may not always incline to the right side, I should be very sorry to lead the Soldan to fight his battles over again. We will take nobody but May.

So saying, we proceeded on our way through winding lanes, between hedgerows tenderly green, till we reached the hatch-gate, with the white cottage beside it embosomed in fruit-trees, which forms the entrance to the Pinge, and in a moment the whole scene was before our eyes.

"Is not this beautiful, Ellen?" The answer could hardly be other than a glowing rapid "Yes!"—A wood is generally a pretty place; but this wood—Imagine a smaller forest, full of glades and sheep-walks, surrounded by irregular cottages with their blooming orchards, a clear stream winding about the brakes, and a road intersecting it, and giving life and light to the picture; and you will have a faint idea of the Pinge. Every step was opening a new point of view, a fresh combination of glade and path and thicket. The accessories too were changing every moment. Ducks, geese, pigs, and children, giving way, as we advanced into the wood, to sheep and forest ponies; and they again disappearing as we became more entangled in its mazes, till we heard nothing but the song of the nightingale, and saw only the silent flowers.

What a piece of fairy land! The tall elms overhead just bursting into tender vivid leaf, with here and there a hoary oak or a silver-barked beech, every twig swelling with the brown buds, and yet not quite stripped of the tawny foliage of autumn; tall hollies and hawthorn beneath, with their crisp brilliant leaves mixed with the white blossoms of the sloe, and woven together with garlands of woodbines and wild-briers; —what a fairy land!

Primroses, cowslips, pansies, and the regular open-eyed white blossom of the wood anemone (or, to use the more elegant Hampshire name, the windflower), were set under our feet as thick as daisies in a meadow; but the pretty weed that we came to seek was coyer; and Ellen began to fear that we had mistaken the place or the season. —At last she had herself the pleasure of finding it under a brake of holly—"Oh, look! look! I am sure that this is the wood sorrel! Look at the pendent white flower, shaped like a snowdrop and veined with purple streaks, and the beautiful trefoil leaves folded like a heart, —some, the young ones, so vividly yet tenderly green that the foliage of the elm and the hawthorn would show dully at their side, —others of a deeper tint, and lined, as it were, with a rich and changeful purple! —Don't you see them?" pursued my dear young friend, who is a delightful piece of life and sunshine, and was half inclined to scold me for the calmness with which, amused by her enthusiasm, I stood listening to her ardent exclamations— "Don't you see them? Oh how beautiful! and in what quantity!

what profusion! See how the dark shade of the holly sets off the light and delicate colouring of the flower! —And see that other bed of them springing from the rich moss in the roots of that old beech-tree! Pray, let us gather some. Here are baskets." So, quickly and carefully we began gathering, leaves, blossoms, roots and all, for the plant is so fragile that it will not brook separation; —quickly and carefully we gathered, encountering divers petty misfortunes in spite of all our care, now caught by the veil in a holly bush, now hitching our shawls in a bramble, still gathering on, in spite of scratched fingers, till we had nearly filled our baskets and began to talk of our departure:—

"But where is May? May! May! No going home without her. May! Here she comes galloping, the beauty!"—(Ellen is almost as fond of May as I am.)—"What has she got in her mouth? that rough, round, brown substance which she touches so tenderly? What can it be? A bird's nest? Naughty May!"

"No! as I live, a hedgehog! Look, Ellen, how it has coiled itself into a thorny ball! Off with it, May! Don't bring it to me!"—And May, somewhat reluctant to part with her prickly prize, however troublesome of carriage, whose change of shape seemed to me to have puzzled her sagacity more than any event I ever witnessed, for in general she has perfectly the air of understanding all that is going forward—May at last dropt the hedgehog; continuing, however, to pat it with her delicate cat-like paw, cautiously and daintily applied, and caught back suddenly and rapidly after every touch, as if her poor captive had been a red-hot coal. Finding that these pats entirely failed in solving the riddle (for the hedgehog shammed dead, like the lamb the other day, and appeared entirely motionless), she gave him so spirited a nudge with her pretty black nose, that she not only turned him over, but sent him rolling some little way along the turfy path, —an operation which that sagacious quadruped endured with the most perfect passiveness, the most admirable non-resistance. No wonder that May's discernment was at fault, I myself, if I had not been aware of the trick, should have said that the ugly rough thing which she was trundling along, like a bowl or a cricket-ball, was an inanimate substance, something devoid of sensation and of will. At last my poor pet, thoroughly perplexed and tired out, fairly relinquished the contest, and came slowly away, turning back once or twice to look at the object of her curiosity, as if half inclined to return and try the event of another shove. The sudden flight of a wood-pigeon effectually diverted her attention; and Ellen amused herself by fancying how the hedgehog was scuttling away, till our notice was also attracted by a very different object.

We had nearly threaded the wood, and were approaching an open grove of magnificent oaks on the other side, when sounds other than of nightingales burst on our ear, the deep and frequent strokes of the woodman's axe, and emerging from the Pinge we discovered the havoc which that axe had committed. Above twenty of the finest trees lay stretched on the velvet turf. There they lay in every shape and form of devastation: some, bare trunks stripped ready for the timber carriage, with the bark built up in long piles at the side; some with the spoilers busy about them, stripping, hacking, hewing; others with their noble branches, their brown and fragrant shoots all fresh as if they were alive—majestic corses, the slain of to-day! The grove was like a field of battle. The young lads who were stripping the bark, the very children who were picking up the chips, seemed awed and silent, as if conscious that death was around them. The nightingales sang faintly and interruptedly—a few low frightened notes like a requiem.

Ah! here we are at the very scene of murder, the very tree that they are felling; they have just hewn round the trunk with those slaughtering axes, and are about to saw it asunder. After all, it is a fine and thrilling operation, as the work of death usually is. Into how grand an attitude was that young man thrown as he gave the final strokes round the root; and how wonderful is the effect of that supple and apparently powerless saw, bending like a riband, and yet overmastering that giant of the woods, conquering and overthrowing that thing of life! Now it has passed half through the trunk, and the woodman has begun to calculate which way the tree will fall; he drives a wedge to direct its course; —now a few more movements of the noiseless saw; and then a larger wedge. See how the branches tremble! Hark how the trunk begins to crack! Another stroke of the huge hammer on the wedge, and the tree quivers, as with a mortal agony, shakes, reels, and falls. How slow, and solemn, and awful it is! How like to death, to human death in its grandest form! Caesar in the Capitol, Seneca in the bath, could not fall more sublimely than that oak.

Even the heavens seem to sympathise with the devastation. The clouds have gathered into one thick low canopy, dark and vapoury as the smoke which overhangs London; the setting sun is just gleaming underneath with a dim and bloody glare, and the crimson rays spreading upward with a lurid and portentous grandeur, a subdued and dusky glow, like the light reflected on the sky from some vast conflagration. The deep flush fades away, and the rain begins to descend; and we hurry homeward rapidly, yet sadly, forgetful alike of the flowers, the hedgehog, and the wetting, thinking and talking only of the fallen tree.

THE DELL

May 2nd. —A delicious evening; —bright sunshine; light summer air; a sky almost cloudless; and a fresh yet delicate verdure on the hedges and in the fields; —an evening that seems made for a visit to my newly-discovered haunt, the mossy dell, one of the most beautiful spots in the neighbourhood, which after passing, times out of number, the field which it terminates, we found out about two months ago from the accident of May's killing a rabbit there. May has had a fancy for the place ever since; and so have I.

Thither accordingly we bend our way; —through the village; —up the hill; —along the common; —past the avenue; —across the bridge; and by the hill. How deserted the road is to-night! We have not seen a single acquaintance, except poor blind Robert, laden with his sack of grass plucked from the hedges, and the little boy that leads him. A singular division of labour! Little Jem guides Robert to the spots where the long grass grows, and tells him where it is most plentiful; and then the old man cuts it close to the roots, and between them they fill the sack, and sell the contents in the village. Half the cows in the street—for our baker, our wheelwright, and our shoemaker has each his Alderney—owe the best part of their maintenance to blind Robert's industry.

Here we are at the entrance of the cornfield which leads to the dell, and which commands so fine a view of the Loddon, the mill, the great farm, with its picturesque outbuildings, and the range of woody hills beyond. It is impossible not to pause a moment at that gate, the landscape, always beautiful, is so suited to the season and the hour, —so bright, and gay, and spring-like. But May, who has the chance of another rabbit in her pretty head, has galloped forward to the dingle, and poor May, who follows me so faithfully in all my wanderings, has a right to a little indulgence in hers. So to the dingle we go.

At the end of the field, which when seen from the road seems terminated by a thick dark coppice, we come suddenly to the edge of a ravine, on one side fringed with a low growth of alder, birch, and willow, on the other mossy, turfy, and bare, or only broken by bright tufts of blossomed broom. One or two old pollards almost conceal the winding road that leads down the descent, by the side of which a spring as bright as crystal runs gurgling along. The dell itself is an irregular piece of broken ground, in some parts very deep, intersected by two or three high banks of equal irregularity, now abrupt and bare, and rocklike, now crowned with tufts of the feathery willow or magnificent old thorns. Everywhere the earth is covered by short, fine turf, mixed with mosses, soft, beautiful, and various, and embossed with the speckled leaves and lilac flowers of the arum, the paler blossoms of the common orchis, the enamelled blue of the wild hyacinth, so splendid in this evening light, and large tufts of oxslips and cowslips rising like nosegays from the short turf.

The ground on the other side of the dell is much lower than the field through which we came, so that it is mainly to the labyrinthine intricacy of these high banks that it owes its singular character of wildness and variety. Now we seem hemmed in by those green cliffs, shut out from all the world, with nothing visible but those verdant mounds and the deep blue sky; now by some sudden turn we get a peep at an adjoining meadow, where the sheep are lying, dappling its sloping surface like the small clouds on the summer heaven. Poor harmless, quiet creatures, how still they are! Some socially lying side by side; some grouped in threes and fours; some quite apart. Ah! there are lambs amongst them—pretty, pretty lambs—nestled in by their mothers. Soft, quiet, sleepy things! Not all so quiet, though! There is a party of these young lambs as wide awake as heart can desire; half a dozen of them playing together, frisking, dancing, leaping, butting, and crying in the young voice, which is so pretty a diminutive of the full-grown bleat. How beautiful they are with their innocent spotted faces, their mottled feet, their long curly tails, and their light flexible forms, frolicking like so many kittens, but with a gentleness, an assurance of sweetness and innocence, which no kitten, nothing that ever is to be a cat, can have. How complete and perfect is their enjoyment of existence! Ah! little rogues! your play has been too noisy; you have awakened your mammas; and two or three of the old ewes are getting up; and one of them marching gravely to the troop of lambs has selected her own, given her a gentle butt, and trotted off; the poor rebuked lamb following meekly, but every now and then stopping and casting a longing look at its playmates; who, after a moment's awed pause, had resumed their gambols; whilst the stately dame every now and then looked back in her turn, to see that her little one was following. At last she lay down, and the lamb by her side. I never saw so pretty a pastoral scene in my life. [1]

---

[1] I have seen one which affected me much more. Walking in the Church-lane with one of the young ladies of the vicarage, we met a large flock of sheep, with the usual retinue of shepherds and dogs. Lingering after them and almost out of sight, we encountered a straggling ewe, now trotting along, now walking, and every now and then stopping to look back, and bleating. A little behind her came a lame lamb, bleating occasionally, as if in answer to its dam, and doing its very best to keep up with her. It was a lameness of both the fore-feet; the knees were bent, and it seemed to walk on the very edge of the hoof—on tiptoe, if I may venture such an expression. My young friend thought that the lameness proceeded from original malformation, I am rather of opinion that it was accidental, and that the poor creature was wretchedly footsore. However that might be, the pain and difficulty with which it took every step were not to be mistaken; and the distress and fondness of the mother, her

Another turning of the dell gives a glimpse of the dark coppice by which it is backed, and from which we are separated by some marshy, rushy ground, where the springs have formed into a pool, and where the moor-hen loves to build her nest. Ay, there is one scudding away now; —I can hear her plash into the water, and the rustling of her wings amongst the rushes. This is the deepest part of the wild dingle. How uneven the ground is! Surely these excavations, now so thoroughly clothed with vegetation, must originally have been huge gravel pits; there is no other way of accounting for the labyrinth, for they do dig gravel in such capricious meanders; but the quantity seems incredible. Well! there is no end of guessing! We are getting amongst the springs, and must turn back. Round this corner, where on ledges like fairy terraces the orchises and arums grow, and we emerge suddenly on a new side of the dell, just fronting the small homestead of our good neighbour Farmer Allen.

This rustic dwelling belongs to what used to be called in this part of the country "a little bargain": thirty or forty acres, perhaps, of arable land, which the owner and his sons cultivated

---

perplexity as the flock passed gradually out of sight, the effort with which the poor lamb contrived to keep up a sort of trot, and their mutual calls and lamentations were really so affecting, that Ellen and I, although not at all lachrymose sort of people, had much ado not to cry. We could not find a boy to carry the lamb, which was too big for us to manage; —but I was quite sure that the ewe would not desert it, and as the dark was coming on, we both trusted that the shepherds on folding their flock would miss them and return for them; —and so I am happy to say it proved.

themselves, whilst the wife and daughters assisted in the husbandry, and eked out the slender earnings by the produce of the dairy, the poultry yard, and the orchard; —an order of cultivators now passing rapidly away, but in which much of the best part of the English character, its industry, its frugality, its sound sense, and its kindness might be found. Farmer Allen himself is an excellent specimen, the cheerful venerable old man with his long white hair, and his bright grey eye, and his wife is a still finer. They have had a hard struggle to win through the world and keep their little property undivided; but good management and good principles, and the assistance afforded them by an admirable son, who left our village a poor 'prentice boy, and is now a partner in a great house in London have enabled them to overcome all the difficulties of these trying times, and they are now enjoying the peaceful evenings of a well-spent life as free from care and anxiety as their best friends could desire.

Ah! there is Mr. Allen in the orchard, the beautiful orchard, with its glorious gardens of pink and white, its pearly pear-blossoms and coral apple-buds. What a flush of bloom it is! How brightly delicate it appears, thrown into strong relief by the dark house and the weather-stained barn, in this soft evening light! The very grass is strewed with the snowy petals of the pear and the cherry. And there sits Mrs. Allen, feeding her poultry, with her three little grand-daughters from London, pretty fairies from three years old to five (only two-and-twenty months elapsed between the birth of the eldest and the youngest) playing round her feet.

Mrs. Allen, my dear Mrs. Allen, has been that rare thing a beauty, and although she be now an old woman I had almost said that she is so still. Why should I not say so? Nobleness of feature and sweetness of expression are surely as delightful in age as in youth. Her face and figure are much like those which are stamped indelibly on the memory of every one who ever saw that grand specimen of woman—Mrs. Siddons. The outline of Mrs. Allen's face is exactly the same; but there is more softness, more gentleness, a more feminine composure in the eye and in the smile. Mrs. Allen never played Lady Macbeth. Her hair, almost as black as at twenty, is parted on her large fair forehead, and combed under her exquisitely neat and snowy cap; a muslin neckerchief, a grey stuff gown and a white apron complete the picture.

There she sits under an old elder-tree which flings its branches over her like a canopy, whilst the setting sun illumines her venerable figure and touches the leaves with an emerald light; there she sits, placid and smiling, with her spectacles in her hand and a measure of barley on her lap, into which the little girls are dipping their chubby hands and scattering the corn amongst the ducks and chickens with unspeakable glee. But those ingrates the poultry don't seem so pleased and thankful as they ought to be; they mistrust their young feeders. All domestic animals dislike children, partly from an instinctive fear of their tricks and their thoughtlessness; partly, I suspect, from jealousy. Jealousy seems a strange tragic passion to attribute to the inmates of the basse cour, —but only look at that strutting fellow of a bantam cock (evidently a favourite), who sidles up to his old mistress with an air half affronted and half tender, turning so scornfully from the barley-corns which Annie is flinging towards him, and say if he be not as jealous as Othello? Nothing can pacify him but Mrs. Allen's notice and a dole from her hand. See, she is calling to him and feeding him, and now how he swells out his feathers, and flutters his wings, and erects his glossy neck, and struts and crows and pecks, proudest and happiest of bantams, the pet and glory of the poultry yard!

In the meantime my own pet May, who has all this while been peeping into every hole, and penetrating every nook and winding of the dell, in hopes to find another rabbit, has returned to my side, and is sliding her snake-like head into my hand, at once to invite the caress which she likes so well, and to intimate, with all due respect, that it is time to go home. The setting sun gives the same warning; and in a moment we are through the dell, the field, and the gate, past the farm and the mill, and hanging over the bridge that crosses the Loddon river.

What a sunset! how golden! how beautiful! The sun just disappearing, and the narrow liny clouds, which a few minutes ago lay like soft vapoury streaks along the horizon, lighted up with a golden splendour that the eye can scarcely endure, and those still softer clouds which floated above them wreathing and curling into a thousand fantastic forms, as thin and changeful as summer smoke, now defined and deepened into grandeur, and edged with ineffable, insufferable light! Another minute and the brilliant orb totally disappears, and the sky above grows every moment more varied and more beautiful as the dazzling golden lines are mixed with glowing red and gorgeous purple, dappled with small dark specks, and mingled with such a blue as the egg of the hedge-sparrow. To look up at that glorious sky, and then to see that magnificent picture reflected in the clear and lovely Loddon water, is a pleasure never to be described and never forgotten. My heart swells and my eyes fill as I write of it, and think of the immeasurable majesty of nature, and the unspeakable goodness of God, who has spread an enjoyment so pure, so peaceful, and so intense before the meanest and the lowliest of His creatures.

THE COWSLIP-BALL

May 16th. —There are moments in life when, without any visible or immediate cause, the spirits sink and fail, as it were, under the mere pressure of existence: moments of unaccountable depression, when one is weary of one's very thoughts, haunted by images that will not depart—images many and various, but all painful; friends lost, or changed, or dead; hopes disappointed even in their accomplishment; fruitless regrets, powerless wishes, doubt and fear, and self-distrust, and self-disapprobation. They who have known these feelings (and who is there so happy as not to have known some of them?) will understand why Alfieri became powerless, and Froissart dull; and why even needle-work, the most effectual sedative, that grand soother and composer of woman's distress, fails to comfort me to-day. I will go out into the air this cool, pleasant afternoon, and try what that will do. I fancy that exercise or exertion of any kind, is the true specific for nervousness.

"Fling but a stone, the giant dies." I will go to the meadows, the beautiful meadows! and I will have my materials of happiness, Lizzy and May, and a basket for flowers, and we will make a cowslip-ball. "Did you ever see a cowslip-ball, my Lizzy?"—"No."—"Come away, then; make haste! run, Lizzy!"

And on we go, fast, fast! down the road, across the lea, past the workhouse, along by the great pond, till we slide into the deep narrow lane, whose hedges seem to meet over the water, and win our way to the little farmhouse at the end. "Through the farmyard, Lizzy; over the gate; never mind the cows; they are quiet enough."—"I don't mind 'em," said Miss Lizzy, boldly and truly, and with a proud affronted air, displeased at being thought to mind anything, and showing by her attitude and manner some design of proving her courage by an attack on the largest of the herd, in the shape of a pull by the tail. "I don't mind 'em."—"I know you don't, Lizzy; but let them alone, and don't chase the turkey-cock. Come to me, my dear!" and, for a wonder, Lizzy came.

In the meantime, my other pet, Mayflower, had also gotten into a scrape. She had driven about a huge unwieldy sow, till the animal's grunting had disturbed the repose of a still more enormous Newfoundland dog, the guardian of the yard. Out he sallied, growling, from the depth of his kennel, erecting his tail, and shaking his long chain. May's attention was instantly diverted from the sow to this new playmate, friend or foe, she cared not which; and he of the kennel, seeing his charge unhurt, and out of danger, was at leisure to observe the charms of his fair enemy, as she frolicked round him, always beyond the reach of his chain, yet always, with the natural instinctive coquetry of her sex, alluring him to the pursuit which she knew to be vain. I never saw a prettier flirtation. At last the noble animal, wearied out, retired to the inmost recesses of his habitation, and would not even approach her when she stood right before the entrance. "You are properly served, May. Come along, Lizzy. Across this wheatfield, and now over the gate. Stop! let me lift you down. No jumping, no breaking of necks, Lizzy!" And here we are in the meadows, and out of the world. Robinson Crusoe, in his lonely island, had scarcely a more complete, or a more beautiful solitude.

These meadows consist of a double row of small enclosures of rich grass-land, a mile or two in length, sloping down from high arable grounds on either side, to a little nameless brook that winds between them with a course which, in its infinite variety, clearness, and rapidity, seems to emulate the bold rivers of the north, of whom, far more than of our lazy southern streams, our rivulet presents a miniature likeness. Never was water more exquisitely tricksy: —now darting over the bright pebbles, sparkling and flashing in the light with a bubbling music, as sweet and wild as the song of the woodlark; now stretching quietly along, giving back the rich tufts of the golden marsh-marigolds which grow on its margin; now sweeping round a fine reach of green grass, rising steeply into a high mound, a mimic promontory, whilst the other side sinks softly away, like some tiny bay, and the water flows between, so clear, so wide, so shallow, that Lizzy, longing for adventure, is sure she could cross unwetted; now dashing through two sand-banks, a torrent deep and narrow, which May clears at a bound; now sleeping, half hidden, beneath the alders, and hawthorns, and wild roses, with which the banks are so profusely and variously fringed, whilst flags, [1] lilies, and other aquatic plants, almost cover the surface of the stream. In good truth, it is a beautiful brook, and one that Walton himself might have sitten by and loved, for trout are there; we see them as they dart up the stream, and hear and start at the sudden plunge when they spring to the surface for the summer flies. Izaak Walton would have loved our brook and our quiet meadows; they breathe the very spirit of his own peacefulness, a soothing quietude that

[1]   Walking along these meadows one bright sunny afternoon, a year or two back, and rather later in the season, I had an opportunity of noticing a curious circumstance in natural history. Standing close to the edge of the stream, I remarked a singular appearance on a large tuft of flags. It looked like bunches of flowers, the leaves of which seemed dark, yet transparent, intermingled with brilliant tubes of bright blue or shining green. On examining this phenomenon more closely, it turned out to be several clusters of dragon-flies, just emerged from their deformed chrysalis state, and still torpid and motionless from the wetness of their filmy wings. Half an hour later we returned to the spot and they were gone. We had seen them at the very moment when beauty was complete and animation dormant. I have since found nearly a similar account of this curious process in Mr. Bingley's very entertaining work, called "Animal Biography."

sinks into the soul. There is no path through them, not one; we might wander a whole spring day, and not see a trace of human habitation. They belong to a number of small proprietors, who allow each other access through their respective grounds, from pure kindness and neighbourly feeling; a privilege never abused: and the fields on the other side of the water are reached by a rough plank, or a tree thrown across, or some such homely bridge. We ourselves possess one of the most beautiful; so that the strange pleasure of property, that instinct which makes Lizzy delight in her broken doll, and May in the bare bone which she has pilfered from the kennel of her recreant admirer of Newfoundland, is added to the other charms of this enchanting scenery; a strange pleasure it is, when one so poor as I can feel it! Perhaps it is felt most by the poor, with the rich it may be less intense—too much diffused and spread out, becoming thin by expansion, like leaf-gold; the little of the poor may be not only more precious, but more pleasant to them: certain that bit of grassy and blossomy earth, with its green knolls and tufted bushes, its old pollards wreathed with ivy, and its bright and babbling waters, is very dear to me. But I must always have loved these meadows, so fresh, and cool, and delicious to the eye and to the tread, full of cowslips, and of all vernal flowers: Shakespeare's "Song of Spring" bursts irrepressibly from our lips as we step on them.

When daisies pied and violets blue

And lady-smocks all silver-white
And cuckoo-buds of yellow hue
Do paint the meadows with delight,
The cuckoo then, on every tree—

"Cuckoo! cuckoo!" cried Lizzy, breaking in with her clear childish voice; and immediately, as if at her call, the real bird, from a neighbouring tree (for these meadows are dotted with timber like a park), began to echo my lovely little girl, "cuckoo! cuckoo!" I have a prejudice very unpastoral and unpoetical (but I cannot help it, I have many such) against this "harbinger of spring." His note is so monotonous, so melancholy; and then the boys mimic him; one hears "cuckoo! cuckoo!" in dirty streets, amongst smoky houses, and the bird is hated for faults not his own. But prejudices of taste, likings and dislikings, are not always vanquishable by reason; so, to escape the serenade from the tree, which promised to be of considerable duration (when once that eternal song begins, on it goes ticking like a clock)—to escape that noise I determined to excite another, and challenged Lizzy to a cowslip-gathering; a trial of skill and speed, to see which should soonest fill her basket. My stratagem succeeded completely. What scrambling, what shouting, what glee from Lizzy! twenty cuckoos might have sung unheard whilst she was pulling her own flowers, and stealing mine, and laughing, screaming, and talking through all.

At last the baskets were filled, and Lizzy declared victor:

and down we sat, on the brink of the stream, under a spreading hawthorn, just disclosing its own pearly buds, and surrounded with the rich and enamelled flowers of the wild hyacinth, blue and white, to make our cowslip-ball. Every one knows the process: to nip off the tuft of flowerets just below the top of the stalk, and hang each cluster nicely balanced across a riband, till you have a long string like a garland; then to press them closely together, and tie them tightly up. We went on very prosperously, CONSIDERING; as people say of a young lady's drawing, or a Frenchman's English, or a woman's tragedy, or of the poor little dwarf who works without fingers, or the ingenious sailor who writes with his toes, or generally of any performance which is accomplished by means seemingly inadequate to its production. To be sure we met with a few accidents. First, Lizzy spoiled nearly all her cowslips by snapping them off too short; so there was a fresh gathering; in the next place, May overset my full basket, and sent the blossoms floating, like so many fairy favours, down the brook; then, when we were going on pretty steadily, just as we had made a superb wreath, and were thinking of tying it together, Lizzy, who held the riband, caught a glimpse of a gorgeous butterfly, all brown and red and purple, and, skipping off to pursue the new object, let go her hold; so all our treasures were abroad again. At last, however, by dint of taking a branch of alder as a substitute for Lizzy, and hanging the basket in a pollard-ash, out of sight of May, the cowslip-ball was finished. What a concentration of fragrance and beauty it was! golden and sweet to satiety! rich to sight, and touch, and smell! Lizzy was enchanted, and ran off with her prize, hiding amongst the trees in the very coyness of ecstasy, as if any human eye, even mine, would be a restraint on her innocent raptures.

In the meanwhile I sat listening, not to my enemy the cuckoo, but to a whole concert of nightingales, scarcely interrupted by any meaner bird, answering and vying with each other in those short delicious strains which are to the ear as roses to the eye: those snatches of lovely sound which come across us as airs from heaven. Pleasant thoughts, delightful associations, awoke as I listened; and almost unconsciously I repeated to myself the beautiful story of the Lutist and the Nightingale, from Ford's "Lover's Melancholy." Here it is. Is there in English poetry anything finer?

> Passing from Italy to Greece, the tales
> Which poets of an elder time have feign'd
> To glorify their Tempe, bred in me
> Desire of visiting Paradise.
> To Thessaly I came, and living private,
> Without acquaintance of more sweet companions
> Than the old inmates to my love, my thoughts,
> I day by day frequented silent groves
> And solitary walks. One morning early
> This accident encounter'd me: I heard

The sweetest and most ravishing contention

That art and nature ever were at strife in.

A sound of music touch'd mine ears, or rather

Indeed entranced my soul; as I stole nearer,

Invited by the melody, I saw

This youth, this fair-faced youth, upon his lute

With strains of strange variety and harmony

Proclaiming, as it seem'd, so bold a challenge

To the clear choristers of the woods, the birds,

That as they flock'd about him, all stood silent,

Wondering at what they heard. I wonder'd too.

A nightingale,

Nature's best skill'd musician, undertakes

The challenge; and for every several strain

The well-shaped youth could touch, she sang him down.

He could not run divisions with more art

Upon his quaking instrument than she,

The nightingale, did with her various notes

Reply to.

Some time thus spent, the young man grew at last

Into a pretty anger, that a bird,

Whom art had never taught cliffs, moods, or notes

Should vie with him for mastery, whose study

Had busied many hours to perfect practice.

To end the controversy, in a rapture

Upon his instrument he plays so swiftly,

So many voluntaries, and so quick,

That there was curiosity and cunning,

Concord in discord, lines of differing method

Meeting in one full centre of delight.

The bird (ordain'd to be

Music's first martyr) strove to imitate

These several sounds; which when her warbling throat

Fail'd in, for grief down dropt she on his lute,

And brake her heart. It was the quaintest sadness

To see the conqueror upon her hearse

To weep a funeral elegy of tears.

He look'd upon the trophies of his art,

Then sigh'd, then wiped his eyes; then sigh'd, and cry'd

"Alas! poor creature, I will soon revenge

This cruelty upon the author of it.

Henceforth this lute, guilty of innocent blood,

Shall never more betray a harmless peace

To an untimely end:" and in that sorrow,

As he was pashing it against a tree,

I suddenly stept in.

When I had finished the recitation of this exquisite passage, the sky, which had been all the afternoon dull and heavy, began to look more and more threatening; darker clouds, like wreaths of black smoke, flew across the dead leaden tint;

a cooler, damper air blew over the meadows, and a few large heavy drops splashed in the water. "We shall have a storm. Lizzy! May! where are ye? Quick, quick, my Lizzy! run, run! faster, faster!"

And off we ran; Lizzy not at all displeased at the thoughts of a wetting, to which indeed she is almost as familiar as a duck; May, on the other hand, peering up at the weather, and shaking her pretty ears with manifest dismay. Of all animals, next to a cat, a greyhound dreads rain. She might have escaped it; her light feet would have borne her home long before the shower; but May is too faithful for that, too true a comrade, understands too well the laws of good-fellowship; so she waited for us. She did, to be sure, gallop on before, and then stop and look back, and beckon, as it were, with some scorn in her black eyes at the slowness of our progress. We in the meanwhile got on as fast as we could, encouraging and reproaching each other. "Faster, my Lizzy! Oh, what a bad runner!"—"Faster, faster! Oh, what a bad runner!" echoed my saucebox. "You are so fat, Lizzy, you make no way!"—"Ah! who else is fat?" retorted the darling. Certainly her mother is right; I do spoil that child.

By this time we were thoroughly soaked, all three. It was a pelting shower, that drove through our thin summer clothing and poor May's short glossy coat in a moment. And then, when we were wet to the skin, the sun came out, actually the sun, as if to laugh at our plight; and then, more provoking still, when the sun was shining, and the shower over, came a maid and a boy to look after us, loaded with cloaks and umbrellas enough to fence us against a whole day's rain. Never mind! On we go, faster and faster; Lizzy obliged to be most ignobly carried, having had the misfortune to lose a shoe in the mud, which we left the boy to look after.

Here we are at home—dripping; but glowing and laughing, and bearing our calamity most manfully. May, a dog of excellent sense, went instantly to bed in the stable, and is at this moment over head and ears in straw; Lizzy is gone to bed too, coaxed into that wise measure by a promise of tea and toast, and of not going home till to-morrow, and the story of Little Red Riding Hood; and I am enjoying the luxury of dry clothing by a good fire. Really getting wet through now and then is no bad thing, finery apart; for one should not like spoiling a new pelisse, or a handsome plume; but when there is nothing in question but a white gown and a straw bonnet, as was the case to-day, it is rather pleasant than not. The little chill refreshes, and our enjoyment of the subsequent warmth and dryness is positive and absolute. Besides, the stimulus and exertion do good to the mind as well as body. How melancholy I was all the morning! how cheerful I am now! Nothing like a shower-bath—a real shower-bath, such as Lizzy and May and I have undergone, to cure low spirits. Try it, my dear readers, if ever ye be nervous— I will answer for its success.

THE OLD HOUSE AT ABERLEIGH

June 25th. —What a glowing glorious day! Summer in its richest prime, noon in its most sparkling brightness, little white clouds dappling the deep blue sky, and the sun, now partially veiled, and now bursting through them with an intensity of light! It would not do to walk to-day, professedly to walk, —we should be frightened at the very sound! and yet it is probable that we may be beguiled into a pretty long stroll before we return home. We are going to drive to the old house at Aberleigh, to spend the morning under the shade of those balmy firs, and amongst those luxuriant rose trees, and by the side of that brimming Loddon river. "Do not expect us before six o'clock," said I, as I left the house; "Six at soonest!" added my charming companion; and off we drove in our little pony chaise, drawn by our old mare, and with the good humoured urchin, Henry's successor, a sort of younger Scrub, who takes care of horse and chaise, and cow and garden, for our charioteer.

My comrade in this homely equipage was a young lady of high family and higher endowments, to whom the novelty of the thing, and her own naturalness of character and simplicity of taste, gave an unspeakable enjoyment. She danced the little chaise up and down as she got into it, and laughed for very glee like a child, Lizzy herself could not have been more delighted. She praised the horse and the driver, and the roads and the scenery, and gave herself fully up to the enchantment of a rural excursion in the sweetest weather of this sweet season. I enjoyed all this too; for the road was pleasant to every sense, winding through narrow lanes, under high elms, and between hedges garlanded with woodbine and rose trees, whilst the air was scented with the delicious fragrance of blossomed beans. I enjoyed it all, —but, I believe, my principal pleasure was derived from my companion herself.

Emily I. is a person whom it is a privilege to know. She is quite like a creation of the older poets, and might pass for one of Shakespeare's or Fletcher's women stepped into life; just as tender, as playful, as gentle, and as kind. She is clever too, and has all the knowledge and accomplishments that a carefully-conducted education, acting on a mind of singular clearness and ductility, matured and improved by the very best company, can bestow. But one never thinks of her acquirements. It is the charming artless character, the bewitching sweetness of manner, the real and universal sympathy, the quick taste and the ardent feeling, that one loves in Emily. She is Irish by birth, and has in perfection the melting voice and soft caressing accent by which her fair countrywomen are distinguished. Moreover she is pretty—I think her beautiful, and so do all who have heard as well as seen her, —but pretty, very pretty, all the world must confess; and perhaps that is a distinction more enviable, because less envied, than the "palmy state" of beauty. Her prettiness is of the prettiest kind—that of which the chief character is youthfulness. A short but pleasing figure, all grace and symmetry, a fair blooming face, beaming with intelligence and good-humour; the prettiest little feet and the whitest hands in the world; —such is Emily I.

She resides with her maternal grandmother, a venerable old lady, slightly shaken with the palsy; and when together (and they are so fondly attached to each other that they are seldom parted), it is one of the loveliest combinations of youth and age ever witnessed. There is no seeing them without feeling an increase of respect and affection for both grandmother and granddaughter—always one of the tenderest and most beautiful of natural connections—as Richardson knew when he made such exquisite use of it in his matchless book. I fancy that grandmamma Shirley must have been just such another venerable lady as Mrs. S., and our sweet Emily—Oh no! Harriet Byron is not half good enough for her! There is nothing like her in the whole seven volumes.

But here we are at the bridge! Here we must alight! "This is the Loddon, Emily. Is it not a beautiful river? rising level with its banks, so clear, and smooth, and peaceful, giving back the verdant landscape and the bright blue sky, and bearing on its pellucid stream the snowy water-lily, the purest of flowers, which sits enthroned on its own cool leaves, looking chastity itself, like the lady in Comus. That queenly flower becomes the water, and so do the stately swans who are sailing so majestically down the stream, like those who

> On St. Mary's lake
> Float double, swan and shadow.

We must dismount here, and leave Richard to take care of our equipage under the shade of these trees, whilst we walk up to the house: —See, there it is! We must cross this stile; there is no other way now."

And crossing the stile we were immediately in what had been a drive round a spacious park, and still retained something of the character, though the park itself had long been broken into arable fields, —and in full view of the Great House, a beautiful structure of James the First's time, whose glassless windows and dilapidated doors form a melancholy contrast with the strength and entireness of the rich and massive front.

The story of that ruin—for such it is—is always to me singularly affecting. It is that of the decay of an ancient and distinguished family, gradually reduced from the highest wealth and station to actual poverty. The house and park, and a small estate around it, were entailed on a distant cousin, and could not be alienated; and the late owner, the last of his name and lineage, after long struggling with debt and difficulty, farming his own lands, and clinging to his magnificent home with a love of place almost as tenacious as that of the younger Foscari, was at last forced to abandon it, retired to a paltry lodging in a paltry town, and died there about twenty years ago, broken-hearted. His successor, bound by no ties of association to the spot, and rightly judging the residence to be much too large for the diminished estate, immediately sold the superb fixtures, and would have entirely taken down the house, if, on making the attempt, the masonry had not been found so solid that the materials were not worth the labour. A great part, however, of one side is laid open, and the splendid chambers, with their carving and gilding, are exposed to the wind and rain—sad memorials of past grandeur! The grounds have been left in a merciful neglect; the park, indeed, is broken up, the lawn mown twice a year like a common hayfield, the grotto mouldering into ruin, and the fishponds choked with rushes and aquatic plants; but the shrubs and flowering trees are undestroyed, and have grown into a magnificence of size and wildness of beauty, such as we may imagine them to attain in their native forests. Nothing can exceed their luxuriance, especially in the spring, when the lilac, and laburnum, and double-cherry put forth their gorgeous blossoms. There is a sweet sadness in the sight of such floweriness amidst such desolation; it seems the triumph of nature over the destructive power of man. The whole place, in that season more particularly, is full of a soft and soothing melancholy, reminding me, I scarcely know why, of some of the descriptions of natural scenery in the novels of Charlotte Smith, which I read when a girl, and which, perhaps, for that reason hang on my memory.

But here we are, in the smooth grassy ride, on the top of a steep turfy slope descending to the river, crowned with enormous firs and limes of equal growth, looking across the winding waters into a sweet peaceful landscape of quiet meadows, shut in by distant woods. What a fragrance is in the air from the balmy fir trees and the blossomed limes! What an intensity of odour! And what a murmur of bees in the lime trees! What a coil those little winged people make over our heads! And what a pleasant sound it is! the pleasantest of busy sounds, that which comes associated with all that is good and beautiful—industry and forecast, and sunshine and flowers. Surely these lime trees might store a hundred hives; the very odour is of a honeyed richness, cloying, satiating.

Emily exclaimed in admiration as we stood under the deep, strong, leafy shadow, and still more when honeysuckles trailed their untrimmed profusion in our path, and roses, really trees, almost intercepted our passage.

"On, Emily! farther yet! Force your way by that jessamine—it will yield; I will take care of this stubborn white rose bough."—"Take care of yourself! Pray take care," said my fairest friend; "let me hold back the branches."—After we had won our way through the strait, at some expense of veils and flounces, she stopped to contemplate and admire the tall, graceful shrub, whose long thorny stems, spreading in every direction, had opposed our progress, and now waved their delicate clusters over our heads. "Did I ever think," exclaimed she, "of standing under the shadow of a white rose tree! What an exquisite fragrance! And what a beautiful flower! so pale, and white, and tender, and the petals thin and smooth as silk! What rose is it?"—"Don't you know? Did you never see it before? It is rare now, I believe, and seems rarer than it is, because it only blossoms in very hot summers; but this, Emily, is the musk rose, —that very musk rose of which Titania talks, and which is worthy of Shakespeare and of her. Is it not?—No! do not smell to it; it is less sweet so than other roses; but one cluster in a vase, or even that bunch in your bosom, will perfume a large room, as it does the summer air."—"Oh! we will take twenty clusters," said Emily. "I wish grandmamma were here! She talks so often of a musk rose tree that grew against one end of her father's house. I wish she were here to see this!"

Echoing her wish, and well laden with musk roses, planted perhaps in the days of Shakespeare, we reached the steps that led to a square summer-house or banqueting-room, overhanging the river: the under part was a boat-house, whose projecting roof, as well as the walls and the very top of the little tower, was covered with ivy and woodbine, and surmounted by tufted barberries, bird cherries, acacias, covered with their snowy chains, and other pendent and flowering trees. Beyond rose two poplars of unrivalled magnitude, towering like stately columns over the dark tall firs, and giving a sort of pillared and architectural grandeur to the scene.

We were now close to the mansion; but it looked sad and desolate, and the entrance, choked with brambles and nettles, seemed almost to repel our steps. The summer-house, the beautiful summer-house, was free and open, and inviting, commanding from the unglazed windows, which hung high above the water, a reach of the river terminated by a rustic mill.

There we sat, emptying our little basket of fruit and country cakes, till Emily was seized with a desire of viewing, from the other side of the Loddon, the scenery which had so much enchanted her. "I must," said she, "take a sketch of the ivied boat-house, and of this sweet room, and this pleasant window; —grandmamma would never be able to walk from the road to see the place itself, but she must see its likeness." So forth we sallied, not forgetting the dear musk roses.

We had no way of reaching the desired spot but by retracing our steps a mile, during the heat of the hottest hour of the day, and then following the course of the river to an equal distance on the other side; nor had we any materials for sketching, except the rumpled paper which had contained our repast, and a pencil without a point which I happened to have about me. But these small difficulties are pleasures to gay and happy youth. Regardless of such obstacles, the sweet Emily bounded on like a fawn, and I followed delighting in her delight. The sun went in, and the walk was delicious; a reviving coolness seemed to breathe over the water, wafting the balmy scent of the firs and limes; we found a point of view presenting the boat-house, the water, the poplars, and the mill, in a most felicitous combination; the little straw fruit basket made a capital table; and refreshed and sharpened and pointed by our trusty lacquey's excellent knife (your country boy is never without a good knife, it is his prime treasure), the pencil did double duty; —first in the skilful hands of Emily, whose faithful and spirited sketch does equal honour to the scene and to the artist, and then in the humbler office of attempting a faint transcript of my own impressions in the following sonnet: —

It was an hour of calmest noon, at day
        Of ripest summer: o'er the deep blue sky
        White speckled clouds came sailing peacefully,
Half-shrouding in a chequer'd veil the ray
Of the sun, too ardent else, —what time we lay
        By the smooth Loddon, opposite the high
        Steep bank, which as a coronet gloriously

Wore its rich crest of firs and lime trees, gay

With their pale tassels; while from out a bower
Of ivy (where those column'd poplars rear

Their heads) the ruin'd boat-house, like a tower,
Flung its deep shadow on the waters clear.

My Emily! forget not that calm hour,
Nor that fair scene, by thee made doubly dear!

THE HARD SUMMER

August 15th. —Cold, cloudy, windy, wet. Here we are, in the midst of the dog-days, clustering merrily round the warm hearth like so many crickets, instead of chirruping in the green fields like that other merry insect the grasshopper; shivering under the influence of the *Jupiter Pluvius* of England, the watery St. Swithin; peering at that scarce personage the sun, when he happens to make his appearance, as intently as astronomers look after a comet, or the common people stare at a balloon; exclaiming against the cold weather, just as we used to exclaim against the warm. "What a change from last year!" is the first sentence you hear, go where you may. Everybody remarks it, and everybody complains of it; and yet in my mind it has its advantages, or at least its compensations, as everything in nature has, if we would only take the trouble to seek for them.

Last year, in spite of the love which we are now pleased to profess towards that ardent luminary, not one of the sun's numerous admirers had courage to look him in the face: there was no bearing the world till he had said "Good-night" to it. Then we might stir: then we began to wake and to live. All day long we languished under his influence in a strange dreaminess, too hot to work, too hot to read, too hot to write, too hot even to talk; sitting hour after hour in a green arbour, embowered in leafiness, letting thought and fancy float as they would. Those day-dreams were pretty things in their way; there is no denying that. But then, if one half of the world were to dream through a whole summer, like the sleeping Beauty in the wood, what would become of the other?

The only office requiring the slightest exertion, which I performed in that warm weather, was watering my flowers. Common sympathy called for that labour. The poor things withered, and faded, and pined away; they almost, so to say, panted for draught. Moreover, if I had not watered them myself, I suspect that no one else would; for water last year was nearly as precious hereabout as wine. Our land-springs were dried up; our wells were exhausted; our deep ponds were dwindling into mud; and geese, and ducks, and pigs, and laundresses, used to look with a jealous and suspicious eye on the few and scanty half-buckets of that impure element, which my trusty lacquey was fain to filch for my poor geraniums and campanulas and tuberoses. We were forced to smuggle them in through my faithful adherent's territories, the stable, to avoid lectures within doors and at last even that resource failed; my garden, my blooming garden, the joy of my eyes, was forced to go waterless like its neighbours, and became shrivelled, scorched, and sunburnt, like them. It really went to my heart to look at it.

On the other side of the house matters were still worse. What a dusty world it was, when about sunset we became cool enough to creep into it! Flowers in the court looking fit for a *hortus siccus*; mummies of plants, dried as in an oven; hollyhocks, once pink, turned into Quakers; cloves smelling of dust. Oh, dusty world! May herself looked of that complexion; so did Lizzy; so did all the houses, windows, chickens, children, trees, and pigs in the village; so above all did the shoes. No foot could make three plunges into that abyss of pulverised gravel, which had the impudence to call itself a hard road, without being clothed with a coat a quarter of an inch thick. Woe to white gowns! woe to black! Drab was your only wear.

Then, when we were out of the street, what a toil it was to mount the hill, climbing with weary steps and slow upon the brown turf by the wayside, slippery, hot, and hard as a rock! And then if we happened to meet a carriage coming along the middle of the road, —the bottomless middle, —what a sandy whirlwind it was! What choking! what suffocation! No state could be more pitiable, except indeed that of the travellers who carried this misery about with them. I shall never forget the plight in which we met the coach one evening in last August, full an hour after its time, steeds and driver, carriage and passengers, all one dust. The outsides, and the horses, and the coachman, seemed reduced to a torpid quietness, the resignation of despair. They had left off trying to better their condition, and taken refuge in a wise and patient hopelessness, bent to endure in silence the extremity of ill. The six insides, on the contrary, were still fighting against their fate, vainly struggling to ameliorate their hapless destiny. They were visibly grumbling at the weather, scolding at the dust, and heating themselves like a furnace, by striving against the heat. How well I remember the fat gentleman without his coat, who was wiping his forehead, heaving up his wig, and certainly uttering that English ejaculation, which, to our national reproach, is the phrase of our language best known on the continent. And that poor boy, red-hot, all in a flame, whose mamma, having divested her own person of all superfluous apparel, was trying to relieve his sufferings by the removal of his neckerchief—an operation which he resisted with all his might. How perfectly I remember him, as well as the pale girl who sat opposite, fanning herself with her bonnet into an absolute fever! They vanished after a while into their own dust; but I have them all before my eyes at this moment, a companion picture to Hogarth's "Afternoon," a standing lesson to the grumblers at cold summers.

For my part, I really like this wet season. It keeps us within, to be sure, rather more than is quite agreeable; but then we are at least awake and alive there, and the world out of doors is so much the pleasanter when we can get abroad. Everything does well, except those fastidious bipeds, men and women; corn ripens, grass grows, fruit is plentiful; there is no lack of birds to eat it, and there has not been such a wasp-season these dozen years. My garden wants no watering, and is more beautiful than ever, beating my old rival in that primitive art, the pretty wife of the little mason, out and out. Measured with mine, her flowers are naught. Look at those hollyhocks, like pyramids of roses; those garlands of the convolvulus major of all colours, hanging around that tall pole, like the wreathy hop-bine; those magnificent dusky cloves, breathing of the Spice Islands; those flaunting double dahlias; those splendid scarlet geraniums, and those fierce and warlike flowers the tiger-lilies. Oh, how beautiful they are! Besides, the weather clears sometimes—it has cleared this evening; and here are we, after a merry walk up the hill, almost as quick as in the winter, bounding lightly along the bright green turf of the pleasant common, enticed by the gay shouts of a dozen clear young voices, to linger awhile, and see the boys play at cricket.

I plead guilty to a strong partiality towards that unpopular class of beings, country boys: I have a large acquaintance amongst them, and I can almost say, that I know good of many and harm of none. In general they are an open, spirited, good-humoured race, with a proneness to embrace the pleasures and eschew the evils of their condition, a capacity for happiness, quite unmatched in man, or woman, or a girl. They are patient, too, and bear their fate as scape-goats (for all sins whatsoever are laid as matters of course to their door), whether at home or abroad, with amazing resignation and, considering the many lies of which they are the objects, they tell wonderfully few in return. The worst that can be said of them is, that they seldom, when grown to man's estate, keep the promise of their boyhood; but that is a fault to come—a fault that may not come, and ought not to be anticipated. It is astonishing how sensible they are to notice from their betters, or those whom they think such. I do not speak of money, or gifts, or praise, or the more coarse and common briberies—they are more delicate courtiers; a word, a nod, a smile, or the mere calling of them by their names, is enough to ensure their hearts and their services. Half a dozen of them, poor urchins, have run away now to bring us chairs from their several homes. "Thank you, Joe Kirby! —you are always first—yes, that is just the place— I shall see everything there. Have you been in yet, Joe?"—"No, ma'am! I go in next."—"Ah, I am glad of that—and now's the time. Really that was a pretty ball of Jem Eusden's! —I was sure it would go to the wicket. Run, Joe! They are waiting for you." There was small need to bid Joe Kirby make haste; I think he is, next to a race-horse, or a greyhound, or a deer, the fastest creature that runs—the most completely alert and active. Joe is mine especial friend, and leader of the "tender juveniles," as Joel Brent is of the adults. In both instances this post of honour was gained by merit, even more remarkably so in Joe's case than in Joel's; for Joe is a less boy than many of his companions (some of whom are fifteeners and sixteeners, quite as tall and nearly as old as Tom Coper), and a poorer than all, as may be conjectured from the lamentable state of that patched round frock, and the ragged condition of those unpatched shoes, which would encumber, if anything could, the light feet that wear them. But why should I lament the poverty that never troubles him? Joe is the merriest and happiest creature that ever lived twelve years in this wicked world. Care cannot come near him. He hath a perpetual smile on his round ruddy face, and a laugh in his hazel eye, that drives the witch away. He works at yonder farm on the top of the hill, where he is in such repute for intelligence and good-humour, that he has the honour of performing all the errands of the house, of helping the maid, the mistress, and the master, in addition to his own stated office of carter's boy. There he works hard from five till seven, and then he comes here to work still harder, under the name of play—batting, bowling, and fielding, as if for life, filling the place of four boys; being, at a pinch, a whole eleven. The late Mr. Knyvett, the king's organist, who used in his own person to sing twenty parts at once of the Hallelujah Chorus, so that you would have thought he had a nest of nightingales in his throat, was but a type of Joe Kirby. There is a sort of ubiquity about him; he thinks nothing of being in two places at once, and for pitching a ball, William Grey himself is nothing to him. It goes straight to the mark like a bullet. He is king of the cricketers from eight to sixteen, both inclusive, and an excellent ruler he makes. Nevertheless, in the best-ordered states there will be grumblers, and we have an opposition here in the shape of Jem Eusden.

Jem Eusden is a stunted lad of thirteen, or thereabout, lean, small, and short, yet strong and active. His face is of an extraordinary ugliness, colourless, withered, haggard, with a look of extreme age, much increased by hair so light that it might rather pass for white than flaxen. He is constantly arrayed in the blue cap and old-fashioned coat, the costume of an endowed school to which he belongs; where he sits still all day, and rushes into the field at night, fresh, untired, and ripe for action, to scold and brawl, and storm, and bluster. He hates Joe Kirby, whose immovable good-humour, broad smiles, and knowing nods, must certainly be very provoking to so fierce and turbulent a spirit; and he has himself (being, except by rare accident, no great player) the preposterous ambition of wishing to be manager of the sports. In short, he is a demagogue in embryo, with every quality necessary to a splendid success in that vocation, —a strong voice, a fluent utterance, an incessant iteration, and a frontless impudence. He is a great "scholar" too, to use the country phrase; his "piece," as our village schoolmaster terms a fine sheet of flourishing writing, something between a valentine and a sampler, enclosed within a border of little coloured prints—his last, I remember, was encircled by an engraved history of Moses, beginning at the finding in the bulrushes, with Pharaoh's daughter dressed in a rose-coloured gown and blue feathers—his piece is not only the admiration of the school, but of the parish, and is sent triumphantly round from house to house at Christmas, to extort halfpence and sixpences from all encouragers of learning—*Montem* in miniature. The Mosaic history was so successful, that the produce enabled Jem to purchase a bat and ball, which, besides adding to his natural arrogance (for the little pedant actually began to mutter against being eclipsed by a dunce, and went so far as to challenge Joe Kirby to a trial in Practice, or the Rule of Three), gave him, when compared with the general poverty, a most unnatural preponderance in the cricket state. He had the ways and means in his hands (for alas! the hard winter had made sad havoc among the bats, and the best ball was a bad one)—he had the ways and means, could withhold the supplies, and his party was beginning to wax strong, when Joe received a present of two bats and a ball for the youngsters in general and himself in particular—and Jem's adherents left him on the spot—they ratted, to a man, that very evening. Notwithstanding this desertion, their forsaken leader has in nothing relaxed from his pretensions, or his ill-humour. He stills quarrels and brawls as if he had a faction to back him, and thinks nothing of contending with both sides, the ins and the outs, secure of out-talking the whole field. He has been squabbling these ten minutes, and is just marching off now with his own bat (he has never deigned to use one of Joe's) in his hand. What an ill-conditioned hobgoblin it is! And yet there is something bold and sturdy about him too. I should miss Jem Eusden.

Ah, there is another deserter from the party! my friend the

little hussar—I do not know his name, and call him after his cap and jacket. He is a very remarkable person, about the age of eight years, the youngest piece of gravity and dignity I ever encountered; short, and square, and upright, and slow, with a fine bronzed flat visage, resembling those convertible signs the Broad-Face and the Saracen's-Head, which, happening to be next-door neighbours in the town of B., I never knew apart, resembling, indeed, any face that is open-eyed and immovable, the very sign of a boy! He stalks about with his hands in his breeches pockets, like a piece of machinery; sits leisurely down when he ought to field, and never gets farther in batting than to stop the ball. His is the only voice never heard in the *mélée*: I doubt, indeed, if he have one, which may be partly the reason of a circumstance that I record to his honour, his fidelity to Jem Eusden, to whom he has adhered through every change of fortune, with a tenacity proceeding perhaps from an instinctive consciousness that the loquacious leader talks enough for two. He is the only thing resembling a follower that our demagogue possesses, and is cherished by him accordingly. Jem quarrels for him, scolds for him, pushes for him; and but for Joe Kirby's invincible good-humour, and a just discrimination of the innocent from the guilty, the activity of Jem's friendship would get the poor hussar ten drubbings a day.

But it is growing late. The sun has set a long time. Only see what a gorgeous colouring has spread itself over those parting masses of clouds in the west, —what a train of rosy light! We shall have a fine sunshiny day to-morrow, —a blessing not to be undervalued, in spite of my late vituperation of heat. Shall we go home now? And shall we take the longest but prettiest road, that by the green lanes? This way, to the left, round the corner of the common, past Mr. Welles's cottage, and our path lies straight before us. How snug and comfortable that cottage looks! Its little yard all alive with the cow, and the mare, and the colt almost as large as the mare, and the young foal, and the great yard-dog, all so fat! Fenced in with hay-rick, and wheat-rick, and bean-stack, and backed by the long garden, the spacious drying-ground, the fine orchard, and that large field quartered into four different crops. How comfortable this cottage looks, and how well the owners earn their comforts! They are the most prosperous pair in the parish— she a laundress with twenty times more work than she can do, unrivalled in flounces and shirt-frills, and such delicacies of the craft; he, partly a farmer, partly a farmer's man, tilling his own ground, and then tilling other people's; —affording a proof, even in this declining age, when the circumstances of so many worthy members of the community seem to have "an alacrity in sinking," that it is possible to amend them by sheer industry. He, who was born in the workhouse, and bred up as a parish boy, has now, by mere manual labour, risen to the rank of a land-owner, pays rates and taxes, grumbles at the times, and is called Master Welles, —the title next to Mister—that by which Shakespeare was called; —what would man have more? His wife, besides being the best laundress in the county, is a comely woman still. There she stands at the spring, dipping up water for to-morrow, —the clear, deep, silent spring, which sleeps so peacefully under its high flowery bank, red with the tall spiral stalks of the foxglove and their rich pendent bells, blue with the beautiful forget-me-not, that gem-like blossom, which looks like a living jewel of turquoise and topaz. It is almost too late to see its beauty; and here is the pleasant shady lane, where the high elms will shut out the little twilight that remains. Ah, but we shall have the fairies' lamps to guide us, the stars of the earth, the glow-worms! Here they are, three almost together. Do you not see them? One seems tremulous, vibrating, as if on the extremity of a leaf of grass; the others are deeper in the hedge, in some green cell on which their light falls with an emerald lustre. I hope my friends the cricketers will not come this way home. I would not have the pretty creatures removed for more than I care to say, and in this matter I would hardly trust Joe Kirby—boys so love to stick them in their hats. But this lane is quite deserted. It is only a road from field to field. No one comes here at this hour. They are quite safe; and I shall walk here to-morrow and visit them again. And now, goodnight! beautiful insects, lamps of the fairies, good-night!

THE SHAW

September 9th. —A bright sunshiny afternoon. What a comfort it is to get out again—to see once more that rarity of rarities, a fine day! We English people are accused of talking overmuch of the weather; but the weather, this summer, has forced people to talk of it. Summer! did I say? Oh! season most unworthy of that sweet, sunny name! Season of coldness and cloudiness, of gloom and rain! A worse November! — for in November the days are short; and shut up in a warm room, lighted by that household sun, a lamp, one feels through the long evenings comfortably independent of the out-of-door tempests. But though we may have, and did have, fires all through the dog-days, there is no shutting out daylight; and sixteen hours of rain, pattering against the windows and dripping from the eaves—sixteen hours of rain, not merely audible, but visible for seven days in the week—would be enough to exhaust the patience of Job or Grizzel; especially if

Job were a farmer, and Grizzel a country gentlewoman. Never was known such a season! Hay swimming, cattle drowning, fruit rotting, corn spoiling! and that naughty river, the Loddon, who never can take Puff's advice, and "keep between its banks," running about the country, fields, roads, gardens, and houses, like mad! The weather would be talked of. Indeed, it was not easy to talk of anything else. A friend of mine having occasion to write me a letter, thought it worth abusing in rhyme, and bepommelled it through three pages of Bath-guide verse; of which I subjoin a specimen: —

> Aquarius surely REIGNS over the world,
> And of late he his water-pot strangely has twirl'd;
> Or he's taken a cullender up by mistake,
> And unceasingly dips it in some mighty lake;
> Though it is not in Lethe—for who can forget
> The annoyance of getting most thoroughly wet?
> It must be in the river called Styx, I declare,
> For the moment it drizzles it makes the men swear.
> "It did rain to-morrow," is growing good grammar;
> Vauxhall and camp-stools have been brought to the hammer;
> A pony-gondola is all I can keep,
> And I use my umbrella and pattens in sleep:
> Row out of my window, whene'er 'tis my whim
> To visit a friend, and just ask, "Can you swim?"

So far my friend. [1] In short, whether in prose or in verse, everybody railed at the weather. But this is over now. The sun has come to dry the world; mud is turned into dust; rivers have retreated to their proper limits; farmers have left off grumbling; and we are about to take a walk, as usual, as far as the Shaw, a pretty wood about a mile off. But one of our companions being a stranger to the gentle reader, we must do him the honour of an introduction.

Dogs, when they are sure of having their own way, have sometimes ways as odd as those of the unfurred, unfeathered animals, who walk on two legs, and talk, and are called rational. My beautiful white greyhound, Mayflower, [2] for instance, is as whimsical as the finest lady in the land. Amongst her other

---

[1]   This friend of mine is a person of great quickness and talent, who, if she were not a beauty and a woman of fortune—that is to say, if she were prompted by either of those two powerful stimuli, want of money or want of admiration, to take due pains—would inevitably become a clever writer. As it is, her notes and "jeux d'esprit" struck off "a trait de plume," have great point and neatness. Take the following billet, which formed the label to a closed basket, containing the ponderous present alluded to, last Michaelmas day: —

"To Miss M.

'When this you see

Remember me,'

Was long a phrase in use;

And so I send

To you, dear friend,

My proxy, 'What?'—A goose!"

[2]   Dead, alas, since this was written.

fancies, she has taken a violent affection for a most hideous stray dog, who made his appearance here about six months ago, and contrived to pick up a living in the village, one can hardly tell how. Now appealing to the charity of old Rachael Strong, the laundress—a dog-lover by profession; now winning a meal from the lightfooted and open-hearted lasses at the Rose; now standing on his hind-legs, to extort by sheer beggary a scanty morsel from some pair of "drouthy cronies," or solitary drover, discussing his dinner or supper on the alehouse-bench; now catching a mouthful, flung to him in pure contempt by some scornful gentleman of the shoulder-knot, mounted on his throne, the coach-box, whose notice he had attracted by dint of ugliness; now sharing the commons of Master Keep the shoemaker's pigs; now succeeding to the reversion of the well-gnawed bone of Master Brown the shopkeeper's fierce house-dog; now filching the skim-milk of Dame Wheeler's cat: — spit at by the cat; worried by the mastiff; chased by the pigs; screamed at by the dame; stormed at by the shoemaker; flogged by the shopkeeper; teased by all the children, and scouted by all the animals of the parish; —but yet living through his griefs, and bearing them patiently, "for sufferance is the badge of all his tribe;" —and even seeming to find, in an occasional full meal, or a gleam of sunshine, or a wisp of dry straw on which to repose his sorry carcase, some comfort in his disconsolate condition.

In this plight was he found by May, the most high-blooded

and aristocratic of greyhounds; and from this plight did May rescue him; —invited him into her territory, the stable; resisted all attempts to turn him out; reinstated him there, in spite of maid and boy, and mistress and master; wore out everybody's opposition, by the activity of her protection, and the pertinacity of her self-will; made him sharer of her bed and of her mess; and, finally, established him as one of the family as firmly as herself.

Dash—for he has even won himself a name amongst us, before he was anonymous—Dash is a sort of a kind of a spaniel; at least there is in his mongrel composition some sign of that beautiful race. Besides his ugliness, which is of the worst sort—that is to say, the shabbiest—he has a limp on one leg that gives a peculiar one-sided awkwardness to his gait; but independently of his great merit in being May's pet, he has other merits which serve to account for that phenomenon— being, beyond all comparison, the most faithful, attached, and affectionate animal that I have ever known; and that is saying much. He seems to think it necessary to atone for his ugliness by extra good conduct, and does so dance on his lame leg, and so wag his scrubby tail, that it does any one who has a taste for happiness good to look at him—so that he may now be said to stand on his own footing. We are all rather ashamed of him when strangers come in the way, and think it necessary to explain that he is May's pet; but amongst ourselves, and those who are used to his appearance, he has reached the point of favouritism in his own person. I have, in common with wiser women, the feminine weakness of loving whatever loves me—and, therefore, I like Dash. His master has found out that he is a capital finder, and in spite of his lameness will hunt a field or beat a cover with any spaniel in England—and, therefore, HE likes Dash. The boy has fought a battle, in defence of his beauty, with another boy, bigger than himself, and beat his opponent most handsomely—and, therefore, HE likes Dash; and the maids like him, or pretend to like him, because we do—as is the fashion of that pliant and imitative class. And now Dash and May follow us everywhere, and are going with us to the Shaw, as I said before—or rather to the cottage by the Shaw, to bespeak milk and butter of our little dairy-woman, Hannah Bint—a housewifely occupation, to which we owe some of our pleasantest rambles.

And now we pass the sunny, dusty village street—who would have thought, a month ago, that we should complain of sun and dust again! —and turn the corner where the two great oaks hang so beautifully over the clear deep pond, mixing their cool green shadows with the bright blue sky, and the white clouds that flit over it; and loiter at the wheeler's shop, always picturesque, with its tools, and its work, and its materials, all so various in form, and so harmonious in colour; and its noise, merry workmen, hammering and singing, and making a various harmony also. The shop is rather empty to-day, for its usual inmates are busy on the green beyond the pond—

one set building a cart, another painting a waggon. And then we leave the village quite behind, and proceed slowly up the cool, quiet lane, between tall hedgerows of the darkest verdure, overshadowing banks green and fresh as an emerald.

Not so quick as I expected, though—for they are shooting here to-day, as Dash and I have both discovered: he with great delight, for a gun to him is as a trumpet to a war-horse; I with no less annoyance, for I don't think that a partridge itself, barring the accident of being killed, can be more startled than I at that abominable explosion. Dash has certainly better blood in his veins than any one would guess to look at him. He even shows some inclination to elope into the fields, in pursuit of those noisy iniquities. But he is an orderly person after all, and a word has checked him.

Ah! here is a shriller din mingling with the small artillery—a shriller and more continuous. We are not yet arrived within sight of Master Weston's cottage, snugly hidden behind a clump of elms; but we are in full hearing of Dame Weston's tongue, raised as usual to scolding pitch. The Westons are new arrivals in our neighbourhood, and the first thing heard of them was a complaint from the wife to our magistrate of her husband's beating her: it was a regular charge of assault—an information in full form. A most piteous case did Dame Weston make of it, softening her voice for the nonce into a shrill tremulous whine, and exciting the mingled pity and anger—pity towards herself, anger towards her husband—of the whole female world, pitiful and indignant as the female world is wont to be on such occasions. Every woman in the parish railed at Master Weston; and poor Master Weston was summoned to attend the bench on the ensuing Saturday, and answer the charge; and such was the clamour abroad and at home, that the unlucky culprit, terrified at the sound of a warrant and a constable, ran away, and was not heard of for a fortnight.

At the end of that time he was discovered, and brought to the bench; and Dame Weston again told her story, and, as before, on the full cry. She had no witnesses, and the bruises of which she made complaint had disappeared, and there were no women present to make common cause with the sex. Still, however, the general feeling was against Master Weston; and it would have gone hard with him when he was called in, if a most unexpected witness had not risen up in his favour. His wife had brought in her arms a little girl about eighteen months old, partly perhaps to move compassion in her favour; for a woman with a child in her arms is always an object that excites kind feelings. The little girl had looked shy and frightened, and had been as quiet as a lamb during her mother's examination; but she no sooner saw her father, from whom she had been a fortnight separated, than she clapped her hands, and laughed, and cried, "Daddy! daddy!" and sprang into his arms, and hung round his neck, and covered him with kisses—again shouting, "Daddy, come home! daddy! daddy!"—and finally nestled her little head in his bosom, with a fulness of contentment, an assurance of tenderness and protection such as no wife-beating tyrant ever did inspire, or ever could inspire, since the days of King Solomon. Our magistrates acted in the very spirit of the Jewish monarch: they accepted the evidence of nature, and dismissed the complaint. And subsequent events have fully justified their decision; Mistress Weston proving not only renowned for the feminine accomplishment of scolding (tongue-banging, it is called in our parts, a compound word which deserves to be Greek), but is actually herself addicted to administering the conjugal discipline, the infliction of which she was pleased to impute to her luckless husband.

Now we cross the stile, and walk up the fields to the Shaw. How beautifully green this pasture looks! and how finely the evening sun glances between the boles of that clump of trees, beech, and ash, and aspen! and how sweet the hedgerows are with woodbine and wild scabious, or, as the country people call it, the gipsy-rose! Here is little Dolly Weston, the unconscious witness, with cheeks as red as a real rose, tottering up the path to meet her father. And here is the carroty-poled urchin, George Coper, returning from work, and singing "Home! sweet Home!" at the top of his voice; and then, when the notes prove too high for him, continuing the air in a whistle, until he has turned the impassable corner; then taking up again the song and the words, "Home! sweet Home!" and looking as if he felt their full import, ploughboy though he be. And so he does; for he is one of a large, an honest, a kind, and an industrious family, where all goes well, and where the poor ploughboy is sure of finding cheerful faces and coarse comforts—all that he has learned to desire. Oh, to be as cheaply and as thoroughly contented as George Coper! All his luxuries a cricket-match! —all his wants satisfied in "home! sweet home!"

Nothing but noises to-day! They are clearing Farmer Brooke's great bean-field, and crying the "Harvest Home!" in a chorus, before which all other sounds—the song, the scolding, the gunnery—fade away, and become faint echoes. A pleasant noise is that! though, for one's ears' sake, one makes some haste to get away from it. And here, in happy time, is that pretty wood, the Shaw, with its broad pathway, its tangled dingles, its nuts and its honeysuckles; —and, carrying away a faggot of those sweetest flowers, we reach Hannah Bint's: of whom, and of whose doings, we shall say more another time.

NOTE. —Poor Dash is also dead. We did not keep him long, indeed I believe that he died of the transition from starvation to good feed, as dangerous to a dog's stomach, and to most stomachs, as the less agreeable change from good feed to starvation. He has been succeeded in place and favour by another Dash, not less amiable in demeanour and far more creditable in appearance, bearing no small resemblance to the pet spaniel of my friend Master Dinely, he who stole the bone from the magpies, and who figures as the first Dash of this volume. Let not the unwary reader opine, that in assigning the same name to three several individuals, I am acting as an humble imitator of the inimitable writer who has given immortality to the Peppers and the Mustards, on the one hand; or showing a poverty of invention or a want of acquaintance with the bead-roll of canine appellations on the other. I merely, with my usual scrupulous fidelity, take the names as I find them. The fact is that half the handsome spaniels in England are called Dash, just as half the tall footmen are called Thomas. The name belongs to the species. Sitting in an open carriage one day last summer at the door of a farmhouse where my father had some business, I saw a noble and beautiful animal of this kind lying in great state and laziness on the steps, and felt an immediate desire to make acquaintance with him. My father, who had had the same fancy, had patted him and called him "poor fellow" in passing, without eliciting the smallest notice in return. "Dash!" cried I at a venture, "good Dash! noble Dash!" and up he started in a moment, making but one spring from the door into the gig. Of course I was right in my guess. The gentleman's name was Dash.

NUTTING

September 26th. —One of those delicious autumnal days, when the air, the sky, and the earth seem lulled into a universal calm, softer and milder even than May. We sallied forth for a walk, in a mood congenial to the weather and the season, avoiding, by mutual consent, the bright and sunny common, and the gay highroad, and stealing through shady, unfrequented lanes, where we were not likely to meet any one, —not even the pretty family procession which in other years we used to contemplate with so much interest—the father, mother, and children, returning from the wheat-field, the little ones laden with bristling close-tied bunches of wheat-ears, their own gleanings, or a bottle and a basket which had contained their frugal dinner, whilst the mother would carry her babe hushing and lulling it, and the father and an elder child trudged after with the cradle, all seeming weary and all happy. We shall not see such a procession as this to-day; for the harvest is nearly over, the fields are deserted, the silence may almost be felt. Except the wintry notes of the redbreast, nature herself is mute. But how beautiful, how gentle, how harmonious, how rich! The rain has preserved to the herbage all the freshness and verdure of spring, and the world of leaves has lost nothing of its midsummer brightness, and the harebell is on the banks, and the woodbine in the hedges, and the low furze, which the lambs cropped in the spring, has burst again into its golden blossoms.

All is beautiful that the eye can see; perhaps the more beautiful for being shut in with a forest-like closeness. We have no prospect in this labyrinth of lanes, cross-roads, mere cart-ways, leading to the innumerable little farms into which this part of the parish is divided. Up-hill or down, these quiet woody lanes scarcely give us a peep at the world, except when, leaning over a gate, we look into one of the small enclosures, hemmed in with hedgerows, so closely set with growing timber, that the meady opening looks almost like a glade in a wood; or when some cottage, planted at a corner of one of the little greens formed by the meeting of these cross-ways, almost startles us by the unexpected sight of the dwellings of men in such a solitude. But that we have more of hill and dale, and that our cross-roads are excellent in their kind, this side of our parish would resemble the description given of La Vendee, in Madame Laroche-Jacquelin's most interesting book. [1] I am sure if wood can entitle a country to be called Le Bocage, none can have a better right to the name. Even this pretty snug farmhouse on the hillside, with its front covered with the rich vine, which goes wreathing up to the very top of the clustered chimney, and its sloping orchard full of fruit—even this pretty quiet nest can hardly peep out of its leaves. Ah! they are gathering in the orchard harvest. Look at that young rogue in the old mossy apple-tree—that great tree, bending with the weight of its golden-rennets—see how he pelts his little sister beneath with apples as red and as round as her own cheeks, while she, with her outstretched frock, is trying to catch them, and laughing and offering to pelt again as often as one bobs against her; and look at that still younger imp, who, as grave as a judge, is creeping on hands and knees under the tree, picking up the apples as they fall so deedily, [2] and depositing them so honestly in the great basket on the grass, already fixed so firmly and opened so widely, and filled almost to overflowing by the

---

[1] An almost equally interesting account of that very peculiar and interesting scenery, may be found in "The Maid of La Vendee," an English novel, remarkable for its simplicity and truth of painting, written by Mrs. Le Noir, the daughter of Christopher Smart, an inheritrix of much of his talent. Her works deserve to be better known.

[2] "Deedily,"—I am not quite sure that this word is good English; but it is genuine Hampshire, and is used by the most correct of female writers, Miss Austen. It means (and it is no small merit that it has no exact synonym) anything done with a profound and plodding attention, an action which engrosses all the powers of mind and body.

brown rough fruitage of the golden-rennet's next neighbour the russeting; and see that smallest urchin of all, seated apart in infantine state on the turfy bank, with that toothsome piece of deformity a crumpling in each hand, now biting from one sweet, hard, juicy morsel and now from another—Is not that a pretty English picture? And then, farther up the orchard, that bold hardy lad, the eldest born, who has scaled (Heaven knows how) the tall, straight upper branch of that great pear-tree, and is sitting there as securely and as fearlessly, in as much real safety and apparent danger, as a sailor on the top-mast. Now he shakes the tree with a mighty swing that brings down a pelting shower of stony bergamots, which the father gathers rapidly up, whilst the mother can hardly assist for her motherly fear— a fear which only spurs the spirited boy to bolder ventures. Is not that a pretty picture? And they are such a handsome family too, the Brookers. I do not know that there is any gipsy blood, but there is the true gipsy complexion, richly brown, with cheeks and lips so red, black hair curling close to their heads in short crisp rings, white shining teeth—and such eyes! — That sort of beauty entirely eclipses your mere roses and lilies. Even Lizzy, the prettiest of fair children, would look poor and watery by the side of Willy Brooker, the sober little personage who is picking up the apples with his small chubby hands, and filling the basket so orderly, next to his father the most useful man in the field. "Willy!" He hears without seeing; for we are quite hidden by the high bank, and a spreading hawthorn bush that overtops it, though between the lower branches and the grass we have found a convenient peep-hole. "Willy!" The voice sounds to him like some fairy dream, and the black eyes are raised from the ground with sudden wonder, the long silky eyelashes thrown back till they rest on the delicate brow, and a deeper blush is burning on those dark cheeks, and a smile is dimpling about those scarlet lips. But the voice is silent now, and the little quiet boy, after a moment's pause, is gone coolly to work again. He is indeed a most lovely child. I think some day or other he must marry Lizzy; I shall propose the match to their respective mammas. At present the parties are rather too young for a wedding—the intended bridegroom being, as I should judge, six, or thereabout, and the fair bride barely five, —but at least we might have a betrothment after the royal fashion, —there could be no harm in that. Miss Lizzy, I have no doubt, would be as demure and coquettish as if ten winters more had gone over her head, and poor Willy would open his innocent black eyes, and wonder what was going forward. They would be the very Oberon and Titania of the village, the fairy king and queen.

Ah! here is the hedge along which the periwinkle wreathes and twines so profusely, with its evergreen leaves shining like the myrtle, and its starry blue flowers. It is seldom found wild in this part of England; but, when we do meet with it, it is so abundant and so welcome, —the very robin—redbreast of flowers, a winter friend. Unless in those unfrequent frosts which destroy all vegetation, it blossoms from September to June, surviving the last lingering crane's-bill, forerunning the earliest primrose, hardier even than the mountain daisy, —peeping out from beneath the snow, looking at itself in the ice, smiling through the tempests of life, and yet welcoming and enjoying the sunbeams. Oh, to be like that flower!

The little spring that has been bubbling under the hedge all along the hillside, begins, now that we have mounted the eminence and are imperceptibly descending, to deviate into a capricious variety of clear deep pools and channels, so narrow and so choked with weeds, that a child might overstep them. The hedge has also changed its character. It is no longer the close compact vegetable wall of hawthorn, and maple, and brier-roses, intertwined with bramble and woodbine, and crowned with large elms or thickly-set saplings. No! the pretty meadow which rises high above us, backed and almost surrounded by a tall coppice, needs no defence on our side but its own steep bank, garnished with tufts of broom, with pollard oaks wreathed with ivy, and here and there with long patches of hazel overhanging the water. "Ah, there are still nuts on that bough!" and in an instant my dear companion, active and eager and delighted as a boy, has hooked down with his walking-stick one of the lissome hazel stalks, and cleared it of its tawny clusters, and in another moment he has mounted the bank, and is in the midst of the nuttery, now transferring the spoil from the lower branches into that vast variety of pockets which gentlemen carry about them, now bending the tall tops into the lane, holding them down by main force, so that I might reach them and enjoy the pleasure of collecting some of the plunder myself. A very great pleasure he knew it would be. I doffed my shawl, tucked up my flounces, turned my straw bonnet into a basket, and began gathering and scrambling—for, manage it how you may, nutting is scrambling work, —those boughs, however tightly you may grasp them by the young fragrant twigs and the bright green leaves, will recoil and burst away; but there is a pleasure even in that: so on we go, scrambling and gathering with all our might and all our glee. Oh, what an enjoyment! All my life long I have had a passion for that sort of seeking which implies finding (the secret, I believe, of the love of field-sports, which is in man's mind a natural impulse)—therefore I love violeting, —therefore, when we had a fine garden, I used to love to gather strawberries, and cut asparagus, and above all, to collect the filberts from the shrubberies: but this hedgerow nutting beats that sport all to nothing. That was a make-believe thing, compared with this; there was no surprise, no suspense, no unexpectedness—it was as inferior to this wild nutting, as the turning out of a bag-fox is to unearthing the fellow, in the eyes of a staunch foxhunter.

Oh, what enjoyment this nut-gathering is! They are in such abundance, that it seems as if there were not a boy in the parish, nor a young man, nor a young woman, —for a basket of nuts is the universal tribute of country gallantry; our pretty damsel Harriet has had at least half a dozen this season; but no one has found out these. And they are so full too, we lose half of them from over-ripeness; they drop from the socket at the slightest motion. If we lose, there is one who finds. May is as fond of nuts as a squirrel, and cracks the shell and extracts the kernel with equal dexterity. Her white glossy head is upturned now to watch them as they fall. See how her neck is thrown back like that of a swan, and how beautifully her folded ears quiver with expectation, and how her quick eye follows the rustling noise, and her light feet dance and pat the ground, and leap up with eagerness, seeming almost sustained in the air, just as I have seen her when Brush is beating a hedgerow, and she knows from his questing that there is a hare afoot. See, she has caught that nut just before it touched the water; but the water would have been no defence, —she fishes them from the bottom, she delves after them amongst the matted grass—even my bonnet—how beggingly she looks at that! "Oh, what a pleasure nutting is! —Is it not, May? But the pockets are almost full, and so is the basket-bonnet, and that bright watch the sun says it is late; and after all it is wrong to rob the poor boys—is it not, May?"—May shakes her graceful head denyingly, as if she understood the question—"And we must go home now—must we not? But we will come nutting again some time or other—shall we not, my May?"

THE VISIT

October 27th. —A lovely autumnal day; the air soft, balmy, genial; the sky of that softened and delicate blue upon which the eye loves to rest, —the blue which gives such relief to the rich beauty of the earth, all around glowing in the ripe and mellow tints of the most gorgeous of the seasons. Really such an autumn may well compensate our English climate for the fine spring of the south, that spring of which the poets talk, but which we so seldom enjoy. Such an autumn glows upon us like a splendid evening; it is the very sunset of the year; and I have been tempted forth into a wider range of enjoyment than usual. This WALK (if I may use the Irish figure of speech called a bull) will be a RIDE. A very dear friend has beguiled me into accompanying her in her pretty equipage to her beautiful home, four miles off; and having sent forward in the style of a running footman the servant who had driven her, she assumes the reins, and off we set.

My fair companion is a person whom nature and fortune would have spoiled if they could. She is one of those striking women whom a stranger cannot pass without turning to look again; tall and finely proportioned, with a bold Roman contour of figure and feature, a delicate English complexion, and an air of distinction altogether her own. Her beauty is duchess-like. She seems born to wear feathers and diamonds, and to form the grace and ornament of a court; and the noble frankness and simplicity of her countenance and manner confirm the impression. Destiny has, however, dealt more kindly by her. She is the wife of a rich country gentleman of high descent and higher attainments, to whom she is most devotedly attached, — the mother of a little girl as lovely as herself, and the delight of all who have the happiness of her acquaintance, to whom she is endeared not merely by her remarkable sweetness of temper and kindness of heart, but by the singular ingenuousness and openness of character which communicate an indescribable charm to her conversation. She is as transparent as water. You may see every colour, every shade of a mind as lofty and beautiful as her person. Talking with her is like being in the Palace of Truth described by Madame de Genlis; and yet so kindly are her feelings, so great her indulgence to the little failings and foibles of our common nature, so intense her sympathy with the wants, the wishes, the sorrows, and the happiness of her fellow-creatures, that, with all her frank-speaking, I never knew her make an enemy or lose a friend.

But we must get on. What would she say if she knew I was putting her into print? We must get on up the hill. Ah! that is precisely what we are not likely to do! This horse, this beautiful and high-bred horse, well-fed, and fat and glossy, who stood prancing at our gate like an Arabian, has suddenly turned sulky. He does not indeed stand quite still, but his way of moving is little better—the slowest and most sullen of all walks. Even they who ply the hearse at funerals, sad-looking beasts who totter under black feathers, go faster. It is of no use to admonish him by whip, or rein, or word. The rogue has found out that it is a weak and tender hand that guides him now. Oh, for one pull, one stroke of his old driver, the groom! how he would fly! But there is the groom half a mile before us, out of earshot, clearing the ground at a capital rate, beating us hollow. He has just turned the top of the hill; —and in a moment—ay, NOW he is out of sight, and will undoubtedly so continue till he meets us at the lawn gate. Well! there is no great harm. It is only prolonging the pleasure of enjoying together this charming scenery in this fine weather. If once we make up our minds not to care how slowly our steed goes, not to fret ourselves by vain exertions, it is no matter what his pace may be. There is little doubt of his getting home by sunset, and that will content us. He is, after all, a fine noble animal; and perhaps when he finds that we are determined to give him his way, he may relent and give us ours. All his sex are sticklers for dominion, though, when it is undisputed, some of them are generous enough to abandon it.

Two or three of the most discreet wives of my acquaintance contrive to manage their husbands sufficiently with no better secret than this seeming submission; and in our case the example has the more weight since we have no possible way of helping ourselves.

Thus philosophising, we reached the top of the hill, and viewed with "reverted eyes" the beautiful prospect that lay bathed in golden sunshine behind us. Cowper says, with that boldness of expressing in poetry the commonest and simplest feelings, which is perhaps one great secret of his originality,

> Scenes must be beautiful, which, daily seen,
> Please daily, and whose novelty survives
> Long knowledge and the scrutiny of years.

Every day I walk up this hill—every day I pause at the top to admire the broad winding road with the green waste on each side, uniting it with the thickly timbered hedgerows; the two pretty cottages at unequal distances, placed so as to mark the bends; the village beyond, with its mass of roofs and clustered chimneys peeping through the trees; and the rich distance, where cottages, mansions, churches, towns, seem embowered in some wide forest, and shut in by blue shadowy hills. Every day I admire this most beautiful landscape; yet never did it seem to me so fine or so glowing as now. All the tints of the glorious autumn, orange, tawny, yellow, red, are poured in profusion among the bright greens of the meadows and turnip fields, till the eyes are satiated with colour; and then before us we have the common with its picturesque roughness of surface tufted with cottages, dappled with water, edging off on one side into fields and farms and orchards, and terminated on the other by the princely oak avenue. What a richness and variety the wild broken ground gives to the luxuriant cultivation of the rest of the landscape! Cowper has described it for me. How perpetually, as we walk in the country, his vivid pictures recur to the memory! Here is his common and mine!

> The common overgrown with fern, and rough
> With prickly gorse, that, shapeless and deform'd
> And dangerous to the touch, has yet its bloom,
> And decks itself with ornaments of gold; —
> ——————————— there the turf
> Smells fresh, and, rich in odoriferous herbs
> And fungous fruits of earth, regales the sense
> With luxury of unexpected sweets.

The description is exact. There, too, to the left is my cricket-ground (Cowper's common wanted that finishing grace); and there stands one solitary urchin, as if in contemplation of its past and future glories; for, alas! cricket is over for the season. Ah! it is Ben Kirby, next brother to Joe, king of the youngsters, and probably his successor—for this Michaelmas has cost us Joe! He is promoted from the farm to the mansion-house, two miles off; there he cleans shoes, rubs knives, and runs on errands, and is, as his mother expresses it, "a sort of 'prentice to the footman." I should not wonder if Joe, some day or other, should overtop the footman, and rise to be butler; and his splendid prospects must be our consolation for the loss of this great favourite. In the meantime we have Ben.

Ben Kirby is a year younger than Joe, and the school-fellow and rival of Jem Eusden. To be sure his abilities lie in rather a different line. Jem is a scholar, Ben is a wag: Jem is great in figures and writing, Ben in faces and mischief. His master says of him, that, if there were two such in the school, he must resign his office; and as far as my observation goes, the worthy pedagogue is right. Ben is, it must be confessed, a great corrupter of gravity. He hath an exceeding aversion to authority and decorum, and a wonderful boldness and dexterity in overthrowing the one and puzzling the other. His contortions of visage are astounding. His "power over his own muscles and those of other people" is almost equal to that of Liston; and indeed the original face, flat and square and Chinese in its shape, of a fine tan complexion, with a snub nose, and a slit for a mouth, is nearly as comical as that matchless performer's. When aided by Ben's singular mobility of feature, his knowing winks and grins and shrugs and nods, together with a certain dry shrewdness, a habit of saying sharp things, and a marvellous gift of impudence, it forms as fine a specimen as possible of a humorous country boy, an oddity in embryo. Everybody likes Ben, except his butts (which may perhaps comprise half his acquaintance); and of them no one so thoroughly hates and dreads him as our parish schoolmaster, a most worthy King Log, whom Ben dumbfounds twenty times a day. He is a great ornament of the cricket-ground, has a real genius for the game, and displays it after a very original manner, under the disguise of awkwardness—as the clown shows off his agility in a pantomime. Nothing comes amiss to him. By the bye, he would have been the very lad for us in our present dilemma; not a horse in England could master Ben Kirby. But we are too far from him now—and perhaps it is as well that we are so. I believe the rogue has a kindness for me, in remembrance of certain apples and nuts, which my usual companion, who delights in his wit, is accustomed to dole out to him. But it is a Robin Goodfellow nevertheless, a perfect Puck, that loves nothing on earth so well as mischief. Perhaps the horse may be the safer conductor of the two.

The avenue is quite alive to-day. Old women are picking up twigs and acorns, and pigs of all sizes doing their utmost to spare them the latter part of the trouble; boys and girls groping for beech-nuts under yonder clump; and a group of younger elves collecting as many dead leaves as they can find to feed the bonfire which is smoking away so briskly amongst the trees, — a sort of rehearsal of the grand bonfire nine days hence; of the loyal conflagration of the arch-traitor Guy Vaux, which is annually solemnised in the avenue, accompanied with as much of squibbery and crackery as our boys can beg or borrow— not to say steal. Ben Kirby is a great man on the 5th of November. All the savings of a month, the hoarded halfpence, the new farthings, the very luck-penny, go off *in fumo* on that night. For my part, I like this daylight mockery better. There is no gunpowder—odious gunpowder! no noise but the merry shouts of the small fry, so shrill and happy, and the cawing of the rooks, who are wheeling in large circles overhead, and wondering what is going forward in their territory—seeming in their loud clamour to ask what that light smoke may mean that curls so prettily amongst their old oaks, towering as if to meet the clouds. There is something very intelligent in the ways of that black people the rooks, particularly in their wonder. I suppose it results from their numbers and their unity of purpose, a sort of collective and corporate wisdom. Yet geese congregate also; and geese never by any chance look wise. But then geese are a domestic fowl; we have spoiled them; and rooks are free commoners of nature, who use the habitations we provide for them, tenant our groves and our avenues, but never dream of becoming our subjects.

What a labyrinth of a road this is! I do think there are four turnings in the short half-mile between the avenue and the mill. And what a pity, as my companion observes—not that our good and jolly miller, the very representative of the old English yeomanry, should be so rich, but that one consequence of his riches should be the pulling down of the prettiest old mill that ever looked at itself in the Loddon, with the picturesque, low-browed, irregular cottage, which stood with its light-pointed roof, its clustered chimneys, and its ever-open door, looking like the real abode of comfort and hospitality, to build this huge, staring, frightful, red-brick mill, as ugly as a manufactory, and this great square house, ugly and red to match, just behind. The old buildings always used to remind me of Woollett's beautiful engraving of a scene in the Maid of the Mill. It will be long before any artist will make a drawing of this. Only think of this redness in a picture! this boiled lobster of a house! Falstaff's description of Bardolph's nose would look pale in the comparison.

Here is that monstrous machine of a tilted waggon, with its load of flour, and its four fat horses. I wonder whether our horse will have the decency to get out of the way. If he does not, I am sure we cannot make him; and that enormous ship upon wheels, that ark on dry land, would roll over us like the car of Juggernaut. Really—Oh no! there is no danger now. I should have remembered that it is my friend Samuel Long who drives the mill team. He will take care of us. "Thank you, Samuel!" And Samuel has put us on our way, steered us safely past his waggon, escorted us over the bridge and now, having seen us through our immediate difficulties, has parted from us with a very civil bow and good-humoured smile, as one who is always civil and good-humoured, but with a certain triumphant masterful look in his eyes, which I have noted in men, even the best of them, when a woman gets into straits by attempting manly employments. He has done us great good though, and may be allowed his little feeling of superiority. The parting salute he bestowed on our steed, in the shape of an astounding crack of his huge whip, has put that refractory animal on his mettle. On we go! past the glazier's pretty house, with its porch and its filbert walk; along the narrow lane bordered with elms, whose fallen leaves have made the road one yellow; past that little farmhouse with the horse-chestnut trees before, glowing like oranges; past the whitewashed school on the other side, gay with October roses; past the park, and the lodge, and the mansion, where once dwelt the great Earl of Clarendon; —and now the rascal has begun to discover that Samuel Long and his whip are a mile off, and that his mistress is driving him, and he slackens his pace accordingly. Perhaps he feels the beauty of the road just here, and goes slowly to enjoy it. Very beautiful it certainly is. The park paling forms the boundary on one side, with fine clumps of oak, and deer in all attitudes; the water, tufted with alders, flowing along on the other. Another turn, and the water winds away, succeeded by a low hedge, and a sweep of green meadows; whilst the park and its palings are replaced by a steep bank, on which stands a small, quiet, village alehouse; and higher up, embosomed in wood, is the little country church, with its sloping churchyard and its low white steeple, peeping out from amongst magnificent yew-trees: —

> Huge trunks! and each particular trunk a growth
> Of intertwisted fibres serpentine
> Up-coiling, and invet'rately convolved.
>
> WORDSWORTH.

No village church was ever more happily placed. It is the very image of the peace and humbleness inculcated within its walls.

Ah! here is a higher hill rising before us, almost like a mountain. How grandly the view opens as we ascend over that wild bank, overgrown with fern, and heath, and gorse, and between those tall hollies, glowing with their coral berries! What an expanse! But we have little time to gaze at present; for that piece of perversity, our horse, who has walked over so much level ground, has now, inspired, I presume, by a desire to revisit his stable, taken it into that unaccountable noddle of his to trot up this, the very steepest hill in the county. Here we are on the top; and in five minutes we have reached the lawn gate, and are in the very midst of that beautiful piece of art or nature (I do not know to which class it belongs), the pleasure-ground of F. Hill. Never was the "prophetic eye of taste" exerted with more magical skill than in these plantations. Thirty years ago this place had no existence; it was a mere undistinguished tract of field and meadow and common land; now it is a mimic forest, delighting the eye with the finest combinations of trees and shrubs, the rarest effects of form and foliage, and bewildering the mind with its green glades, and impervious recesses, and apparently interminable extent. It is the triumph of landscape gardening, and never more beautiful than in this autumn sunset, lighting up the ruddy beech and the spotted sycamore, and gilding the shining fir-cones that hang so thickly amongst the dark pines. The robins are singing around us, as if they too felt the magic of the hour. How gracefully the road winds through the leafy labyrinth, leading imperceptibly to the more ornamented sweep. Here we are at the door amidst geraniums, and carnations, and jasmines, still in flower. Ah! here is a flower sweeter than all, a bird gayer than the robin, the little bird that chirps to the tune of "mamma! mamma!". the bright-faced fairy, whose tiny feet come pattering along, making a merry music, mamma's own Frances! And following her guidance, here we are in the dear round room time enough to catch the last rays of the sun, as they light the noble landscape which lies like a panorama around us, lingering longest on that long island of old thorns and stunted oaks, the oasis of B. Heath, and then vanishing in a succession of gorgeous clouds.

October 28th. —Another soft and brilliant morning. But the pleasures of to-day must be written in shorthand. I have left myself no room for notes of admiration.

First we drove about the coppice: an extensive wood of oak, and elm, and beech, chiefly the former, which adjoins the park-paling of F. Hill, of which demesne, indeed, it forms one of the most delightful parts. The roads through the coppice are studiously wild; so that they have the appearance of mere cart-tracks: and the manner in which the ground is tumbled about, the steep declivities, the sunny slopes, the sudden swells and falls, now a close narrow valley, then a sharp ascent to an eminence commanding an immense extent of prospect, have a striking air of natural beauty, developed and heightened by the perfection of art. All this, indeed, was familiar to me; the colouring only was new. I had been there in early spring, when the fragrant palms were on the willow, and the yellow tassels on the hazel, and every twig was swelling with renewed life; and I had been there again and again in the green leafiness of midsummer; but never as now, when the dark verdure of the fir-plantations, hanging over the picturesque and unequal paling, partly covered with moss and ivy, contrasts so remarkably with the shining orange-leaves of the beech, already half fallen, the pale yellow of the scattering elm, the deeper and richer tints of the oak, and the glossy stems of the "lady of the woods," the delicate weeping birch. The underwood is no less picturesque. The red-spotted leaves and redder berries of the old thorns, the scarlet festoons of the bramble, the tall fern of every hue, seem to vie with the brilliant mosaic of the ground, now covered with dead leaves and strewn with fir-cones, now, where a little glade intervenes, gay with various mosses and splendid *fungi*. How beautiful is this coppice to-day! especially where the little spring, as clear as crystal, comes bubbling out from the old "fantastic" beech root, and trickles over the grass, bright and silent as the dew in a May morning. The wood-pigeons (who are just returned from their summer migration, and are cropping the ivy berries) add their low cooings, the very note of love, to the slight fluttering of the falling leaves in the quiet air, giving a voice to the sunshine and the beauty. This coppice is a place to live and die in. But we must go. And how fine is the ascent which leads us again into the world, past those cottages hidden as in a pit, and by that hanging orchard and that rough heathy bank! The scenery in this one spot has a wildness, an abruptness of rise and fall, rare in any part of England, rare above all in this rich and lovely but monotonous county. It is Switzerland in miniature.

And now we cross the hill to pay a morning visit to the family at the great house, —another fine place, commanding another fine sweep of country. The park, studded with old trees, and sinking gently into a valley, rich in wood and water, is in the best style of ornamental landscape, though more according to the common routine of gentlemen's seats than the singularly original place which we have just left. There is, however, one distinctive beauty in the grounds of the great house; —the magnificent firs which shade the terraces and surround the sweep, giving out in summer odours really Sabaean, and now in this low autumn sun producing an effect almost magical, as the huge red trunks, garlanded with ivy, stand out from the deep shadows like an army of giants. Indoors—Oh I must not take my readers indoors, or we shall never get away! Indoors the sunshine is brighter still; for there, in a lofty, lightsome room, sat a damsel fair and arch and *piquante*, one whom Titian or Velasquez should be born again to paint, leaning over an instrument[1] as sparkling and fanciful as herself, singing pretty French romances, and Scottish Jacobite songs, and all sorts of graceful and airy drolleries picked up I know not where—an English improvisatrice! a gayer Annot Lyle! whilst her sister, of a higher order of beauty, and with an earnest kindness in her smile that deepens its power, lends to the piano, as her father to the violin, an expression, a sensibility, a spirit, an eloquence almost superhuman—almost divine! Oh to hear these two instruments accompanying my dear companion (I forgot to say that she is a singer worthy to be so accompanied) in Haydn's exquisite canzonet, 'She never told her love,'—to hear her voice, with all its power, its sweetness, its gush of sound, so sustained and assisted by modulations that rivalled its intensity of expression; to hear at once such poetry, such music, such execution, is a pleasure never to be forgotten, or mixed with meaner things. I seem to hear it still.

> As in the bursting spring time o'er the eye
>   Of one who haunts the fields fair visions creep
>   Beneath the closed lids (afore dull sleep
> Dims the quick fancy) of sweet flowers that lie

---

[1]   The dital harp.

On grassy banks, oxlip of orient dye,

    And palest primrose and blue violet,

    All in their fresh and dewy beauty set,

Pictured within the sense, and will not fly:

So in mine ear resounds and lives again

    One mingled melody, —a voice, a pair

    Of instruments most voice-like! Of the air

Rather than of the earth seems that high strain,

A spirit's song, and worthy of the train

    That soothed old Prospero with music rare.

HANNAH BINT

The Shaw, leading to Hannah Bint's habitation, is, as I perhaps have said before, a very pretty mixture of wood and coppice; that is to say, a tract of thirty or forty acres covered with fine growing timber—ash, and oak, and elm, very regularly planted; and interspersed here and there with large patches of underwood, hazel, maple, birch, holly, and hawthorn, woven into almost impenetrable thickets by long wreaths of the bramble, the briony, and the brier-rose, or by the pliant and twisting garlands of the wild honeysuckle. In other parts, the Shaw is quite clear of its bosky undergrowth, and clothed only with large beds of feathery fern, or carpets of flowers, primroses, orchises, cowslips, ground-ivy, crane's-bill, cotton-grass, Solomon's seal, and forget-me-not, crowded together with a profusion and brilliancy of colour, such as I have rarely seen equalled even in a garden. Here the wild hyacinth really enamels the ground with its fresh and lovely purple; there,

On aged roots, with bright green mosses clad,

Dwells the wood sorrel, with its bright thin leaves

Heart-shaped and triply folded, and its root

Creeping like beaded coral; whilst around

Flourish the copse's pride, anemones,

With rays like golden studs on ivory laid

Most delicate; but touch'd with purple clouds,

Fit crown for April's fair but changeful brow.

The variety is much greater than I have enumerated; for the ground is so unequal, now swelling in gentle ascents, now dimpling into dells and hollows, and the soil so different in different parts, that the sylvan Flora is unusually extensive and complete.

The season is, however, now too late for this floweriness; and except the tufted woodbines, which have continued in bloom during the whole of this lovely autumn, and some lingering garlands of the purple wild vetch, wreathing round the thickets, and uniting with the ruddy leaves of the bramble, and the pale festoons of the briony, there is little to call one's attention from the grander beauties of the trees—the sycamore, its broad leaves already spotted—the oak, heavy with acorns— and the delicate shining rind of the weeping birch, "the lady of the woods," thrown out in strong relief from a background of holly and hawthorn, each studded with coral berries, and backed with old beeches, beginning to assume the rich tawny hue which makes them perhaps the most picturesque of autumnal trees, as the transparent freshness of their young foliage is undoubtedly the choicest ornament of the forest in spring.

A sudden turn round one of these magnificent beeches brings us to the boundary of the Shaw, and leaning upon a rude gate, we look over an open space of about ten acres of ground, still more varied and broken than that which we have passed, and surrounded on all sides by thick woodland. As a piece of colour, nothing can be well finer. The ruddy glow of the heath-flower, contrasting, on the one hand, with the golden-blossomed furze—on the other, with a patch of buck-wheat, of which the bloom is not past, although the grain be ripening, the beautiful buck-wheat, whose transparent leaves and stalks are so brightly tinged with vermilion, while the delicate pink-white of the flower, a paler persicaria, has a feathery fall, at once so rich and so graceful, and a fresh and reviving odour, like that of birch trees in the dew of a May evening. The bank that surmounts this attempt at cultivation is crowned with the late foxglove and the stately mullein; the pasture of which so great a part of the waste consists, looks as green as an emerald; a clear pond, with the bright sky reflected in it, lets light into the picture; the white cottage of the keeper peeps from the opposite coppice; and the vine-covered dwelling of Hannah Bint rises from amidst the pretty garden, which lies bathed in the sunshine around it.

The living and moving accessories are all in keeping with the cheerfulness and repose of the landscape. Hannah's cow grazing quietly beside the keeper's pony; a brace of fat pointer puppies holding amicable intercourse with a litter of young pigs; ducks, geese, cocks, hens, and chickens scattered over the turf; Hannah herself sallying forth from the cottage-door, with her milk-bucket in her hand, and her little brother following with the milking-stool.

My friend, Hannah Bint, is by no means an ordinary person. Her father, Jack Bint (for in all his life he never arrived at the dignity of being called John, indeed in our parts he was commonly known by the cognomen of London Jack), was a drover of high repute in his profession. No man, between Salisbury Plain and Smithfield, was thought to conduct a flock of sheep so skilfully through all the difficulties of lanes and commons, streets and high-roads, as Jack Bint, aided by Jack Bint's famous dog, Watch; for Watch's rough, honest face, black, with a little white about the muzzle, and one white ear, was as well known at fairs and markets as his master's equally honest and weather-beaten visage. Lucky was the dealer that could secure their services; Watch being renowned for keeping a flock together better than any shepherd's dog on the road—Jack, for delivering them more punctually, and in better condition. No man had a more thorough knowledge of the proper night stations, where good feed might be procured for his charge, and good liquor for Watch and himself; Watch, like other sheep dogs, being accustomed to live chiefly on bread and beer. His master, though not averse to a pot of good double X, preferred gin; and they who plod slowly along, through wet and weary ways, in frost and in fog, have undoubtedly a stronger temptation to indulge in that cordial and reviving stimulus, than we water-drinkers, sitting in warm and comfortable rooms, can readily imagine. For certain, our drover could never resist the gentle seduction of the gin-bottle, and being of a free, merry, jovial temperament, one of those persons commonly called good fellows, who like to see others happy in the same way with themselves, he was apt to circulate it at his own expense, to the great improvement of his popularity, and the great detriment of his finances.

All this did vastly well whilst his earnings continued proportionate to his spendings, and the little family at home were comfortably supported by his industry: but when a rheumatic fever came on, one hard winter, and finally settled in his limbs, reducing the most active and hardy man in the parish to the state of a confirmed cripple, then his reckless improvidence stared him in the face; and poor Jack, a thoughtless, but kind creature, and a most affectionate father, looked at his three motherless children with the acute misery of a parent who has brought those whom he loves best in the world to abject destitution. He found help, where he probably least expected it, in the sense and spirit of his young daughter, a girl of twelve years old.

Hannah was the eldest of the family, and had, ever since her mother's death, which event had occurred two or three years before, been accustomed to take the direction of their domestic concerns, to manage her two brothers, to feed the pigs and the poultry, and to keep house during the almost constant absence of her father. She was a quick, clever lass, of a high spirit, a firm temper, some pride, and a horror of accepting parochial relief, which is every day becoming rarer amongst the peasantry; but which forms the surest safeguard to the sturdy independence of the English character. Our little damsel possessed this quality in perfection; and when her father talked of giving up their comfortable cottage, and removing to the workhouse, whilst she and her brothers must go to service, Hannah formed a bold resolution, and without disturbing the sick man by any participation of her hopes and fears, proceeded after settling their trifling affairs to act at once on her own plans and designs.

Careless of the future as the poor drover had seemed, he had yet kept clear of debt, and by subscribing constantly to a benefit club, had secured a pittance that might at least assist in supporting him during the long years of sickness and helplessness to which he was doomed to look forward. This his daughter knew. She knew also, that the employer in whose service his health had suffered so severely, was a rich and liberal cattle-dealer in the neighbourhood, who would willingly aid an old and faithful servant, and had, indeed, come forward with offers of money. To assistance from such a quarter Hannah saw no objection. Farmer Oakley and the parish were quite distinct things. Of him, accordingly, she asked, not money, but something much more in his own way—"a cow! any cow! old or lame, or what not, so that it were a cow! she would be bound to keep it well; if she did not, he might take it back again. She even hoped to pay for it by and by, by instalments, but that she would not promise!" and, partly amused, partly interested by the child's earnestness, the wealthy yeoman gave her, not as a purchase, but as a present, a very fine young Alderney. She then went to the lord of the manor, and, with equal knowledge of character, begged his permission to keep her cow on the Shaw common. "Farmer Oakley had given her a fine Alderney, and she would be bound to pay the rent, and keep her father off the parish, if he would only let it graze on the waste;" and he too, half from real good nature—half, not to be outdone in liberality by his tenant, not only granted the requested permission, but reduced the rent so much, that the produce of the vine seldom fails to satisfy their kind landlord.

Now Hannah showed great judgment in setting up as a dairy-woman. She could not have chosen an occupation more completely unoccupied, or more loudly called for. One of the most provoking of the petty difficulties which beset people with a small establishment in this neighbourhood, is the trouble, almost the impossibility, of procuring the pastoral luxuries of milk, eggs, and butter, which rank, unfortunately, amongst the indispensable necessaries of housekeeping. To your thoroughbred Londoner, who, whilst grumbling over his own breakfast, is apt to fancy that thick cream, and fresh butter, and new-laid eggs, grow, so to say, in the country—form an actual part of its natural produce—it may be some comfort to learn, that in this great grazing district, however the calves and the farmers may be the better for cows, nobody else is; that farmers' wives have ceased to keep poultry; and that we unlucky villagers sit down often to our first meal in a state of destitution, which may well make him content with his thin milk and his Cambridge butter, when compared to our imputed pastoralities.

Hannah's Alderney restored us to one rural privilege. Never was so cleanly a little milkmaid. She changed away some of the cottage finery, which, in his prosperous days, poor Jack had pleased himself with bringing home, the china tea-service, the gilded mugs, and the painted waiters, for the useful utensils of the dairy, and speedily established a regular and gainful trade in milk, eggs, butter, honey, and poultry—for poultry they had always kept.

Her domestic management prospered equally. Her father, who retained the perfect use of his hands, began a manufacture of mats and baskets, which he constructed with great nicety and adroitness; the eldest boy, a sharp and clever lad, cut for him his rushes and osiers; erected, under his sister's direction, a shed for the cow, and enlarged and cultivated the garden (always with the good leave of her kind patron the lord of the manor) until it became so ample, that the produce not only kept the pig, and half kept the family, but afforded another branch of merchandise to the indefatigable directress of the establishment.

For the younger boy, less quick and active, Hannah contrived to obtain an admission to the charity-school, where he made great progress—retaining him at home, however, in the hay-making and leasing season, or whenever his services could be made available, to the great annoyance of the schoolmaster, whose favourite he is, and who piques himself so much on George's scholarship (your heavy sluggish boy at country work often turns out quick at his book), that it is the general opinion that this much-vaunted pupil will, in process of time, be promoted to the post of assistant, and may, possibly, in course of years, rise to the dignity of a parish pedagogue in his own person; so that his sister, although still making him useful at odd times, now considers George as pretty well off her hands, whilst his elder brother, Tom, could take an under-gardener's place directly, if he were not too important at home to be spared even for a day.

In short, during the five years that she has ruled at the Shaw cottage, the world has gone well with Hannah Bint. Her cow, her calves, her pigs, her bees, her poultry, have each, in their several ways, thriven and prospered. She has even brought Watch to like butter-milk, as well as strong beer, and has nearly persuaded her father (to whose wants and wishes she is most anxiously attentive) to accept of milk as a substitute for gin. Not but Hannah hath had her enemies as well as her betters. Why should she not? The old woman at the lodge, who always piqued herself on being spiteful, and crying down new ways, foretold from the first she would come to no good, and could not forgive her for falsifying her prediction; and Betty Barnes, the slatternly widow of a tippling farmer, who rented a field, and set up a cow herself, and was universally discarded for insufferable dirt, said all that the wit of an envious woman could devise against Hannah and her Alderney; nay, even Ned Miles, the keeper, her next neighbour, who had whilom held entire sway over the Shaw common, as well as its coppices, grumbled as much as so good-natured and genial a person could grumble, when he found a little girl sharing his dominion, a cow grazing beside his pony, and vulgar cocks and hens hovering around the buck-wheat destined to feed his noble pheasants. Nobody that had been accustomed to see that paragon of keepers, so tall and manly, and pleasant looking, with his merry eye, and his knowing smile, striding gaily along, in his green coat, and his gold-laced hat, with Neptune, his noble Newfoundland dog (a retriever is the sporting word), and his beautiful spaniel Flirt at his heels, could conceive how askew he looked, when he first found Hannah and Watch holding equal reign over his old territory, the Shaw common.

Yes! Hannah hath had her enemies; but they are passing away. The old woman at the lodge is dead, poor creature; and Betty Barnes, having herself taken to tippling, has lost the few friends she once possessed, and looks, luckless wretch, as if she would soon die too! —and the keeper?—why, he is not dead, or like to die; but the change that has taken place there is the most astonishing of all—except, perhaps, the change in Hannah herself.

Few damsels of twelve years old, generally a very pretty age, were less pretty than Hannah Bint. Short and stunted in her figure, thin in face, sharp in feature, with a muddled complexion, wild sunburnt hair, and eyes whose very brightness had in them something startling, over-informed, super-subtle, too clever for her age, —at twelve years old she had quite the air of a little old fairy. Now, at seventeen, matters are mended. Her complexion has cleared; her countenance has developed itself; her figure has shot up into height and lightness, and a sort of rustic grace; her bright, acute eye is softened and sweetened by the womanly wish to please; her hair is trimmed, and curled and brushed, with exquisite neatness; and her whole dress arranged with that nice attention to the becoming, the suitable both in form and texture, which would be called the highest degree of coquetry, if it did not deserve the better name of propriety. Never was such a transmogrification beheld. The lass is really pretty, and Ned Miles has discovered that she is so. There he stands, the rogue, close at her side (for he hath joined her whilst we have been telling her little story, and the milking is over!)—there he stands—holding her milk-pail in one hand, and stroking Watch with the other; whilst she is returning the compliment by patting Neptune's magnificent head. There they stand, as much like lovers as may be; he smiling, and she blushing—he never looking so handsome nor she so pretty in all their lives. There they stand, in blessed forgetfulness of all except each other; as happy a couple as ever trod the earth. There they stand, and one would not disturb them for all the milk and butter in Christendom. I should not wonder if they were fixing the wedding day.

THE FALL OF THE LEAF

November 6th. —The weather is as peaceful to-day, as calm, and as mild, as in early April; and, perhaps, an autumn afternoon and a spring morning do resemble each other more in feeling, and even in appearance, than any two periods of the year. There is in both the same freshness and dewiness of the herbage; the same balmy softness in the air; and the same pure and lovely blue sky, with white fleecy clouds floating across it. The chief difference lies in the absence of flowers, and the presence of leaves. But then the foliage of November is so rich, and glowing, and varied, that it may well supply the place of the gay blossoms of the spring; whilst all the flowers of the field or the garden could never make amends for the want of leaves, —that beautiful and graceful attire in which nature has clothed the rugged forms of trees—the verdant drapery to which the landscape owes its loveliness, and the forests their glory.

If choice must be between two seasons, each so full of

charm, it is at least no bad philosophy to prefer the present good, even whilst looking gratefully back, and hopefully forward, to the past and the future. And of a surety, no fairer specimen of a November day could well be found than this, — a day made to wander

> By yellow commons and birch-shaded hollows,
> And hedgerows bordering unfrequented lanes;

nor could a prettier country be found for our walk than this shady and yet sunny Berkshire, where the scenery, without rising into grandeur or breaking into wildness, is so peaceful, so cheerful, so varied, and so thoroughly English.

We must bend our steps towards the water side, for I have a message to leave at Farmer Riley's: and sooth to say, it is no unpleasant necessity; for the road thither is smooth and dry, retired, as one likes a country walk to be, but not too lonely, which women never like; leading past the Loddon—the bright, brimming, transparent Loddon—a fitting mirror for this bright blue sky, and terminating at one of the prettiest and most comfortable farmhouses in the neighbourhood.

How beautiful the lane is to-day, decorated with a thousand colours! The brown road, and the rich verdure that borders it, strewed with the pale yellow leaves of the elm, just beginning to fall; hedgerows glowing with long wreaths of the bramble in every variety of purplish red; and overhead the unchanged green of the fir, contrasting with the spotted sycamore, the tawny beech, and the dry sere leaves of the oak, which rustle as the light wind passes through them; a few common hardy yellow flowers (for yellow is the common colour of flowers, whether wild or cultivated, as blue is the rare one), flowers of many sorts, but almost of one tint, still blowing in spite of the season, and ruddy berries glowing through all. How very beautiful is the lane!

And how pleasant is this hill where the road widens, with the group of cattle by the wayside, and George Hearn, the little post-boy, trundling his hoop at full speed, making all the better haste in his work, because he cheats himself into thinking it play! And how beautiful, again, is this patch of common at the hilltop with the clear pool, where Martha Pither's children, —elves of three, and four, and five years old, —without any distinction of sex in their sunburnt faces and tattered drapery, are dipping up water in their little homely cups shining with cleanliness, and a small brown pitcher with the lip broken, to fill that great kettle, which, when it is filled, their united strength will never be able to lift! They are quite a group for a painter, with their rosy cheeks, and chubby hands, and round merry faces; and the low cottage in the background, peeping out of its vine leaves and china roses, with Martha at the door, tidy, and comely, and smiling, preparing the potatoes for the pot, and watching the progress of dipping and filling that useful utensil, completes the picture.

But we must go on. No time for more sketches in these

short days. It is getting cold too. We must proceed in our walk. Dash is showing us the way and beating the thick double hedgerow that runs along the side of the meadows, at a rate that indicates game astir, and causes the leaves to fly as fast as an east-wind after a hard frost. Ah! a pheasant! a superb cock pheasant! Nothing is more certain than Dash's questing, whether in a hedgerow or covert, for a better spaniel never went into the field; but I fancied that it was a hare afoot, and was almost as much startled to hear the whirring of those splendid wings, as the princely bird himself would have been at the report of a gun. Indeed, I believe that the way in which a pheasant goes off, does sometimes make young sportsmen a little nervous, (they don't own it very readily, but the observation may be relied on nevertheless), until they get as it were broken in to the sound; and then that grand and sudden burst of wing becomes as pleasant to them as it seems to be to Dash, who is beating the hedgerow with might and main, and giving tongue louder, and sending the leaves about faster than ever—very proud of finding the pheasant, and perhaps a little angry with me for not shooting it; at least looking as if he would be angry if I were a man; for Dash is a dog of great sagacity, and has doubtless not lived four years in the sporting world without making the discovery, that although gentlemen do shoot, ladies do not.

The Loddon at last! the beautiful Loddon! and the bridge, where every one stops, as by instinct, to lean over the rails, and gaze a moment on a landscape of surpassing loveliness, —the fine grounds of the Great House, with their magnificent groups of limes, and firs, and poplars grander than ever poplars were; the green meadows opposite, studded with oaks and elms; the clear winding river; the mill with its picturesque old buildings, bounding the scene; all glowing with the rich colouring of autumn, and harmonised by the soft beauty of the clear blue sky, and the delicious calmness of the hour. The very peasant whose daily path it is, cannot cross that bridge without a pause.

But the day is wearing fast, and it grows colder and colder. I really think it will be a frost. After all, spring is the pleasantest season, beautiful as this scenery is. We must get on. Down that broad yet shadowy lane, between the park, dark with evergreens and dappled with deer, and the meadows where sheep, and cows, and horses are grazing under the tall elms; that lane, where the wild bank, clothed with fern, and tufted with furze, and crowned by rich berried thorn, and thick shining holly on the one side, seems to vie in beauty with the picturesque old paling, the bright laurels, and the plumy cedars, on the other; —down that shady lane, until the sudden turn brings us to an opening where four roads meet, where a noble avenue turns down to the Great House; where the village church rears its modest spire from amidst its venerable yew trees: and where, embosomed in orchards and gardens, and backed by barns and ricks, and all the wealth of the farmyard, stands the spacious and comfortable abode of good Farmer Riley, —the end and object of our walk.

And in happy time the message is said and the answer given, for this beautiful mild day is edging off into a dense frosty evening; the leaves of the elm and the linden in the old avenue are quivering and vibrating and fluttering in the air, and at length falling crisply on the earth, as if Dash were beating for pheasants in the tree-tops; the sun gleams dimly through the fog, giving little more of light and heat than his fair sister the lady moon; —I don't know a more disappointing person than a cold sun; and I am beginning to wrap my cloak closely round me, and to calculate the distance to my own fireside, recanting all the way my praises of November, and longing for the showery, flowery April, as much as if I were a half-chilled butterfly, or a dahlia knocked down by the frost.

Ah, dear me! what a climate this is, that one cannot keep in the same mind about it for half an hour together! I wonder, by the way, whether the fault is in the weather, which Dash does not seem to care for, or in me? If I should happen to be wet through in a shower next spring, and should catch myself longing for autumn, that would settle the question.

Bilingual Classics

双语经典

——

我们的村庄

〔英国〕玛丽·拉塞尔·米特福德 著

张方方 译

译林出版社

目 录

序

安妮·萨克雷·里奇[①]

一

米特福德小姐有许多值得称道的文学作品，数量之多足以令这篇序文的作者对那些依然记得她作品的人感到愧疚，因为在和米特福德小姐本人既不熟识也未曾谋面的情况下，仅凭坊间的传闻她就斗胆提笔，介绍起《我们的村庄》的作者。然而，那个朴素又和善的身影是如此鲜活，那个"如钟声一样"的嗓音是如此清亮，它传达着热情而友好的问候，以至于她几乎难以相信，她们之间的相识仅仅存在于一个假想的世界里。

对于那些不再期盼来日，而开始怀念旧时光的人来说，没有比读我们可能曾亲眼见过或者当面有过交谈的男女主人公的回忆录和趣闻逸事更让人愉快的了。我们读着读着，就会被引入某个美好的旧日世界——就像杜莫里耶先生在

---

① 安妮·萨克雷·里奇（Anne Thackeray Ritchie，1837—1919），英国女作家，《名利场》作者威廉·萨克雷（William Makepeace Thackeray，1811—1863）之女。（译者注。以下除特别说明，均为译注）

《彼得·以贝特森》①中所描述的一样——在那个世界里，我们，和我们的故交旧友，重新回到青年时代，再度变得年轻，活力十足，满怀憧憬。那里有我们爱的人，还有我们记得的人。音乐响起，我们又一次翩翩起舞，开怀大笑，在田野里欢呼雀跃；我们的父母也再度变得年轻，也在开怀大笑。或许时不时地还会有某个老友，同样是活力十足、满怀希望的样子，突然从书里冒出来，开始和我们交谈，或是写来了一封信；往日的情景和声音又一次浮现在眼前，我们拥有现在，我们也拥有昨天，两者和谐融洽，毫不违和。对于读过米特福德小姐回忆录的那一代文人学子，有多少这样熟悉的场景和名字会一而再，再而三地在眼前浮现！这当中一定少不了她传记的作者哈内斯先生②，他总是受到朋友们的一致赞扬。坎布尔夫人、萨特里斯夫人、查尔斯·奥斯顿·考林斯提到他的时候总是满怀敬意和深情。我一度认为，他们在说起他的名字时，都带着一种特别的音调。他并非我们最亲密的朋友，但在我的印象中那是两个多么熟悉的身影啊，哈内斯先生和他的妹妹兼管家哈内斯小姐，他们总是沿着繁忙的肯辛顿大街一起走着。这对兄妹就像是从某本书里走出来的人物，脸上总是带着和善的表情，过着简单而注重精神追求的生活；他们被身边那

---

① 乔治·杜莫里耶（George Louis Palmella Busson du Maurier，1834—1896），法籍英国漫画家、作家，《彼得·以贝特森》（*Peter Ibbetson*，1891）是他的第一部小说。

② 威廉·哈内斯（William Harness，1790—1869），英国牧师、作家，米特福德的挚友。在米特福德去世后，他不顾外界的反对，完成了《米特福德小姐传》（*The Life of Mary Russell Mitford*，1870）。

么多有趣和浪漫的事情打动，对那么多遭受苦难的人深怀同情。我记得他头发灰白，脸上总是带着微笑。他个子不高，走起路来还有些跛；哈内斯小姐也是个小个子，总是仰望着她周围的世界，她圆圆的脸庞显得很和善，浓密的睫毛下一双眼睛闪闪发光。玛丽·米特福德与她的朋友们在一起时确实非常幸福，就像她与自己的至亲在一起时非常不幸一样。

尽管有诸多的不如意，米特福德小姐的生活中还是充满了美和喜悦。对于她来说，物质享受的缺失可以借由热烈的情感、满腔的热情和对父母的爱来弥补。她长年的坚持与忍耐，对父母的孝顺与虔敬，实在让人望尘莫及！是她那充满爱意的心灵让她安享天年，而且，她在自己对生活莫名的热爱中找到了慰藉。她丝毫没有那种会将和谐毁于一旦的躁动难安的情绪；她坚持始终如一，动机单纯且一致，这就是她的魅力所在，也正是查尔斯·金斯利[1]不吝溢美之词，称之为"一心无二"的精神。她热爱她的家，她的树，她周围的小路和公地。她热爱她的朋友。书籍和鲜花是她生活中真实而重要的陪伴，总是在生活带给她烦忧时，让她得到安慰和排遣。"我可以很客观地说，"她曾在给巴雷特小姐[2]的信中写道，"从我还是一个小姑娘的时

---

① 查尔斯·金斯利（Charles Kingsley，1819—1875），英国牧师、大学教授、社会改革家、历史学家、作家，著有小说《水孩子》（*The Water Babies*，1863）。

② 伊丽莎白·巴雷特·勃朗宁（Elizabeth Barrett Browning，1806—1861），英国著名女诗人，玛丽·米特福德的挚友。

候起，我就从未（尽管有些年生活貌似比较宽裕）有过不为金钱烦恼的时刻——这种烦扰无时无刻不在压迫着我的神经，晚上入睡前萦绕在心头的，早上醒来所要面对的，都是这种无休止的折磨和困扰，我感到自己已经不堪重负，几乎要被压垮了。"

玛丽·拉塞尔·米特福德出生于一七八七年十二月十六日，是家里唯一的孩子。她的父母都家境良好，母亲是家产的继承人，父亲来自北方的米特福德家族。她形容自己是"一个瘦弱的孩子，一头浓密的鬈发使她看上去就像是自己那个大娃娃的孪生姐妹"。她三岁的时候就会认字，而在她几乎还不认字的时候，她就已经把珀西民谣①全背会了。许多年后，她曾这样描述当初学习这些她所钟爱的民谣的情形：那是在一间摆满了书的早餐室里，地上铺着暖和的土耳其地毯，壁炉里烧着明亮的炉火，屋子里摆着安乐椅，窗外是一个开满了花的花园——开着紫罗兰、忍冬和石竹。让人为之动容的是，尽管她一生艰难困苦，但她的路上总是（名副其实地）缀满了鲜花，自始至终，对于花的热爱总是能带给她安慰和激励。在最难过的时候，芬芳美丽的天竺葵，她最爱的花，尽管短暂易逝，却总是能给她激励，帮助她重新振作起来。即使在母亲去世的时候，她也从她们共同照料的花草中找到了慰藉，并最终将

---

① 指托马斯·珀西（Thomas Percy，1729—1811）编著的《古诗拾遗》（*Reliques of Ancient English Poetry*，1765），包含一百八十首英格兰和苏格兰民谣，甫一出版便受到广泛关注，启发了包括柯勒律治和华兹华斯在内的许多浪漫主义诗人。

它们描绘进她的文字里，宣泄内心的情感。

　　一七九八年她被送往汉斯广场 22 号去读书，受教于一位叫作圣昆汀的夫人。那似乎是一家相当不错的学校，玛丽在那里学习了竖琴和天文，她的文学爱好也得到了鼓励。那些求学的年轻小姐穿着牧羊女的服装，会在老师的教导下接触很多复杂的活动，但是她从未在穿着牧羊女服装的学习中有过特别的建树。她更大的成功来源于她在文学上的努力，她的一篇"关于气球"的作文得到了广泛好评。她在一八〇二年回到了家里。"尽管身材、长相都不突出，但她看上去绝非平庸之辈。"哈内斯先生说。他对她的描述相当可爱，"绝非寻常小孩，她甜美的微笑，风趣的谈话，积极乐观的生活态度，温柔的嗓音，为她赢得了诸多朋友（无论长幼）的爱和赞美"。哈内斯先生主要是用米特福德小姐自己信中的话来讲述她的故事，读者在阅读的过程中，可以追随她心绪的演进和变化，而这些心绪正是她真正的历史：童年时的刻苦勤奋，年轻时的意气风发，后半生与日俱增的忧虑，愈加成熟的判断，偶尔考验她乐观天性的绝望和恐惧，以及与所有这些相伴的、从未真正抛弃过她的、纯真而执着的对未来的憧憬。她坚忍顽强的品格来源于她的父亲，那位屡教不改的老斯金普尔[①]。"总的来说我到哪儿都很开心。"她在年轻的时候写道。后来她写道："我在热爱和赞美中找

────────────

① 老斯金普尔（Harold Skimpole），查尔斯·狄更斯（Charles Dickens，1812—1870）的小说《荒凉山庄》（*Bleak House*，1852）中的人物，自私贪婪，善于钻营牟利。

到了巨大的乐趣，这是让我得以在冰霜和暴风雨中幸存的法宝。"她的确曾在某个地方加上了一句问话，"你可曾注意到过去的欢愉胜过新近的太多太多？"她如是问道。

她在与友人的通信中会不自觉地描述自己英俊潇洒的父亲，和相貌平平、忍辱负重的母亲。"医生[①]举止随和、自然、热情，显得相当直率，"哈内斯先生说，"然而，他遇事总是随心所欲，随时准备为了一时的权益，做出有悖真诚的举动。他不仅挥霍无度，而且嗜好赌博。他妻子的大笔财产，他女儿的，还有他自己的家产，都在短得不可思议的时间里被他挥霍一空，但从未听到他的妻子或是女儿对他的行为进行抱怨，她们对他的爱戴似乎也不曾减损。"

米特福德小姐那两万英镑的故事在女作家的离奇故事中可谓独一无二。米特福德医生不仅花光了妻子的财产，还被迫放弃原来那个遍布鲜花和铺着土耳其地毯的舒适之家，让一家人搬进了布莱克福瑞尔大桥附近的一座小屋，在这种情况之下，他决定在女儿十岁生日的时候送给她一张昂贵的彩票券作为礼物。米特福德小姐对 2224 这个号码情有独钟，因为这四个数字相加之和正好是 10。这组数字最后中了两万英镑的头奖，这笔奖金让这个家重新过上了相对富裕的生活。米特福德医生随即就盖起了一座体面的新房，他称之为伯特勒姆大屋，房子所在的地方原本有一座漂亮的老农舍，他事先就找人给拉倒了。他还找人定

---

① 指玛丽的父亲乔治·米特福德，他是一名执业医生。

做了一套印有米特福德家族徽章的甜品餐具；米特福德太太添置了一辆马车，她还订阅了一项流动图书馆的服务。

她当时为女儿借书的清单现在依然能看到，每个月大约五十五册，大都是些没有多大价值的消遣类读物:《维琴察》《水手的友情和战士的爱情》《克莱伦缇娜》《罗伯特与阿黛拉》《维尔蒙伯爵》《三个西班牙人》和《德·克利福德》（四卷本），还有诸如此类的种种。

接下来的两三年日子过得足够风光，全家人过着每年三四千英镑开销的生活。他们热情好客，家里有用人、马车，添置了不少画和家具，还宴请宾朋。科贝特[①]算得上他们的密友。很自然地米特福德医生花了一大笔钱买彩票，但没有获得任何回报。

家里的女士们把他投机赌博的行为看成天经地义的事，实际上他心血来潮时所做的任何事都被看作天经地义的事，她们只是恳求他至少应该到那些体面的俱乐部里去。他经常不在家。他的女儿试图用盛开的风信子劝诱他回家。"它们多么渴望能再见到他！"她说，"每天到雷丁去的马车都空载而归，它们是多么失望！到雷丁的驿站车夫已经习惯了总是被他们家的马车拦下。"后来她又告诉他报春花的期盼，但不管是风信子还是报春花都无法让医生远离牌桌。最后，杜鹃花和映山红也开了，但它们同样对他毫无吸引力。

米特福德小姐后来不止一次被送到伦敦求学，到圣昆

---

① 威廉·科贝特（William Cobbett，1763—1835），英国作家、记者。

汀那里和别处的学校。她去看过戏剧表演，去过威斯敏斯特大厅，她见到了自己心目中的英雄查尔斯·詹姆斯·福克斯[1]，并有幸目睹了他被人搀扶上马的情形。她很开心见到了罗米利先生，但她最喜欢的人物是惠特布雷德先生。[2]"你知道我一直是个热情洋溢的人，"她写道，"但是现在我对这位卓越人物的敬仰竟然无以言表。"她说到他的声音，"即使是在说一门不为人知的语言，她也能听得欣喜若狂"！她专门为他写了一首十四行诗，"即兴之作，因听到惠特布雷德先生在威斯敏斯特大厅宣称自己有信心流芳后世而作"。

> 你壮怀激烈渴望声名远扬，
>
> 你热情睿智点燃了希望之光；
>
> 只要英国人依旧向往纯净，
>
> 只要自由还有一方立足之境，
>
> 历史的缪斯定会为你做证，
>
> 你的不朽之名必定万世流芳！

她写给家里的信中多次提及当世的名人——所有人都认为谢里丹的滑稽戏愚蠢至极，欧佩夫人被誉为一颗冉冉

---

① 查尔斯·詹姆斯·福克斯（Charles James Fox，1749—1806），英国资深政治家、辉格党成员。

② 塞缪尔·罗米利（Samuel Romilly，1757—1818），英国司法改革家；塞缪尔·惠特布雷德（Samuel Whitbread，1764—1815），英国政治家、议会议员。

升起的文坛新星，等等。[①]

奥斯汀小姐[②]过去常常到汉斯广场 23 号去，米特福德小姐曾一直待在 22 号，但不是在同一时期。米特福德夫人在奥斯汀小姐还是个孩子的时候就认识她了。她后来对奥斯汀小姐的印象难免带有偏见和作为母亲的嫉妒，这并非不可原谅，但是玛丽·米特福德则总是怀着最大的热情爱戴简·奥斯汀。她从伦敦给母亲写信的时候，总是滔滔不绝地讲起发生在她身边的每一件事，她遇见的每一个人，每一本书，还有每一次经历——在布朗普顿享用的优雅晚餐，希腊式的灯，巴克先生的俊朗，普拉默先生的平淡无奇，还有她的紫色长裙被弄坏的事。

米特福德夫人给她的回信中描述的是雷丁的节庆活动，"在瓦尔皮医生家中享用可口的晚餐，沃曼夫人和皮科克小姐都在，议员 J. 辛普森先生也来了；晚餐相当不错，两道主菜和一道替菜，汤撤下去后上了一只羊腿"。米特福德夫人会把她出去吃的每顿饭的菜单都详细地跟女儿讲一遍。

一八〇六年，米特福德医生带着当时快要十九岁的女儿回到了北方，走访亲戚。他们受到了来自特里维廉和斯温伯恩家族的祖父母，还有现今的奥格尔和米特福德家族

---

① 理查德·谢里丹（Richard Sheridan，1751—1816），爱尔兰剧作家、讽刺作家，代表作有《造谣学校》（*The School for Scandal*，1777）；欧佩夫人（Amelia Opie，1769—1853），英国小说家。

② 简·奥斯汀（Jane Austen，1775—1817），英国小说家，代表作有《理智与情感》（*Sense and Sensibility*，1811）、《傲慢与偏见》（*Pride and Prejudice*，1813）、《爱玛》（*Emma*，1816）等。

的款待。他们在约翰·斯温伯恩爵士家的湖中垂钓，参观了阿尼克城堡。米特福德小姐在到达阿尼克之前一直将前面的头发卷在卷发带中，因而尽管有三十英里的行程，但她到达的时候，装束和衣裙都纹丝不乱。他们坐下一起用餐，席上高朋满座，所有的食物"当然"（她不无惊讶地说道）都是用盘子端上来的。可怜的玛丽因为父亲突然不见而兴致大减，米特福德医生习惯了不分场合和地点的意气用事，完全不顾及给别人造成的不便。虽然当时人们在北方特地安排了欢迎他的聚会，而且他的女儿也指望着在他的陪伴下回家（当时人们是通过邮寄，而不是随身将车票从纽卡斯尔带到伦敦），但是米特福德医生还是在某个早晨留下口信，说他已经动身前往雷丁去参加选举了，但他根本就没有必要出席。这是他女儿人生中第一次，显然也是唯一一次，向他表示了抗议。"奥格尔先生大发雷霆；您只有立刻回来才能得到他的谅解！我恳求您回来，我希望您能像妈妈那样顾及体面，赶紧回来。我绝不相信我的父亲，我亲爱的父亲，会在离家如此遥远的地方将我抛下不管！每个人都目瞪口呆。"米特福德医生最终被劝了回来，回到了诺森伯兰郡接他的女儿。

常伴女儿左右的米特福德医生一定让他正直善良的女儿看待生活的方式发生了微妙的变化。她如此崇拜自己的父亲，肯定很快就习惯于把他的美好言辞当作美好的行动了，并不顾良心的不安坦然接受了他的自满。她给人的印象是个情感热烈的女人，有着强烈的是非观念。然而，可怜的人儿，在她的日常经验中，从未见到过那些未曾成就伟业但同样能尽职尽责的人；而她也从不指望那些不会慷慨陈词的人会有正直、勇敢和自我反省的品格。当时，高调的言论受到人们追捧，高调的生活被人们视作浪漫。现在我们的生活中依然有它们的身影，但人们不再崇尚那样的生活，对于米特福德医生之流，人们有了一套不一样的说辞。[①]这基本可以解释为什么米特福德小姐对她称之为"冷漠自私的"一代会有那样的判断，她对他们的看法实在是有失公允。

二

作为作家所要付出的代价之一就是，他们很容易把头脑中形成的生动形象和鲜活的画面太过当真，会把想象误认为现实。在讲故事的时候这自然很好，与任何人都无涉；然而，在真实的历史中，尤其是在一个人自己的历史中，这种能力很容易因循个人的经历幻化出一些妖魔鬼怪和噩梦；当一个人只顾着和臆想中的魔鬼搏斗时，那些真实而美好的东西就会在不经意间从身边溜走，最美好的现实生活反而被忽略了……

但是，毕竟玛丽·拉塞尔·米特福德一生中大量的时间都花在采集无花果和应对艰难困苦上，因而和许多人相比，她很少沉迷于想象中的烦恼。

---

① 如今，在听到狮子吼叫时，人们更倾向于发笑而不是羡慕。我想，恐怕是因为人们现在更欣赏的是猫咪和小羊那样的叫声，这种趋势越来越明显。（安妮·萨克雷·里奇注）

当她的第一本诗集出版的时候，她才二十三岁，因而我们在她的信中读到，她恳请父亲不要删减任何她献给他的诗。她说，除非是他极度谦逊，否则找不到任何理由删减其中的诗作。她这样说，不仅是出于女儿对父亲的喜爱，更是出于一个诗人的敏感。尽管已经有作品问世，但我们这位年轻的女诗人表现得相当谦虚；她感到自己和克雷布①相比（简·奥斯汀可能也会这么做），就如同"一线烛火要面对一轮太阳的光华"。随后，她居然收到了出版商寄来的五十九英镑的账单，她倍感震惊，因为这实在是一笔不小的数额！米特福德小姐在接下来的一封信里提醒父亲，税款尚未支付，而在此后的一封来信中，有人说可以选一幅医生收藏的画作来支付税款。当时医生一直待在伦敦，整日吃喝玩乐，在外逍遥。大家都在猜测弗朗西斯·波蒂特爵士②会不会被关到伦敦塔里去。③"哦，我亲爱的爸爸，我多么羡慕你能在这样有趣的时刻，处在信息的源头地！我甚至羡慕波蒂特夫人，她竟能有这样的机会来展示我们女性的英雄气概！"女儿如此写道，而她只能在家里

① 乔治·克雷布（George Crabbe，1754—1832），英国诗人、牧师，他擅长以写实的手法描绘乡村的日常生活，其诗歌多以英雄双韵体（heroic couplets）写成。

② 弗朗西斯·波蒂特爵士（Sir Francis Burdett，1770—1844），英国政治改革家，因与议会发生争执，1810 年被关进伦敦塔，后在议会休会期间被释放。

③ 我们在温布尔登的郊区小花园中有一段老树篱的残余，那原本是长在弗朗西斯·波蒂特爵士居住的庄园里的，位于后厨的花园里。据说当年他光荣被捕，被人带走时，正在那个花园的小径上散步。（安妮·萨克雷·里奇注）

面对怒气冲冲的税务官……反正不管怎样，账单还是付清了，家里的各项安排又恢复如初。

除了给自己家里人写信，米特福德小姐很早就开始给另外一个人写信。那人就是威廉·埃尔福德爵士[1]，她向他描述自己的出游和冒险经历，她参观塔维斯多克大宅的情形，当时她的好朋友佩里一家在那里接待了她。佩里先生是《早晨纪事报》的主编，他和他美丽的太太几乎结交了当时所有最有趣的人。在此，我们又一次看到，这位作家的亲身经历为她笔下的文字做了很好的诠释。她对伦敦人和伦敦社会最初的认识来自切舍姆街区的一所小房子，住在那里的是她父亲的老朋友弗雷德里克·艾略特夫人和佩里小姐，也就是米特福德小姐那两位朋友的女儿们。她们和一群很出名又很有趣的人构成了一个社交中心，他们都充满了善意，不需要太多刻意的安排，便很自然地就聚在了一起，这是一种无法言明的默契。他们彼此能很快地心领神会，能体贴入微地互相挑剔（我不得不使用这种让人匪夷所思的字眼），而这些都是成为好客主人的必备品质。现在人们寻求的是一种截然不同的标准，过来敲门的是成长起来的一代新人，而房门后面那些曾经的峥嵘岁月已然倾颓，像邓肯王[2]一样僵硬无比了。

米特福德小姐还有其他的休闲娱乐活动，比如她去参

---

① 威廉·埃尔福德爵士（Sir William Elford，1749—1837），英国银行家、政治家、业余画家。

② 邓肯王（Duncan I, 1001—1040），苏格兰国王，莎士比亚悲剧《麦克白》中邓肯王的原型。

加了庆祝维多利亚大捷①的游乐会；她还有幸见到了斯塔尔夫人②，斯塔尔夫人是佩里夫妇很要好的朋友。"她在花园中，如同公主一样被人们追随着。"她说，毫不掩饰自己的惊奇、快乐和痴迷。她带着年轻人的欣喜开始阅读彭斯③的诗歌，并不吝笔墨地论述他那汪洋恣肆的想象，他的丰富多变，随后她给出了一个十分中肯的评价。"那种世上罕有的被称作天才的人物，"她说，"他们身上真正稀有的特点不就是丰富多变吗？——丰富多变和活泼谐趣。"后来她接着说到两本刚刚出版、据称为莫利夫人④所作的广受赞誉的小说——《傲慢与偏见》和《理智与情感》。

她依然从伯特勒姆大屋往外写信，然而她愉快的闲谈不断地被写给父亲的信打断，那些信件虽更为紧急却不那么令人开心。律师事务所的职员又不断地送来通知与警告，

<hr>

① 维多利亚大捷（Battle of Vittoria），指 1813 年 6 月 21 日，英国、葡萄牙和西班牙的联军在威灵顿公爵阿瑟·韦尔斯利（Arthur Wellesley，1769—1852）的指挥下在西班牙的维多利亚盆地打败了约瑟夫·波拿巴（Joseph Bonaparte，1768—1844）率领的法国军队。这次大捷奠定了联军在半岛战争（Peninsular War，1807—1814）中的胜局，彻底击溃了拿破仑在西班牙的势力。

② 斯塔尔夫人（Mme. de Staël，1766—1817），法国作家、历史学家，受到拿破仑的迫害长期流亡海外。她的作品洋溢着激情和鲜明的个人主义色彩，是法国浪漫主义的先驱。

③ 罗伯特·彭斯（Robert Burns，1759—1796），苏格兰诗人，一生致力于收集整理苏格兰民谣，为后世留下了大量经典诗篇。

④ 莫利夫人（Lady Morley），指莫利伯爵约翰·帕克（John Parker，1772—1840）的第二任妻子弗朗西斯·塔伯特（Frances Talbot，1782—1857)，她是位业余艺术家，也是社交界的名流。因《傲慢与偏见》和《理智与情感》当时是匿名出版，有传言认为她就是那位匿名作者。

税务官也开始过来找麻烦。米特福德医生依旧跟之前一样，没有留下任何地址，因而她只能把信都寄到"星星办公室"（父亲原来的通信地址）去碰碰运气。"妈妈也送上最温柔的爱"，无一例外，每封信都以这样一句结尾。

尽管家中的女士对这位父亲不乏崇敬和溢美之词，但哈内斯先生在提到这位英俊的医生时却很不客气！他对他的行事做派、道德观念、自我为重，以及夸夸其谈的表现都颇有微词。"这个老东西从来不向朋友们透露任何信息。他们对他和他的那些丑事的了解，不管他是想让他们信以为真还是一笑置之，都是他不小心说漏了嘴吐露出来的。"

一八一四年，米特福德小姐依旧和她的父母住在伯特勒姆大屋，但家里已经发生了变化；仆人们都走了，石子路上长出了青苔，草坪无人打理，已经成了牧场，灌木丛成了枝杈横生的树丛，房子还算新，但已经成了"部分有人居住的废墟，而且还有一桩官司悬在他们的头上"。与此同时，美国传来了一些让她感到振奋的消息。她的诗集的两个版本都已付梓并且开始售卖。那首《女性角色的叙事诗》大获成功。"所有有感知心和判别力的人，一定都希望您能葆有健康和闲暇，去完成您的计划。"出版商们在那段美好的日子里为她送上样书的时候，如是写道……

这一时期发生了许多大事。战事不断，捷报频传，拿破仑正一步步地走向圣赫勒拿岛[①]；伦敦城成了一片欢乐的海洋，处处张灯结彩，歌舞升平。对于玛丽·米特福德

---

① 圣赫勒拿岛（St. Helena），南大西洋中的一个小岛。在滑铁卢战败被俘后，拿破仑被流放于此。

来说，《威弗利》①这本小说的问世，是和波旁王朝复辟同样重要的事件。她确信《威弗利》的作者就是沃尔特·司各特爵士，但她认为《占星人》②的作者另有其人。她满怀着对书和文学真诚而又浪漫的热爱，一门心思地沉迷于其中。到了一八一六年的春天，她甚至更为欣喜。米特福德医生或许身无分文，他们父女之间的纠葛或许又在老调重弹，但是这个迷人的季节已经到来，万物重焕生机，又一次变得美丽而丰饶。灌木林中的报春花像地毯一样铺了一地，其中还点缀着三色堇和野生的草莓花，酢浆草和银莲花娇嫩的花朵在树林中闪耀夺目，黄花九轮草为草地披上了亮丽的彩衣……当然，没有人比米特福德小姐更适合眼前这个世界，也没有人比她更懂得如何欣赏和享受它的美，而她曾经在某个场合说过，她唯一的愿望就是让自己变得美丽，这样她就完全满足了。

三

大多数人的一生都可以分成三个阶段，当我们阅读米特福德小姐的个人历史时，发现她也不例外。早年的第一阶段是热情洋溢的，她有着自己的期许和不受约束的判断，

---

① 《威弗利》（*Waverley*，1814），沃尔特·司各特（Sir Walter Scott，1771—1832）创作的第一本历史小说，于1814年匿名出版，开创了西方历史小说的先河。
② 《占星人》（*The Astrologer*，1815），又名《盖伊·曼纳林》（*Guy Mannering*），司各特的第二部小说，于1815年匿名出版。

她那时的衣着古板老旧，遣词造句也是一样的风格；接下来的第二阶段，她的生活被切实的工作和严肃的任务占据，她要赡养两个孩子一样的父母，尽管他们都一把年纪了，却依然处于被人照顾的阶段。米特福德小姐的最后一个阶段是回顾性的，尽管身体每况愈下，但她依旧勇敢地坚持着，她相当笃定，自己艰苦付出换来的成就是当之无愧的；除了悲剧在舞台上的成功给她带来的名望，我们发现她也为自己赢得了在外界读者和作家心目中应得的地位。

从某些方面来看，十九世纪早期从事写作的女性是适逢其时的。一卷诗抄，一本小游记，几次茶会，屋角的一把竖琴，还有斜戴在一边的羽毛帽，似乎已经足以引领潮流、激发灵感了。她们有脚凳可以把缎面鞋搁在上面歇脚，她们有仰慕者和致颂词者来讨她们的欢心，最重要的是她们享有那种独特的志得意满的感觉（除了几个人所共知的例外），那是我们这个时代独独没有的。我们热切，我们大胆，我们独树一帜，但我们从未有过志得意满的感觉。或许她们都是玩偶，但她们是生活在玩偶之家的玩偶；而我们则是无家可归的游魂，我们来去都被裹挟在几张报纸之中，手中捧着火光闪烁的煤油灯，并借由这点微光寻找属于我们自己的一片天地。可怜这些忧郁的魂灵！我们不再属于旧世界！新世界尚未为我们而来。甚至连格莱斯顿先生①都不允许我们进入下议院；地理协会将我们拒之门外，皇家艺术学院也是一样。然而，谁又能说是他们把门

①　威廉·尤尔特·格莱斯顿（William Ewart Gladstone，1809—1898），英国政治家，曾四度出任英国首相。

槛抬得太高了呢！有那么一两个幸运儿，她们单独被出版业的天使带上了狭小的祭坛和塔楼，似乎可以高枕无忧了；但是，大多数勤苦的知识女性"感恩着点滴所得，准备着去迎接更多"。难道她们不能在绝望的时刻畅想一下，假设自己早出生半个世纪，将会有怎样的人生际遇？

米特福德小姐尽管有诸多的不如意（据说她曾说过，她宁愿当一个洗衣工而不是文学女性），但她当时拥有的机会当今没有几个女性能获得。当你尝试着阅读祖辈们喜爱的悲剧时，只顾着赞叹他们的品位如何可靠，却不知《黎恩济》[①]当时售出了四千册，上演了四十五场。曾经一度米特福德小姐有两部悲剧同时在舞台上排演，一出在考文特花园，另一出在德鲁里剧院，查尔斯·肯布尔和麦克雷迪[②]为了演出她的剧目还发生了争执。难道你们没有读过汉娜·摩尔或者乔安娜·贝利[③]的作品获得成功时类似的报道吗？热情的观众鼓掌欢呼，就连男人都感动到落泪。[④]

《朱利安》是米特福德小姐第一部被搬上舞台的剧目。一八二三年，该剧在考文特花园上演，那年她三十六岁。

---

① 《黎恩济》（*Rienzi*, 1828），米特福德创作的一部五幕历史剧，故事取材于爱德华·吉本（Edward Gibbon, 1737—1794）的《罗马帝国衰亡史》（*The History of the Decline and Fall of the Roman Empire*, 1788）。

② 查尔斯·肯布尔（Charles Kemble, 1775—1854）和麦克雷迪（William Charles Macready, 1793—1873），均为英国演员，两人都出演过多部莎翁剧作，是名噪一时的舞台剧演员。

③ 汉娜·摩尔（Hannah More, 1745—1833），英国作家、慈善家；乔安娜·贝利（Joanna Baillie, 1762—1851），苏格兰剧作家、诗人。

④ 根据汉娜·摩尔的《回忆录》第 124 页。（安妮·萨克雷·里奇注）

麦克雷迪担当主角。"如果能连演九天，"米特福德小姐在写给麦克雷迪的信中说，"将是对肯布尔先生的完美反驳。他的名言是'没有哪个演员能单独撑起整场演出'。我们的剧中除了美丽的阿方索（富特小姐饰演），就只有朱利安了，唯一且仅有的主角。我们对他的操劳和善心是怎样感恩戴德，让他自己去想吧。"[①]

　　让她倍感失望的是，《朱利安》在第八天停演了，但是她已经投身于另外一部——几部——悲剧的创作中了。她迫切地需要钱，因为她供稿的那家杂志的编辑已经跑路，还欠着她五十英镑。查尔斯·肯布尔和麦克雷迪随后又发生了一些难堪和莫名其妙的争吵，这不仅拖延了她的悲剧上演，还大大影响了可怜的米特福德小姐的神经和收益。她获得了一丝安慰。她说，她的父亲，部分是因为不忍心看到可怕的责任感和权力欲对于她身心的压迫，最终下定决心要去试一试，看看能否亲自找到什么差事，来减轻一点家庭的重担。米特福德医生鼓起勇气做出这般英勇的决定实在是好事一桩。"每年家里微薄的收入如果能增加两百甚至一百英镑，再加上我，只要笔耕不辍总能想办法挣到一点，这样就能卸下我心头的部分负担，这样的重担我简直不知道该如何向你描述……即使是《朱利安》也是

①　我们在麦克雷迪的日记中找到了与此相关的一则，他的记录没有太多客套。《朱利安》在三月十五日上演，只能算是小小的成功。考文特花园剧院已经不再那么支持包含道德角色的剧目了。女作家在献词中对我大加感谢和赞赏，但是演出没有给观众留下什么印象，很快就被忘记了。"（安妮·萨克雷·里奇注）

在不容我有片刻喘息的焦虑压力下写成的……"因而她总是要动情地多想想这些让人愉快的前景。接着,我们在她写给威廉·埃尔福德爵士的下一封信中读到,她亲爱的父亲,"秉着天赐的乐观心态,依旧指望我来苦苦撑持,我想,谋差事这档子事,他连问都没问,尽管我巴不得他快点找,但也不会去催促;我倒是更愿意在剧院里再试试运气"。

米特福德小姐不止一次地写信给她的委托人,请求他卖掉自己剩余的那一丁点儿财产,有一次她在信中写道:"我亲爱的父亲,许多年来,一直缺乏远见,现在依然是个爱发脾气、难以相处的人,但他也是一个有着无数美德的人……在这个纷杂的世界上,能比得上他一半好的人可谓寥寥无几;眼下之所以需要这笔钱,都是我造成的,完全是我的错,而且如果拿不到这笔钱,我亲爱的父亲一定会难以支撑,身心都受到重创,那样的话我将再也享受不到片刻的欢乐。"

难怪了解幕后详情的哈内斯先生反对这样的愚孝。米特福德小姐为了满足医生一时的奇想和妄念,不惜牺牲自己的健康、睡眠和内心的安宁。当时,在她夜以继日、片刻不休地辛苦劳作以便支付生活的必要开销之时,米特福德医生还坚持要求拥有一头奶牛、一间牛棚,以及专门为他添置的各种制奶器具,他去世的时候给这个生活节俭的女儿留下了一千英镑的债务,要她去偿还。她决意要把钱还上,就算是变卖自己的衣服也在所不惜。医生依然健在的时候,米特福德小姐殚精竭虑地想要他安享天年。她正(带着绝对的信心)专注于一个宏大的历史题材,有关查理一世和克伦威尔[①]，她说，这是英国历史中最好看的剧情。然而，她在这件事上遇到了新的麻烦。这一次是戏剧审查官过来插手了，他认为触及这样的题材会危害到国家安全。乔治·考曼先生仔细斟酌了一下这个主题，尽管他认为米特福德女士没有任何不良企图，但是眼下，她必须停止与之相关的所有工作。正当米特福德小姐使尽浑身解数对抗焦虑与困顿交织的生活之际（她最终收到了萨里郡的一家剧院因《朱利安》一剧付给她的二百英镑），一家名为惠特克的新公司打算重新出版《乡村素描》，这原本是她写给那位跑路的编辑的书稿。这本书将以"我们的村庄"这一名字面世。

四

"你书中的人物和描写都是真实的吗？"有人曾这样问过我们的女作者。"是的，没错，没错，能有多真就有多真，"她回答说，"作为一个伟大的风景画家，你知道，在画你最喜欢的场景时，你会不自觉地略加修饰；你会利用那些渲染气氛的愉快的插曲；如果有什么丑陋的东西，你会将它剔除出去，如果有需要添加的东西，你会把它加

---

① 查理一世（Charles I，1600—1649），英国斯图亚特王朝国王，1625 年登基，为了对抗议会对其王权的限制，于 1642 年发动英国内战，战败后又于 1647 年挑起第二次内战，战败后被俘，1649 年 1 月被公开处死；奥利弗·克伦威尔（Oliver Cromwell，1599—1658），英国资产阶级革命家、政治家，在两次内战中战胜王党的军队，将查理一世推上了断头台。1653 年，他遣散议会，出任护国主。

进去。但是整幅画还是和实际场景非常相像。"

米特福德小姐如是写道。尽管我对她和威廉·埃尔福德爵士，那位伟大的风景画家尊敬有加，但我还是忍不住会想，她书中值得称赞的部分，并非她对于那些善解人意的村民和猎狗如实的描绘和刻画，而是那些更具想象力的东西；是她传达出的关于空间、自然和进步的体悟，她对此得心应手；她总是能以真挚的笔触，扣动人们心中温柔而感性的心弦。就拿她对于落日的描写来说吧，虽然语言简单平实，但总是能传达出细腻微妙的感情。透过文字，我们能感受到她由衷的喜悦，并深受感染。这不是修饰出来的效果，或者对事实的夸大，而是自然流露出的真实而欢悦的情感……"太阳正在隐去，余晖将几条狭长的云带渲染得金光闪耀，晃得人眼睛几乎无法直视。那些云带几分钟之前还是横卧在地平线上的柔软的水汽条痕，而那些飘浮在它们上面的更为柔软的云层，则环绕、卷曲，变幻出千百种不可思议的形状，就像夏日里的轻烟一样缥缈，富于变化，此刻难以形容的耀眼光线勾勒出它们的轮廓，加深了它们的颜色，给它们镶上了金边，绘制出一幅壮丽的画面。一转眼的工夫，那一轮耀眼的光球就完全消失了，上面的天空每时每刻都在变幻，变得无比绚丽多姿，炫目的金色光芒与彤亮的红色、璀璨的紫色交织、融合，小的暗色黑斑点缀其间，这些色彩又一起融进如篱雀蛋一般的青空里。抬头仰望，可见辉煌灿烂的天空，低头俯视又能看见清澈可爱的洛登河水中这幅恢宏画面的倒影，这样的喜悦简直无法言说，永难忘怀。在写下这段文字的时候，我不禁心潮澎湃，眼眶湿润，我想到了大自然无与伦比的雄浑壮阔，上帝无法言表的仁慈，他如此慷慨，不吝将这样纯粹、这样祥和又这样热烈的图景，展现在那最为卑微、渺小的生灵面前。"

但此刻我们无须再继续赞美《我们的村庄》，或重述这本小书所获得的成功。那些经得起时间检验的书自有其缘由和魅力，它们天经地义地成了每个人生活的一部分。它们并不是常常被人阅读，但它们不声不响地在我们中间占据着一席之地。这本书在我们这里和美国都是一版再版，艺术家们纷纷为其中的场景绘制插图。米特福德小姐生前很喜欢巴克斯特先生[1]绘制的图画，但她真应该活到现在，看看汤姆森先生[2]笔下的乡村生活是多么富有情趣。"我不在乎它们。"莉兹对奶牛们说道，它们都精神抖擞，正以牛特有的优雅姿势站在牛棚门后面。"根本不在乎它们！"

我想作者一定会喜欢那幅面包师、车匠和鞋匠各自赶着自己的奥尔德尼奶牛回村子的画作，或者是农夫赶着车载着自己老伴儿的那幅……有一幅，就是一位女士穿着木套鞋的那幅画，真是摸透了作者写这段文字的心思，因为她可能是健在的女作家中唯一一位曾经着木套鞋出门散步的。她七岁那年，有一位曾姑母送给她一双这样的木套

---

[1] 托马斯·巴克斯特（Thomas Baxter，1782—1821），英国瓷器画家、水彩画家、插画家。

[2] 休·汤姆森（Hugh Thomson，1860—1920），爱尔兰插画家，以钢笔墨水插画著称，曾为简·奥斯汀、查尔斯·狄更斯和 J. M. 巴利的作品绘制插图。他创作插图的《我们的村庄》于 1893 年由麦克米兰公司出版。

鞋，那位慈祥的老太太住在罕布什尔郡菲尔汉姆村，他们那里的人都还在穿这种鞋子。穿上木套鞋在泥路上踩出一个个小圆圈是多么有趣啊，而每走一步都差不多要鼻子着地的样子是多么好玩儿！

尽管取得了这些成功，米特福德小姐的生活依然是麻烦不断。她写信给哈内斯先生说："你想象不到我是怎样的心烦意乱。家里的情况实在是不忍详述，这些问题由来已久，让人痛苦不堪。我的双亲，父亲大手大脚，挥霍无度，与我更亲密的母亲，则记忆力和身体每况愈下，他们让我倍感忧虑和担心，恐怕我总有一天会难以支撑。"她的困难还远不止这些。新的出版商不再付钱给她，所以眼下就连《我们的村庄》也没有给她带来什么收益；查尔斯·肯布尔没有为《福斯卡里》[①]出价。她心急火燎地赶到伦敦，想从几个出版商那里讨回一些欠款，但是，据哈内斯先生所说，除了稿约和恭维，她从债主那里所获寥寥。她构思了一部小说，并打算创作一部歌剧，《丘比特和塞姬》。

最后，情况总算有了改观，她收到了一笔一百五十英镑的新小说稿酬，还有布莱克伍德公司支付的十几尼的定金。随后，查尔斯·肯布尔的来信给她的悲剧带来了新的希望，那部剧不久以后得以在考文特花园上演。

悲剧是以悲剧的英语写成的，当然，那是舞台上的语言，但也不乏简洁和它特有的韵律。一八五四年，赫斯特和布莱凯特出版社出版了几卷本的米特福德作品集，在悲

---

① 《福斯卡里》(*Foscari*, 1826)，米特福德创作的一部悲剧，这部剧最终在 1826 年由查尔斯·肯布尔担当主角在考文特花园上演。

剧作品的序言中，米特福德小姐描述说："演出前的混乱场面是无法描述的，朦朦胧胧地让人感到晦暗又迷惑。悲剧演员们戴着帽子，披着外套，不停地跳来跳去，聊着天，开着玩笑，唯一一个异常严肃的人是演丑角的李斯顿[1]。跳芭蕾的女孩子们在排练方阵舞步，给她们伴奏的是一把孤单的提琴，琴声仿佛是自成一体的曲调，从乐队的高凳和音乐桌中间传来，也不知为何，这声音竟然能从这无休无止的嘈杂声中穿透而出。哦，那一片嘈杂！声音来自四面八方，上面、下面，前后左右，有各种音高和声调。重物在这里滚动，从那边跌落。铃声不明来由地响个不停，催场员无处不在，到处都是他们的身影。"

演出成功的时候，她难掩惊讶之情。"我并没有什么胆量亲临自己首部悲剧演出的现场，而是在附近某个安静的寓所中，静静地坐着，不停地发抖。演出结束后，有个朋友飞奔到那里，让我悬着的心放了下来。通常，传递好消息的使者都是可怜的海顿[2]，他机智伶俐又为人热情，格外适合这样的场合。"

我们能看到她写给母亲的关于《福斯卡里》的信，我刚刚引用的段落就出自此信。《黎恩济》在德鲁里剧院上演的时候（也就是两年后的一八二八年十月），从她写给威廉·埃尔福德爵士的信中我们也能知道，那时她可怜的

---

① 约翰·李斯顿（John Liston，1776—1846），英国喜剧演员，代表作为《保罗·普莱》（*Paul Pry*，1825）。

② 本杰明·海顿（Benjamin Robert Haydon，1786—1846），英国画家，擅长创作宏大的历史题材画作。

老母亲已经不在人世，无法分享女儿成功的喜悦了。

米特福德小姐满怀感激地记录下了来自朋友们的支持，他们是那天热心肠的缪斯。特罗洛普夫人[①]、兰登小姐、埃奇沃思小姐[②]、波登小姐、霍夫兰德夫人[③]、欧佩夫人都来向她登门道贺。

米特福德小姐说，在偏爱宏大的历史场面这一点上，她和海顿最是心有戚戚焉。古典主义时期、西班牙、意大利、中世纪的罗马，这些都是她钟爱的场景和时期。公爵和护民官是她心目中的英雄；短剑匕首、地牢和刽子手则是她用来营造气氛的手段。

她非常谨慎地看待自己在戏剧上获得的成功。她说："它并不像我们心中默默期许的那样甘甜，那般荣耀，那样给人以全然的满足。它并没有带来心灵的慰藉——只是让人获得一时的沉醉，随后低落的反面情绪就会接踵而至。"她对一个朋友说，她第一部真正成功的戏剧《黎恩济》上演之后，她经历了人生中从未有过的绝望和消沉。她又顺带暗示说自己的父亲心绪不佳，不是发脾气就是生闷气，这或许能部分解释事情的原委。会不会是医生在那些不合

---

① 特罗洛普夫人（Francis Milton Trollope，1779—1863），英国小说家，著有多部社会小说。她的大儿子、三儿子也都是小说家，维多利亚时代的小说家安东尼·特罗洛普（Anthony Trollope，1815—1882）正是她的第三子。

② 埃奇沃思小姐（Maria Edgeworth，1767—1849），爱尔兰小说家，著有多部小说和儿童文学作品。

③ 霍夫兰德夫人（Barbara Hofland，1770—1844），英国作家，著有儿童寓言故事和多部小说。

时宜的毛病之外又增添了小气和嫉妒？他看不惯任何一个作家或者演员，简言之，看不惯任何不属于这个乡村之家的人。他对女儿现在难免要结交的朋友十分反感，这自然可以解释她为什么会如此情绪低落了。她总是处于过分紧张、负担过重、神经紧绷的状态，每一次的写作都让她精疲力竭。她后来从王室的奖励津贴中获得了一小笔抚恤金，对于这个饱受磨难的可怜女人来说，这笔钱实在是难以形容的恩惠。

悲剧创作带来的收入让米特福德小姐添置了一匹结实的小马和一辆柳条马车，同时她还收到了各式各样的邀约（其中不乏来自塔尔福德家族①的），她像名人一样受到款待，被左右簇拥着。塔尔福德大律师一定是在这样的场合，气愤地抱怨起一篇当时针对《离子》的剧评。他的一位宾客为了安慰他，竟毫不避讳地说："如果她的悲剧遭遇这样的批评，她是不会放在心上的。"

"您的《黎恩济》，当然！我想是不用放在心上的，"大律师说道，"但《离子》可不一样。"正像莱斯特兰奇先生描述的那样，塔尔福德家族是一个滑稽的大杂烩。他们既是诗书之家，热情好客，同时又邋遢懒散，乖张任性；他们既有发自内心的善良，也有最真实的人性流露。

F. 波洛克爵士所著的《麦克雷迪传》中也多次提及米

---

① 指托马斯·努恩·塔尔福德爵士（Sir Thomas Noon Talfourd, 1795—1854）一家，塔尔福德爵士是英国律师、法官，曾出任代表雷丁地区的国会议员，业余从事文学创作。他的悲剧《离子》（*Ion*）在 1835 年由他个人自费出版，并于次年在考文特花园剧院上演。

特福德小姐。那位伟大的悲剧演员似乎对她并没有多少真诚的好感，但是他愉快地记述了一次晚餐会上的逸事。那是为《离子》而举办的聚会，米特福德小姐也在场，她在席间问麦克雷迪是否暂时不出演她的悲剧了。悲剧演员未置可否，但是坐在一旁的华兹华斯[①]插嘴道："啊，可别放过他。"

五

除了哈内斯先生和莱斯特兰奇先生合著的《米特福德小姐传》外，还有一本叫作《玛丽·拉塞尔·米特福德和朋友们》的书，该书收录了她收到的友人来信，而不是她写的信。你如果看过印刷体的名人书信，一定会意识到手写的书信和印刷体书信有多么不同。透过手写的信纸，你能听见朋友的声音，望见朋友的眼睛，即使是墨渍和涂改的痕迹都会让你想起写信的那个人。但是，在行距均匀的印刷体书信中，这种魅力会消失不见。每个人的字体看起来都一模一样，每个人都用着一样的字体，一样的表述。你的眼睛浏览过一页又一页的书信，可是不会有丝毫被触动、被说服的感觉。我能想象每一封这样的来信都能给米特福德小姐带来莫大的喜悦，而写给她的信总是源源不断。这些信来自那些声名显赫的女士，她们素来受人尊敬。特罗洛普夫人、霍夫兰德夫人、豪威特夫人、S. C. 霍尔夫人、

[①] 威廉·华兹华斯（William Wordsworth，1770—1850），英国诗人，浪漫主义文学巨擘。

斯特里克兰小姐、欧佩夫人，此外，还有巴雷特小姐、贾米森夫人和从美国寄来信件的塞奇威克小姐，她们都是十分有趣的人物，但也必须承认她们的书信并不十分有趣。巴雷特小姐是个例外，她的信读来就和手稿一样亲切。但是，毫无疑问，给其他女作家的恭维之词，读来总是略感乏味，比不上自己写的或收到的那些漂亮话。还有些是致歉信，为未能尽早写信表示歉意，但是这些信不管给受到冒犯的收信人带来了怎样的宽慰，或给良心不安的寄信人带来怎样的解脱，一旦变成了印刷体，读来都是索然无味的。

　　"我看上去一定像个忘恩负义的小人，我亲爱的米特福德小姐"，云云。"你，我亲爱的朋友，一定再清楚不过一本书急于完稿的情形，因而断不会责备我没有写信"，等等。"这是从昨天早上起我写的第三十九封信，"哈丽特·马蒂诺①说道，"哦，我简直无法控制自己手中的笔！我不会允许没有给你写信的羞愧来阻止我此刻给你写信。"所有这些人似乎和现在的人一样忙，一样有趣，也一样无聊。只不过他们要额外花些工夫自己盖上邮资已付的邮戳，而且还要洋洋洒洒写满四页纸，而不是一张明信片。我们的信虽然也可能枯燥无味，但不管怎样不会写那么长。我们能更快地切入正题，避免那些客气的婉转措辞。但即使不说别的，让人印象深刻的除了那个年代更为炽热的文学热情，还有传阅的手稿和悲剧作品的巨大数量，作者们都

---

① 哈丽特·马蒂诺（Harriet Martineau，1802—1876），英国社会理论家、作家，通常被看作英国第一位女性社会学家。

很放心地把手稿和作品交于另一个人传阅。与此同时，还有大量的诗歌作品踏上了流浪之旅，它们振翅高飞，一路高歌不停歇。

一位热情的美国批评家在造访英国时对这种情形印象颇深。这位威利斯先生"无以复加的仰慕之情"似乎很能说明当时的情况和人们高涨的热情。即使奥斯汀小姐笔下的德伯格小姐一试身手创作了一部手稿，那位总是对她溜须拍马的柯林斯①也不可能形容得更加殷切了……如果能够任由——威利斯先生——选择的话，他每年都会从米特福德小姐笔下拿去一部悲剧。"这是多么让人沉醉的生活啊，"他惊呼道，"在昨天的晚餐会上我遇见了简·波特、艾金小姐、汤姆·摩尔②，还有一大批拥有美丽心灵的人！再没有比此处更让人心驰神往的地方了。"

米特福德小姐在自己的信中有更为自然的描述。

"我怎么也弄不明白人们到底在我的书信中找到了什么让他们喜爱的东西，"米特福德小姐写道，"除非他们对这些信有特别的感情。"这种感情就来自她那颗善良的心。米特福德小姐或许缺少识人的慧眼，但她绝不缺乏同情心。她天性善良，似乎对所有人都一视同仁地怀有爱心，就好像他们都是她头脑中创造出来的人物：但不管是回报他人

① 德伯格小姐和柯林斯是简·奥斯汀的小说《傲慢与偏见》中的人物，柯林斯在贵妇德伯格小姐的帮助下当上了牧师，因此人前人后都不忘阿谀奉承她。

② 简·波特（Jane Porter，1776—1850），英国历史小说家、戏剧家；露西·艾金（Lucy Aikin，1781—1864），英国历史和传记作家；托马斯·摩尔（Thomas Moore，1779—1852），爱尔兰诗人。

的善意，还是救朋友于水火，她总是不遗余力，尽力而为。如果她生活的方方面面透过这层玫瑰色的纱幕而变得多姿多彩，谁又会为此而抱怨呢？

"在我所享的诸多恩惠之中——我亲爱的父亲，我敬爱的母亲，我那些患难与共且出类拔萃的朋友——有一样是我最应该真诚地感谢上帝恩赐的，那就是我与生俱来的、昂扬向上的精神，始终心存希望的态度和实现幸福的意愿，这些都是我从父亲那里继承来的。"她写道。难道所有的孝道都像她这样让人感到愤慨？不管有怎样的耐心，她对米特福德医生的夸赞还是让人难以忍受。他那些不切实际的妄念既是他本性的流露，也是他女儿天性的投射，他们一个是以自我为中心、绝对的自私自利的人，一个是慷慨、谦卑、美丽善良的人。她几乎从没有真正地生过气，仅有的例外是当她在报纸上读到关于自己婚姻的报道时。那是一则声明，声称她和家族中的某位亲戚已经订了婚，这则消息很快就在她的朋友圈中不胫而走。让米特福德小姐大为光火的是，这条消息竟然是天性浪漫的霍夫兰德夫人杜撰的。据说霍夫兰德夫人也用同样的方式把埃奇沃思小姐给嫁出去了。

玛丽·米特福德在友情而非爱情中找到了自己真正的浪漫。她待在伦敦的那段日子里，有一天肯尼恩先生[1]来看她，并提出要带她到动物园去看看。路上，他提议拐到格洛斯特广场接上一位年轻的女士，那是他的一位亲戚，

---

[1] 约翰·肯尼恩（John Kenyon，1784—1856），英国诗人、慈善家，诗人罗伯特·勃朗宁（Robert Browning，1812—1889）的恩主。

巴雷特小姐。米特福德小姐就这样结识了勃朗宁夫人，她们的友谊是她一生中最感幸福的事情之一。那确实是一次幸福的浪漫邂逅，两人随后的实际交往使得这份浪漫得以天长地久。的确，交一个新朋友就像学习一门新的语言。我自己的一位朋友曾经说过，我们每个人都有属于自己的特定听众，我们会本能地找他们倾诉，在他们面前演练自己头脑中的想法；他们的想法会影响我们，而他们的赞许则是我们心中秘密的期许。勃朗宁夫人之于米特福德小姐似乎正是一位这样的听众。

"我坐下来想着你还有你即将要写的诗，以及那被称作名声的像彩虹一样光怪陆离的皇冠，直到眼前浮现出这样的场景……我的自豪和希望似乎都与你融为一体。我在这有生之年，所爱者寥寥，因而急切地想将那欢乐的图景化为现实，你大约难以想象满怀憧憬给我带来的喜悦……"这位年长的女士是怀着这样浪漫的情愫写信给那位年轻小姐的。米特福德小姐曾经说过，她对幸福有着蜜蜂从花丛中采蜜那样的本能，此言不虚。不管遇到怎样的甜蜜和欢乐，她总是径直而去，毫不迟疑。

只有对巴雷特小姐，她才会偶尔抱怨一下。"我理应去挣钱，但我完全做不到，我跟你说说我眼下的处境，应该就能帮助你明白我的苦衷了。我今天不只收到你的来信，还收到另外十六封信；随即父亲拿了份报纸来到我的房间，让我念第十到十二栏来自印度的消息给他听；之后我吃了饭，这既是午餐又是早餐；然后起床，这个时候花园里已经来了三拨人，还有另外八个人正在赶来……我不得不走了，因为约好了要去拜访玛德琳·帕尔默夫人。她带我在帕尔默先生美丽的种植园里徒步走了六英里，寻找一种叫睡菜的精美野花，你知道这种花吗？非常美的一种花，不管是野生的，还是像 K 说的那样，'驯养的'。经过好一番寻找，我们发现这种植物还没有开花。"

米特福德医生为女儿如此操劳伤心流泪，逢人便说她这样散步和坐车会要了她的命。他希望她永远不要走出花园的范围，不要涉足他的报纸专栏之外的领域。她回应说只有出门置身田野间，她才能忍受紧迫的工作和焦虑持续交替带来的压力。大自然实在是她的第二天性。查尔斯·金斯利对于东风的描写也难出其右……

"我们曾经有连续九周的干旱，东风不停地刮着，几乎一朵花也看不到，草地上没有一丝翠色，树丛中看不到一片绿叶；即使是偶然冒出一朵可怜的紫罗兰或者报春花，也没有丝毫香气。我一次也不曾听到我所讨厌的杜鹃的叫声……此地因燕子而得名，显然是燕子的栖居地，然而就是在这里，迄今还未曾见过任何一只燕子。我唯一一次听到夜莺的叫声，是在一个温暖的晴日，我坐车到树林里去，那里曾有着大片大片的酢浆草。到了才发现那里也不过才开了两朵小花，但是在我驱车驶进树林的时候，有一群夜莺齐声和唱向我致意。"

这段对于自然景物的生动描写颇有赛威尼夫人[①]的风范。

[①] 赛威尼夫人（Madame de Sévigné，1626—1696），法国女作家，贵族出身，有与女儿的书信集传世，文笔生动、幽默。

她的父亲久病不愈，她一直在病榻前侍奉陪伴。父亲去世时，她发现自己孑然一身，身体状况堪忧，除了王室微薄的奖励津贴之外，生活几乎无以为继。米特福德医生留下了一千英镑的债务，这位可敬的女士当即就着手开始偿还。她的勇气和执着让她的许多朋友和读者都深受感动，最后这笔钱实际上由他们认捐了。女王、主教、公爵和侯爵夫人，诸多人士都参与了这场认捐，从事写作的文学女性也在其中，巴利夫人、埃奇沃思小姐，还有特罗洛普夫人。欧佩夫人决意要至少拿出二十英镑，尽管她有言在先，表示只要这笔钱不是给医生还债，可以用作任何支出。

　　到了一八四四年，我们读到她饱经磨难的人生终于有了些许安逸，这实在让人感到开心。这位善良的女士组织了一场校园宴会，安排了面包点心，还布置了彩旗，孩子们乘着用月桂装饰的马车，由米特福德小姐领头，其余八到十辆马车紧随其后，一行人都来到燕子地的大道上等着看维多利亚女王和阿尔伯特亲王，他们在拜访过威灵顿公爵后回转会经过此地。"我们的公爵没花什么钱。"米特福德小姐说道。（米特福德医生若是健在，定然不会同意这种说法。）公爵确实买了一条地毯，但其余的家具都是他出了一周的租金从雷丁租借来的。几个敲钟的工人，辛苦工作了四个小时，他们送了一个罐子到公爵的府上讨要啤酒喝，结果那罐子居然空着被送回来了。

　　米特福德小姐直到生命中的最后几年才离开三里口，来到燕子地定居下来。"那个破旧的小屋在我们周围摇晃，我们要是再待上些日子,怕是已经被埋在废墟里了。"她说,"我在那里辛苦过,奋斗过,品尝过苦涩的焦虑、恐惧和希望,这是众多女性都会经历的。"接着有一段精彩的描述,写的是三里口那条笔直而布满尘土的道路。"我在一个秋日的黄昏从一栋房子走到另一栋,迁徙的候鸟在我的头顶盘旋。这些鸟儿习惯了聚集在此处开始它们每年一次的旅行。我猜,这就是这个村子被称作燕子地的缘由。我不禁吟诵起海利[1]那几行悲怆的诗句,那是他在最后的病痛中,看见同样的鸟儿聚集在他的屋顶时写下的:

'温柔的鸟儿,高高栖上我的屋脊,
细细地啄理你的羽翅……

准备着行将开始的别离,
趁着寒冬的怒气尚未威胁到此地;
我也像你一样啄理着灵魂的羽翼,
准备着飞越坟墓去往更远的天地。

愿上帝垂目侧耳,
眷顾
远行的人们,流浪的鸟儿,
愿他的慈悲将我们佑护,

---

① 威廉·海利(William Hayley,1745—1820),英国作家、诗人,以他为诗人威廉·考珀(William Cowper,1731—1800)所作的传记闻名。

引我们去向那未知的国度！'"

　　这些动人的诗行可以让人的思绪变得平静而温柔，更为欢快的景象不觉随之而来……

　　她正是在燕子地写下了下面的文字："我感到自己最近又能活跃地与新朋友交流了，这真是上天对我的眷顾。要知道在这个残酷的春天，我失去了许多老友与故交。我带着比感谢上帝赠予我面包还要诚恳的心，感谢他给予我这样的眷顾，因为友谊就是心灵的面包。"

　　尽管已经到了生命的最后阶段，但从三里口搬离之后她结识了许多让人感到温暖的新朋友，她生命中一些最真诚的友谊正是从这时开始的。她对詹姆斯·佩恩先生和菲尔茨先生①的爱就如同母亲对儿子的疼爱，住在附近一座大宅里的拉塞尔夫人成了她亲近又挚爱的朋友。

六

　　我们前几日来到了雷丁，就像之前许多米特福德小姐的朋友那样，要亲眼看一看"我们的村庄"，看一看她住了许多年的小屋。一辆配有一匹快马的轻型马车来车站接我们，它带着我们从热闹的城镇飞驰而过，之后就沿着那条笔直而布满尘土的大路径直走去。我们在透过云层的柔

---

① 詹姆斯·佩恩（James Payn，1830—1898），英国小说家；詹姆斯·托马斯·菲尔茨（James Thomas Fields，1817—1881），美国出版商、编辑、诗人。

和日光下一路前行，我越过道路两旁的树篱向远处望去，可以看见田野和树丛，还有这儿一片那儿一片的红色屋顶，画面底部的背景是地平线上绵延不绝的青色远山。这是一幅朴实无华的寻常景致，但每分钟都会有可恶的药品广告牌从眼前闪过，宣传这家或那家的药片。确实是"树木的言语"①，只不过和那位被流放的公爵的感受大相径庭！很快我们就看到了奔流的小溪，尚未受到污染的溪水淙淙流淌，清冽而湍急，再也没有那些江湖庸医的广告来污人眼目。不久我们就来到了惠特利，见到了那里带着漂亮山墙的旅店（米特福德小姐过去兜风的时候会驾车到惠特利，然后再折返）。清新的凉风扬起了阵阵尘土，空气中可以闻到成熟玉米的香气，几头奶牛在榆树下面俯首而立，看起来和汤姆森先生精美画作中的一模一样，它们的身上长着褐色的斑点，腿和头上的角显得很精致。我们一路上几乎没有遇到什么人，只见过一个坐在车里被人拉着的婴儿，还有围在他身边的兄弟姐妹；有一条猎狐犬跑过来冲着我们的车轮叫了几声；最后，马车在路旁的两三栋房子前猛然停了下来，车夫用鞭子指着说："那就是'米特福德家'，太太。——那就是米特福德小姐过去住的地方！"

仅此而已？我看到尘土飞扬的马路边上有两三栋普通的民居，还看到一棵榆树旁有一个舒适的小酒馆，它的边

① 树木的言语（tongues in trees）出自莎士比亚喜剧《皆大欢喜》第二幕第一场。剧中被流放的公爵安慰随从说："虽然远离尘嚣，但我们可以去发现树木的言语、溪流的教诲、顽石的箴言和万物中的美好。"此处指的是树上的广告牌。

上是另一间毫不起眼的灰色小房子，石板瓦的屋顶，方正的围墙，大门的上方油漆着"米特福德"几个大字……

我并不知道自己一直期盼的是什么——一座尖塔，一个水泵，一片绿地，一条弯弯曲曲的街道——我之前凭空设想的村庄瞬间随风飘散，取而代之的是眼前这个挂着招牌的小酒馆，还有这六七间砖房，差不多都是四四方方的样子！仅此而已！这就是作者笔下隽永迷人的"我们的村庄"！这就是那双善良的眼睛曾经注视过的风景，那双眼睛所见的不仅是单调的砖头瓦片，还有隐匿于其中的灵魂，她总是能洞悉一切。倘若不是为了这个记忆，三里口将会是最缺乏生机与趣味的乡间一隅……

我们姑且来看看米特福德小姐自己的描述。"感谢上帝，三里口并不是一个市镇，既不腐朽也不独立。这里的居民既安静又平和，他们甚至想不起来要拜访我们，即使我们装了门环，期待有人敲门。我们居住的是一间小房子"（她在写给威廉·埃尔福德爵士的信中写道），"不，不是小房子，它甚至还配不上这个名字——只能算是一间农宅或者棚户，就像一个靠着攒下的一千四百英镑过活的小农民退休之后所居住的地方。房子里有好几个小房间，最大的一间大约八英尺见方，它们分别被叫作客厅、厨房和食品储藏室，它们中有的房间还会缺一个角，那是特别给烟囱留出的空间，还有一些少了半边，那是被倾斜的屋顶占了的地方。屋后有一个花园，大小只有一个像样的起居室那么大，里面有一个凉亭，差不多就是一棵女贞树搭起来的岗哨。房子一侧是一间酒馆，另一侧是村子里的商店，正对面是鞋匠的摊铺。尽管如此，'这间小屋，'正像布阿卜迪勒①所说，'还是很方便的。'正好在我原来散步的范围之内，距离我发现紫罗兰的那片山坡，长满黄花九轮草的草地，还有开满酢浆草的树林都不远……爸爸已经在整顿周边秩序的过程中获得了满足，并正准备把三里口一名扰乱治安的害群之马送到感化院……妈妈刚刚给一间旧的乳品作坊添置了器具；我弄丢了自己唯一的钥匙，但在花园里塞满了花……"这位知足的年轻女士这样记述这里的生活。

　　这样的描述可比惯常用的格子窗和山墙的叙述效果高明多了；作者在写这封信的时候描绘了那些并不在场的东西，她将开满紫罗兰的山坡请进单调的房间里，让那里芳香四溢，这种下意识的让人感到愉悦的手法是多么非同一般。这封信的附言也是十足的米特福德小姐的风格。"请原谅信中的墨水渍和补于行间的文字。当时窗外有一只夜莺啾鸣婉转，将一个音乐的世界倾泻进我的窗棂，让我不觉失了神。"

　　"你难道不想成为朋友心目中贴心的伴侣吗？"米特福德小姐曾在某处说过，这话用在她自己身上再合适不过。

---

① 布阿卜迪勒（Boabdil），格拉纳达最后的国王穆罕默德十二世（Abu Abdallah Muhammad XII，1459—1533）。1491 年，格拉纳达被西班牙人攻陷，他于次年投降，后来逃亡到摩洛哥。十九世纪时出现了多部根据这段历史创作的小说和戏剧，比如美国文学家华盛顿·欧文（Washington Irving，1783—1859）的小说《攻陷格拉纳达》（*The Chronicles of the Conquest of Granada*，1829），此处的引文当出自此类改编故事，具体篇目不详。

她有一颗仁慈的心，她永远是最贴心的伴侣，用赛威尼夫人的话说就是"值得放入背篓的花"①。

我们走进了一个四方的小厅，这是米特福德医生生病期间安置病榻的地方，访客和家里的其他人都要经厨房门往来探视。在一度只为他个人所用的客厅里，此刻正坐着一批从雷丁来的普通朋友，他们一边休憩一边喝茶。主人也为我们奉上了热茶，并斟上薄酒供我们祭奠曾经在这个安静的地方操持的米特福德小姐。随后房东太太带我们四处走走看看，她带我们参观了厨房，里面的角落布置得很舒适，窗框都很低——"我猜这里几乎没有什么变化吧？"我们中的一个人问道。

"哦，不，夫人，"管家说，"我们用的是封闭炉灶，米特福德小姐过去一直用开放式的炉子。"

花园，连同那个女贞树搭起来的岗哨一样的凉亭，都已经不复存在；那里现在是一间铁皮布道厅，里面有风琴和一排排稻草编的椅子，还有桌子和特定场合会用到的烛台。墙上挂着米特福德小姐的画像，那是一幅手工上色的复制肖像画。画上，她面带微笑，慈祥而亲切，透过油彩依然能看出她性情平和、神情专注且才思敏捷。今天人们的所思所想当然应该在事物的精神而非外在的符号上得到体现……我们当中的任何一个想必都见过路边为了纪念中世纪的某个圣徒而设立的圣祠，祠堂中的神像常常衣着华丽，头后面还有一顶光轮，身上披着拖地的斗篷，脸上

---

① 出自赛威尼夫人的书信集，意指可敬可爱之人。

戴着面纱，其中的浪漫气息不言而喻……这里，说来说去，也是一样的情形，不过是以十九世纪的风貌呈现的，用的是瓦楞铁皮搭成的小屋，一杯杯待客的茶水和填絮席垫。"帕尔默先生买下了这个地方，"房东太太说，"他把这里变成了一家禁酒旅店，并在花园里建造了这间禁酒厅。"……

这里没有什么浪漫的大理石神庙，有的是出于善意建起的一间四四方方的礼拜堂，虽然只是简单的方形建筑，没有哥特式的拱门和曲线，但虔敬之心并没有丝毫减损。这里所要宣扬的，并不是一个神圣且神秘的圣徒，而是一位善良且热心的女士，一位天生慈悲而乐观的终身苦修者，以及她给无数后辈带来的天真快乐的甜蜜想象和温暖祝福！

七

这里有一封短笺，字迹细密娟秀，介于沃尔特·司各特爵士和勃朗宁夫人之间，笔者已将它珍藏多年，一直夹在书里，和早年的其他贵重之物放在一起：

最亲爱的普利西拉小姐，感谢您的一片好意。我奉还给您第九卷的×××（模糊不清）和随后的四卷，我这里只有这几卷了，或许这本书只出版了这几卷。我若是有了其他卷册，定会拿给您看。请转告乔治先生（我最好不要叫他韦尔-韦尔），我想起来那位作者的名字了，就是那本有趣的小说《红与黑》（这就是正确的书名，跟作者本人的名字无关）的作者，他叫司汤达，至少他是这么称呼自己的。我想他要么是个音乐家，要么是个音乐批评家，而且已经去世了……我的访客还没到（约的下午六点），昨天早上我一连回了她两封短信，太过突然，她一定是给吓到了；的确，没人能想到回信会那么快就写完，这都是迫于走路送信的速度……

请代我向昨天来访的客人致以诚挚的爱意，他们将这世间所有的善意都给予了我，事实上您家里的每个人都是这样对我的。

永远对您，亲爱的普利西拉小姐，充满深情挚爱的，

M. R. 米特福德

笔者自己早年的时候，也就是燕子地现今的主人还是个年幼的小男孩的时候，曾听到他和他的姐姐，布拉肯伯里夫人（也就是短笺中的普利西拉小姐），深情地回忆这位新近故去的老友，她过去就住在他们对门。通过这两扇友谊之门，这位女士在漫长而辛劳的人生行将结束之际，体会到了愉快的陪伴和深情的关爱所带来的欢欣鼓舞，这

真让人感到高兴和宽慰。当麦克米伦先生们①建议我写这篇序言的时候，我找到了米特福德小姐原来的手写记录本，并遵照上面的提示写信给相关人士（不确定这些联系是否还继续维系着），询问与米特福德小姐相关的讯息，笔者这才发现原来自己也曾在燕子地被盛情款待过，还应邀参观过作者在《我们的村庄》里欣然描绘过的场景。

我想我愿意把那句关于读书与行路的老话倒过来说，按照我自己独特的想法，应该是先读书再去行路。鲜有比遇见一个鲜活的人物更让人开心的事了，听着他在印刷的书页里侃侃而谈，讲得头头是道，或者含沙射影，你会随着时间的流逝越发了解他，他也会越发变得生动具体，好似真人一样的存在；接着，你在他的感召之下，突然发现自己已经置身他所处的生活场景中，周围是你感到熟悉的印象和经历，你意识到自己仿佛通过某种奇异的轮回，有了另一种迥然不同的生存经验，那是假设可能——或者毋宁说是必然如此——的情形。当你有了这样的经历，你便不再只是读书，而是融入书本，融入书中的世界。

位于燕子地庄园里的那幢房子是一座老旧的英式乡村住宅，经历了岁月的洗礼而依旧屹立不倒，雄伟的外墙和屋内的厅堂，还有庄园外美丽的百年老树，都记录着那些伟大的时代和那些杰出的人物。这个庄园是亨利八

---

① 指创立麦克米伦出版公司的丹尼尔·麦克米伦（Daniel Macmillan，1813—1857）和亚历山大·麦克米伦（Alexandra Macmillan，1818—1896）兄弟。

世[①]的某一位不幸的王后的一部分陪嫁，现代风格的住宅是克拉伦登[②]建造的，掩映在榆树林中的老教堂可以追溯至一二〇〇年，里面有雕刻的标记和符号，还有骑士与普通市民的黄铜画像，以及发音古怪的名字和过去的风尚。

拉塞尔夫人，就是她派了配着快马的马车到车站去接我们的，我们的车子进来的时候，她正在园子里散步，因而她没有先带我们去宅子里，而是领着我们穿过草地，沿着溪流去了老教堂。站在教堂那植被修剪得齐整而美丽的墓园中，令人感到连死神看起来都面带微笑，不那么可怕了，这就是善良的玛丽·米特福德那颗炽热的心安息的地方，"她忙碌的双手，"用她自己的话说，"在那里静静地安歇，阳光正透过高大的榆树，凝视着燕子地这片美丽的教堂墓园。"

查尔斯爵士，这里的最后一位准男爵，曾经参加过克里米亚战争，从父亲亨利爵士那里继承了爵位，他将分隔的栅栏拆去，以便他的老朋友也能享受到这些榆树的阴凉。拉塞尔夫人带我们看了这片宁静的绿地，给我们讲述了它的故事。听她说老教堂曾一度要被拆毁，幸而金斯利碰巧来访，在他的恳求之下，这座教堂才幸免于难。后来，教堂的垃圾和外部残败的印记被清除干净，修缮者们的虔诚

---

① 亨利八世（Henry VIII，1491—1547），英格兰国王（1509—1547 年在位），在位期间结婚六次，有过六位王后。
② 克拉伦登，指克拉伦登伯爵（Earl of Clarendon），英国世袭的贵族封号，历史上有过两次授封，分别是在 1661 年和 1776 年，继承封号的有十余人，具体所指不详。

也得到了回报，他们发现虽然年深日久，但那些贵重的橡木屋梁竟完好无损，他们还发现了被埋藏在地下、保存良好的纪念碑、铜制画像和铭牌。今天人们依然能够在父辈们跪拜祈福的祠堂中对着这些物品祷告，传统似乎并没有被清除殆尽。庄园现任的女主人对旧传统钟爱有加，尽力为她的孩子们保留了这些历史的印记。

因而，当米特福德小姐离开三里口来到燕子地度过她最后的岁月时，她有这些善良的朋友给她鼓励和安慰。她刚刚搬到这里的时候，亨利·拉塞尔爵士还健在，但是已经开始时不时地受到病痛突然发作的折磨。她还是像以往一样冲动，写信的时候把这些情况描述成一种常年的困扰。他去世后，他的遗孀，当时的拉塞尔夫人，成了她最贴心的朋友和安慰者。

玛丽·米特福德离开三里口搬到燕子地后所居住的小屋位于一个三岔路口，现在像其他小屋一样，扩建出了一两间房，但是其他的部分，我想并没有什么可以改动的。当时有许多有趣的人到访，米特福德小姐就是在这里接待了他们，她那时就坐在"金合欢树的流穗"下那张大书桌旁写作。庄园的现任女主人把我们带到大门口的时候，金合欢树的花已经落尽，但是夏日馥郁芬芳的气息四处弥散。窗户下面的墙壁上攀附着一朵美丽的蔷薇花（它一定是经过许多年才长到了这样的高度），花园的围栏外面是广阔的田地，此时正值七月末，田里的庄稼开始成熟，呈现出金黄的色泽。农夫和他的儿子正挥动着镰刀，忙于劳作；鸟儿还在天上飞，甜甜的香气在空气中飘散。

那天，从一位与她熟识的、在信中被她称作"我自己的安妮小姐"的女士那里，我们得知了更多关于《我们的村庄》的作者的事，关于她让人着迷的智慧，她说话的天赋，易于冲动的性情，爱热闹的天性，还有她敏捷思维的魅力。她也有自己的缺点，会轻易得出结论，会受制于与她一起生活的人的影响。她生来就是一个受害者——即使是在她暴君一样的老父亲去世之后，她多多少少又受到仆人们的牵制。邻居们看 K 和本总有些不放心，但他们对她很好，总的来说，把她照顾得很周到。拉塞尔夫人说，她和自己的弟弟有一天早上到她的小屋里去避雨，当他们在炉火边烤干身子的时候，他们看见仆人们将精心准备的饭食端给老太太，有腰花和蛋奶糕，那是她的简便早餐。

米特福德小姐去世的时候，将她所有的一切都留给了她喜爱的 K 和本，唯一的例外是她希望她的每位朋友都能从她藏书丰富的图书馆中得到一本书。米特福德医生尽管有诸多缺点，却是一个爱书之人，他买过许多装帧精美、价值不菲的名家首版书。K 和本似乎也很喜欢这些书籍和首版书。对于曾经照顾过、安慰过米特福德小姐，和她比邻而居，并最终怀抱着她离世的拉塞尔一家，本给他们带去的是一本 G. P. R. 詹姆斯[①]的小说，聊作纪念，那是一本一先令一卷的旧书，而这竟然是本仅能割舍的东西。一件略微美好一点的事情是拉塞尔夫人告诉我的，她有一次去米特福德小姐的陵前拜谒，看见一个她并不认识的年轻

---

① G. P. R. 詹姆斯（George Payne Rainsford James，1799—1860），英国小说家、历史作家。

人站在那里。"您不认识我了吗？"他说道，"我是亨利，夫人。我刚刚从澳大利亚回来。"他是在小木屋里暂住过的一对夫妻的一个孩子，他回国后拜访的第一个地方竟是他昔日的女保护人的陵墓。

我也听过一个朋友向我描述她在米特福德小姐去世前几个月去拜访时的情形，这位朋友是在米特福德小姐最后的那段日子里与她结识的。据她说，米特福德小姐当时尽管已经病得很重了，但依然跟原来一样，精神矍铄，反应敏捷。这位年轻的来访者自己生病卧床休息了一阵子，已经有些日子没来她的病榻前探望了。她们谈论了许多事情，其间提到一位女作家，米特福德小姐似乎对她写作一本书的能力很是怀疑。在她的访客离开之后，这位病痛缠身的女士写了一封她特有的隽永美丽的短笺，盖上一枚小小的印章（印章至今完好无损，M. R. M 三个字还是她当初盖上去的样子）之后就送出去了。这封短笺的内容如下：

谢谢您，最亲爱的 ×× 小姐，又一次让我看到您美丽的面孔，而且我最最亲爱的朋友（拉塞尔夫人）也一起来了，对于她的好意我无以言谢，无法形容。在我的生命要走到尽头的时候，我依然在犯错，在懊悔。您走之后我一直深感内疚，为自己对 ×× 夫人说过的那些不客气的话感到难过……愿上苍宽恕我，保佑她能获得比开头所预示的结局更为完满的人生。如果你有一位虚度光阴的爱人，亲爱的，请将我刚才的话转赠予他，因为那才是有价值的箴言。

愿上帝保佑你们所有人！永远，最忠实，最深情的，

M. R. 米特福德

周日于暮色中

八

当你把目光从米特福德小姐的作品转向传记辞典中的介绍（米特福德小姐和米特拉达梯[①]在同一页上）时，你会发现她的声望是如此稳固。"作家女士，"我忠实的顾问《传记大全》上说，"被认为是英格兰乡村生活最忠实的描绘者。""她是《朱利安》这部非凡悲剧的作者，麦克雷迪在剧中担任主角，其后还有《福斯卡里》《黎恩济》等其他作品。"这是《英国传记辞典》中的记载。

"我被我的新小屋迷住了，"她在最后一次搬家之后这样写道，"邻居们都特别和善。"金斯利是最早来拜访她的客人之一。"他对这里超乎寻常的喜爱让我倍感吃惊。"老太太这样写道。

菲尔茨先生，那位美国出版商，也到燕子地来看望米特福德小姐，并立刻就成了她的一个忠实盟友。米特福德小姐那幅出自卢卡斯之手的肖像画就是赠送给了他。菲尔茨先生在他的《旧时与作家旧友》一书中留下了一段有趣

---

① 米特拉达梯（Mithridates），位于小亚细亚半岛的古国本都国的国王。

的描述——"她的几条狗和几丛天竺葵，"他写道，"是最令她感到与有荣焉的东西！她曾给我写过好几封长信聊她的芳淑，那是之前我到小木屋拜访她时见到的一条狗。她将天底下所有的美德都赋予了这条犬类朋友。我只好在回信中承认，自我们的星球开始旋转之日起，就没有哪只四条腿走路的动物能与芳淑相比。我之前和芳淑的先辈富莱茜[①]也很熟悉，也听惯了关于她的精彩故事，但芳淑自有她的风度和天赋。米特福德小姐一定会赞同汉默顿[②]所说的那番话：'我怀着谦卑之心感谢圣主造就了狗这种动物，并对那些生活中没有狗相伴的人深怀怜悯。'"

米特福德小姐的另一位挚友是约翰·罗斯金[③]，你很容易就能想到，他们之间有多少共同之处。罗斯金这样评价米特福德小姐的作品："它们有着《威克菲尔德的牧师》[④]的轻松诙谐与纯净，却没有其中故作幽默的机锋，或者说

---

① 富莱茜（Flush），勃朗宁夫妇的爱犬，一条英国猎犬，勃朗宁夫人曾为其赋诗（"To Flush，My Dog"）。英国现代主义小说家弗吉尼亚·伍尔芙（Virginia Woolf，1882—1941）曾以这条狗的视角创作小说《富莱茜传记》（*Flush: A Biography*，1933）。

② 菲利普·吉尔伯特·汉默顿（Philip Gilbert Hamerton，1834—1894），英国艺术家、艺术批评家、作家。

③ 哈内斯先生在写到罗斯金和米特福德小姐时说，"他的关爱使她在生命的最后一程备受鼓舞。他把她可能感兴趣的每本书，可能有助她恢复的每一种美味，都找来给她。"（安妮·萨克雷·里奇注）约翰·罗斯金（John Ruskin，1819—1900），英国维多利亚时代首屈一指的艺术批评家、画家、社会思想家、慈善家。

④ 《威克菲尔德的牧师》（*The Vicar of Wakefield*，1766），爱尔兰小说家奥利弗·戈德斯密斯（Oliver Goldsmith，1730？—1774）的成名作，也是十八世纪英国最为畅销的小说之一。

树篱另一侧世俗大道上的尘土……"

世俗的尘土和男人世界的道德标准都不是米特福德小姐写作的天赋之所在。她笔下描写自然的文字总是如行云流水，自在而甜美，毕竟那是她成长并本能地游弋其间的大自然。与之相比，她臧否人物的笔触却让人不敢恭维，比如她赞颂路易·拿破仑，她把狄更斯先生描述为一个乏味的伙伴，或者她对家父的看法，认为他是一个无情无义的世俗之人。每每从这些评判回到她描绘的自然之中都让人倍感宽慰。

在所有描述《我们的村庄》的作者的文字中，詹姆斯·佩恩先生的描述或许是最让人着迷的。他有不少她的信件可供摘引。"纸上是七零八落的文字，"他说，"没有一次不被覆盖或涂划过。即使是信封的盖口和外封也会传达出不少讯息。"

佩恩先生到燕子地去看望她，并描述了那个从地板到天花板都堆着书、飘着花香的小屋。"房间的住客艰难地从扶手椅中站起身，带着灿烂的微笑和迷人的姿态对我表示欢迎。我的父亲曾是她的一位老友，她用只有女人才会有的方式说起我的家和家里的摆设，不一会儿我们就径直说到了男人和书。她给我的印象是，她似乎认识每一个值得认识的人，从威灵顿公爵到刚刚崭露头角的诗人。她说起话来像天使一样，但是她对于把诗歌作为毕生事业的看法着实让我吃了一惊。她说她喜欢权宜的婚姻胜过因爱情而结合的婚姻，因为前者往往有更好的结局。'让你感到吃惊了，'她笑着说道，'不过我以为我是剧作家中最不浪漫的那个。'虽然当时她的剧作几乎已经被人忘记了，但她还是更为自己的戏剧感到自豪，而不是那些她被人熟知、引得人们从天涯海角跑来看她的那些作品……

"没有什么能摧毁她对自己所爱的执着信念。我若不是从自己家人那里了解到她父亲的事，我会以为他是个爱国者和殉道者。她谈到他的样子，就好像从来没有这样一个父亲——在某种意义上的确如此。"

佩恩先生还摘录了米特福德小姐对 K 的迷人描述："她对她佩服得五体投地。""K 是一个了不起的奇人，在某些方面她是我迄今见过的最聪明的女人，不是在文学方面（这并不让我感到失望），而是在任何实用的方面。她能给公爵夫人缝制一件宫廷礼服，可以给市长大人烹制晚餐，但她最主要的天赋是能把她身边的每个人都摆弄得服服帖帖，尤其是她的丈夫还有我。我们两人的钱都由她掌管，她决不允许我们当中任何一个在她不知情的情况下花上六便士……你真应该看看她让本跟她对账时的样子，还有她对那些管不住丈夫的女人的鄙夷。"

另一处有趣的摘录来自查尔斯·金斯利写给佩恩先生的一封信。它从另一个角度将过去展现在我们眼前。

"我永远也忘不了在燕子地的小房间里，那个蜷缩在两把椅子上的小身影，周围是一直堆到天花板的书——那个小小的身躯，裹在那些辨别不出，也无法辨别样式的衣服里，而就在这堆衣服顶端的某处，在圆润的宽大额头下面，闪烁着两只我大约从未在任何别的英国女人脸上看到过的眼睛——虽然我相信她一定是有法国人的血统，才会长出这样的眼睛，具有这样的口才，美丽的言辞出自那长相丑陋之人（确实如此），还有那双像燃烧着的炭一样闪烁、深邃的眼睛——当时还带着十足的诚恳……"真想一直这样摘录、引述下去，但我的序言必须就此打住了，因为这毕竟只是一篇序言，不过是在尘埃落定之后，依照过往而写就的许多篇序言中的一篇而已。

乡村图景

在所有常住居所中最让我感到愉快的莫过于远僻乡间的一个小村落。乡里乡亲比邻而居，不是住在大户人家的府宅大院里，而是庇身于茅屋村舍之中，我的一个朋友把这种毫不起眼的朴素住宅称作"农宅或棚户"，其中的居民和我们彼此熟识，就像我们熟识自家花园里的花儿一样。这是我们自己的一片小天地，我们聚在一起，与世隔绝，就像蚁穴中的蚂蚁，蜂巢中的蜜蜂，羊圈里的羊群，或者修道院里的修女，轮船上的水手；我们认识每个人，每一个人也都认识我们，我们关注每一个人，并理所当然地希望每一个人也同样关注我们。我们会出于习惯下意识地对彼此满怀善意，真诚相待，这真是让人身心愉悦的事。我们学着去了解、去关爱我们身边那些充满个性的人，就像我们学着去了解、去喜欢我们每天经过的林荫小道和晒场空地的角角落落。即使是在书里，我也偏爱封闭的生活环境，批评家们在谈论三一律时也有此偏爱。坐在主人公的马车轮子上飞驰而过大半个欧洲，在维也纳睡下，在马德里醒来，实在是让人厌烦透顶。这容易让人疲惫不堪，意志消沉。话说回来，最让人惬意的事是在奥斯汀小姐甜美的小说中，找一处乡间村落坐定，心里有十足的把握，知道我们会在离开之前对这里的每一处角落、每一个人都了如指掌；或者和怀特先生[①]一起在他塞尔伯恩的教区里漫步，与那里的田野、树林，还有栖身其间的鸟儿、老鼠和松鼠，结识交好；再或者和鲁滨孙·克鲁索[②]扬帆出海，到他的小岛上，和他、他的山羊，还有他的奴隶星期五，一起生活；——我们可不想有任何不速之客加入，不管是新近上岸的野人还是水手。我们从来不会因为主人公形单影只、少人陪伴而对他心怀同情，反而会因为他摆脱了这种境况而苦闷不已；或者和费迪南德一起遭遇沉船事故，登上另一个更为美妙的小岛——那个普洛斯彼罗、米兰达、卡里班和艾瑞尔栖居的小岛[③]，岛上再没有别的人，没有德莱顿[④]笔下那些新奇的发明——这样才美妙至极。一个

---

① 怀特的《塞尔伯恩博物志》（*The Natural History and Antiquities of Selborne*，1789）是迄今为止最迷人的书之一。我怀疑还没有自然学家采用过这种写法。（作者注）吉尔伯特·怀特（Gilbert White，1720—1793），英国十八世纪著名博物学家、教区牧师，现代生态学鼻祖，他以书信体形式记录家乡自然风物的著作《塞尔伯恩博物志》，以科学严谨的态度、质朴率性的行文，描绘自然，渲染闲适清雅的生活趣味，对后世影响深远。

② 丹尼尔·笛福《鲁滨孙漂流记》（*Robinson Crusoe*,1719）的主人公。

③ 莎士比亚剧作《暴风雨》（*The Tempest*，1611）中的人物和场景设置。

④ 约翰·德莱顿（John Dryden，1631—1700），英国著名诗人、文学评论家，英国历史上第一位桂冠诗人（1668）。他和威廉·大卫南特（William D'Avenant，1606—1668）一起改编了莎剧《暴风雨》，增加了许多新奇的角色。

鸡犬之声相闻的小村落不管是在真实存在的现实中，还是在诗歌或散文的字里行间都同样美好；一个小村落，譬如我在其间写作的伯克郡村庄，那里有一个平缓的山丘，山丘的谷底有一条蜿蜒的小路，还有一条大路横贯其中，常常有轻便马车、骑手和四轮马车出没，最近还因为有了从 B 地到 S 地的驿马车队而热闹了起来，十天前刚刚过去一班，我猜他们不日就会返程。时下的马车可谓多种多样，或许这是专门为每月往返或者每两周一趟的行程设计的。可敬的读者，你可愿意与我一起到我们的村庄里走走看看？路程并不长。我们将从地势低洼的那头出发，一路沿着山势向上。

我们的右手边是一幢整洁方正的红色小屋，靠路边的地方是它狭长而茂盛的花园，它的主人是隔壁镇上一位退休的酒馆老板，他家境殷实，有位长相秀丽的太太。他时常夸耀自己独立而闲散，喜欢谈论政治、阅读报纸，对牧师恨之入骨，呼吁要进行改革。他在王后①被赦罪的那天

---

① 指英王乔治四世的妻子卡罗琳王后（Caroline of Brunswick，1768—1821）。乔治和卡罗琳于 1795 年成婚，1796 年正式分居。乔治在 1820 年妄图通过议会废止两人的婚姻，剥夺卡罗琳的王后头衔，但最终因遭到托利党的阻挠而失败。乔治提议议会通过《痛苦和刑罚草案》，实际上是对卡罗琳的一次公开审判，受到了民众的广泛关注。该草案虽然在上议院勉强通过，但最终因引发民怨而被废止，卡罗琳因此被赦罪，仍保留王后头衔。

晚上，为我们介绍了亮灯仪式[①]，给我们这个宁静的村寨带来了颠覆性的新鲜体验。大家的抗议和劝说都徒劳无益；他津津乐道的是自由，甚至扬言要打碎窗户——因而我们都被鼓动起来，点亮了蜡烛。哦！那个夜晚他真是出尽了风头，烛光摇曳，月桂飘香，他家的窗户上装饰着白色蝴蝶结和金纸，还镶上了一张透明画片[②]（那原本是为口袋巾设计的），画片上正是王后本人的肖像，头戴着插有赤色羽毛的火红帽子，在烛光的照射下彤彤欲燃。我们都承认，他在村子里独领风骚，无人能及，熊熊的篝火在他面前都黯然失色；男孩子们特意为他点燃了他们最好的爆竹，而他给他们的纯银六便士比任何人都多。他恨不得每个月都举行一次亮灯仪式，因为显而易见，尽管需要料理花园，阅读报纸，坐着小车四处游玩，经常光顾教堂和聚会，但我们这位值得敬重的邻居已经开始对闲散生活感到厌倦了。他在自己家门口兜兜转转，总设法引诱路人停下脚步，与他攀谈。他自告奋勇四处帮忙，给人烟熏樱桃树治愈虫害，还追踪并消灭了整个教区里所有的胡蜂窝。我今天在我们的花园里还看到一大群胡蜂，回头一定告诉他这个消

① 亮灯仪式（illumination）是十五世纪起源于伦敦的一项习俗，当时政府要求主干道两侧的居民在特定的日子在窗户外悬挂灯笼，以方便议政晚归的议员；十六世纪时这项规定在英国广泛施行，人们在临街的窗户里面点上蜡烛，来庆祝皇室婚礼、加冕、战事大捷等重大事件，有时还伴有篝火和焰火活动；十七世纪时，这项习俗得到更广泛的推广和强化；十八世纪晚期，政党、社团和工会，甚至居民们，自发地开始利用这项活动表达他们的心愿和诉求。

② 透明画片（transparency），印制在亚麻纸上的图像画，多为人物肖像，放置在光源前面时，可以呈现半透明的效果。

息，让他找点乐子。他甚至还会帮助他太太打扫、擦洗、整理房间。可怜的人儿！他真算得上一个体面人，倘若他能在体面之余再从事一份工作，那他一定也会成为一个幸福的人。那才是他生命中至关重要的事。

与他比邻而居的是鞋匠，一个面色苍白、头发黝黑，看起来病恹恹的人，正是那种做事一丝不苟的楷模。两家之间隔着另一个狭长的花园，花园的一头有一间紫杉凉棚。鞋匠家的房子看起来相当不错，他每天都坐在自家的小店里，从清晨一直到深夜，就算是地震也很难撼动他：亮灯仪式也不能。他一直纹丝不动地坚持到最后，从第一盏灯亮起，经过漫长的燃烧到缓慢熄灭，最后他那根孤零零的巨大蜡烛成为那一带唯一的光亮。那天晚上这两位邻居，一位侍弄着透明画片，一位固执地与鞋履为伴，两人对彼此怀有的轻蔑简直到了无以复加的地步。在虚荣这一点上，辛勤劳作的那一位丝毫不亚于游手好闲的那一位，因为鞋匠也是个有产业的人。他手下有三个出了师的学徒工，两个是瘸子，一个是矮子，所以他的鞋铺看起来就像是医院。他花钱买下了他那间宽敞住宅的租契，也有人说他已经将那房子都买下了；他膝下只有一个可爱的女儿，年方十四，生得肤白貌美，一头金发。她是个孩子王，整天陪着街坊里三岁以下的小孩蹦蹦跳跳，载歌载舞，她逗弄孩子，给他们吃的，既是他们的守护天使，又是他们的玩伴。这个喜欢孩子的姑娘魅力十足。我从未见过任何一个与她身份相仿的人有如此与生俱来又难以名状的魅力和淑女风范。星期天的时候，我看到她穿着白色连衣裙，一身素雅的打扮，还以为她是一位伯爵的女儿呢。她也喜欢花草，她的窗前就种着一大丛白色的紫罗兰，和她一样纯洁美好。

路对面的第一所房子是铁匠家的，那是一幢阴森森的建筑，好像终年都见不到太阳似的，里里外外都黑咕隆咚、乌烟瘴气的，俨然一个冶炼厂。铁匠在我们这里还算是一位高级官员，级别和治安官不相上下；不过，呜呼哀哉！每次发生争端，治安官被请到现场的时候就会发现，他总是事端中牵涉最深的那一个。如果这个世界上没有酒馆，他的妻子和八个孩子该是何等幸运啊：治安官先生唯一的缺点就是，总会难以克制地要到那些充满诱惑的地方去。

这幢官员住宅的隔壁是一座整洁悦目的红砖小楼，高高的，窄窄的，傲视一方，楼面上一层接一层，一共有三扇可以上下拉动的框格窗，它们是村子里仅有的框格窗。楼的一侧种着一株铁线莲，另一侧是一株蔷薇，都生得细细高高的，像这座小楼一样。这座纤细的房子看起来相当雅致、有品位。小小的门厅似乎是专门为贺加斯笔下的老处女还有她发育不良的童仆①设计的，这里可以喝茶，可以设牌局——只能摆下一张桌子；褪色的丝绸衣服簌簌作响，老旧的瓷器散发着温润的光泽；四个人喜笑颜开，发牌斗点，洗牌的间隙还要说上几句温馨的悄悄话，聊聊别家的飞短流长；有人扭捏作态、装腔作势，有人肚子空空

---

① 威廉·贺加斯（William Hogarth，1697—1764），英国著名画家、版画家、讽刺漫画家，他在《浪子生涯》（*A Rake's Progress*，1735）系列版画中绘有一幅《迎娶老处女》（*Marries an Old Maid*）的画作，画面中的老处女身材矮小，她的前面还有一位更为矮小的童仆。

如也、饥饿难耐。这本是这个门厅该有的命运，但是阴差阳错：它属于一个体态丰腴、乐乐呵呵、吵吵闹闹的夫人，她带着四个胖乎乎、粉嘟嘟、闹哄哄的孩子，他们的确是粗俗和富足所孕育的精华。

接下来就是村子里的商店了，像其他村子里的店铺一样，这里如同集市一样琳琅满目，储备着各式各样的商品：面包、鞋子、茶叶、奶酪、扎带、彩带和熏肉。简言之，就是应有尽有，可是偏巧没有你一时急需却无论如何也找不到的那样东西。店主一家都待人很和善，他们生意做得红红火火，却依然很节俭。他们把房子的上面一层租给了两个年轻女人（其中一个是位蓝眼睛的漂亮姑娘），她们教年幼的孩子学习认字，给他们的妈妈做帽子和长袍——一边做学校老师，一边做裁缝。我相信她们一定会发现，修饰身体是一项远比修饰头脑更为赚钱的营生。

和商店隔着一个狭长的院子并正对着鞋匠家的，也是一处住宅，不过对于住在其中的人我将只字不提。那是一座小屋——不——一座微型房子，有许多附属的搭建，犄角旮旯儿的小地方都被利用了起来，有食品储藏室，还有其他诸如此类的空间。每个角落都物尽其用，让人分不清内外左右，却也别具魅力。半边房子前面是一个砖块砌成的小院子，另一半的前面是个小花圃；院墙久经风霜，已经颇为老旧，被蜀葵、玫瑰、忍冬，还有一株高大的杏树，遮住了。窗台上摆满了天竺葵（啊，我们那只了不起的白猫正栖身其间，眯着眼朝外张望呢）；隔间（我们的房主总是自信地把它们称作房间）里摆满了各种各样的器具和角柜;屋后的花园里种满了常见的花花草草:郁金香、石竹、飞燕草、芍药、紫罗兰和康乃馨,还有一座女贞树的枝条搭成的凉亭,不能不说像一个岗哨。当你坐在里面,会有绿色的光自然洒下,清爽宜人,在这里可以守望着花圃里百花争妍,花开花谢。这座房子建造的初衷,似乎就是为了展示一个奇小的空间里可以被安置得有多舒服。好了,我不能在此处再逗留了。

下一栋房子是一处重要场所——玫瑰酒馆:粉刷的白色外墙,房子离开大路一段距离,位于它那块精致的随风摆动的招牌后面。有一间带着一小扇凸窗的房间从房子的一侧凸出来,和我们马厩所在的另一边围成了一处开阔地带,时常停放着拉货的马车、四轮马车和返程的轻便马车。这会儿那里停放着两辆拉货的马车,我们的店主正穿着他那件永不离身的红马甲招待车夫们喝啤酒。他现在生意兴隆,人也发了福,从他身上的那件马甲就可以看出来,在过去的一年里,这件马甲被拆开线脚放宽了两次。我们的店主有一位精力充沛的妻子,一个前途无量的儿子,还有一个女儿,那可是村子里的大美女。这个姑娘并不像鞋匠家的那位仙女那般清秀,也远不如她优雅,但是打扮得要比她精巧十倍。她一大早就满头的卷发棒,活像一头豪猪,下午的时候顶一头卷发,活像一只卷毛狗,裙子上的褶边比卷发棒还要多,身边的情郎比发卷更多。菲比小姐更适合生活在城里,而不是乡村,正巧她自己对此也深有体会,因而得了空就往城里跑。她今天去了 B 城,带着她那位新近结交的、常伴左右的情郎,一位负责征兵的军士——这位就和凯特中士①一样高，也一样的厚颜无耻。总有一天他要把菲比小姐给拐走。

　　和那间带凸窗的房间并排的是一堵低矮的花园隔墙，墙的里面是一幢正在维修的房屋。这幢白色房屋正对着马轭匠的店铺，房子前面有四棵椴树，门口还堆着一车砖头。这幢房子是一个有钱人的玩物，那人热心肠，怪脾气，住在一英里之外。他对砖头和砂浆着了迷，但还没有头脑发热到要在自己的住所里折腾，于是就在这里捣鼓起来，改造再改造，翻修再翻修，一会儿建起来，一会儿再拆掉，忙得不亦乐乎。这真是一个完美的珀涅罗珀之网②。木匠和瓦工已经在这里工作了一年半，但有时我站在这里总是忍不住纳闷他们到底做了什么。然而，去年六月里他们倒是完成了一项壮举，这是毋庸置疑的。我们的这位芳邻突发奇想，认为那些椴树遮挡了太阳，使房间里昏暗无光（房间里除了工人并没有人居住），因而让工人把每棵树上的树叶都扒了个精光。那些树还站在原地，像一具具可怜兮兮的骷髅，它们从烈日炎炎的仲夏季节，突然过渡到了圣诞节，树干光秃秃的，片叶不存。大自然用她自己温和而

----

① 凯特中士（Sergeant Kite），爱尔兰剧作家乔治·法克尔（George Farquhar，1677—1707）的剧作《征兵军士》（*The Recruiting Officer*，1706）里的角色，该剧在当时风靡一时，广受欢迎，一直到世纪末都经演不衰。

② 珀涅罗珀之网（Penelope's Web），古希腊英雄奥德修斯的妻子珀涅罗珀在丈夫远赴战场未归之际，不堪追求者的烦扰，便承诺要在自己编织的长袍完成之日做出选择，但为了拖延时日，她白天编织，夜晚拆除，长袍便永远无法完成。

亲切的方式进行了报复，新叶重新在枝条上萌出，到了快圣诞节的时候，枝头上的绿叶已经和当初暴行实施之前一样茂密繁盛了。

隔壁住的是个木匠，他"盛名十里，名副其实"——没有几个打柜子的手艺能赶上他，他的太太出色能干，他们有一个小女儿莉兹。小莉兹是村子里的活宝，人见人爱，被宠得像女王一样，按照出生记录来看她只有三岁，可是看个头、体力和智力，以及掌控力和意志力，则完全是六岁孩子水平。她总是能掌控全局，调动差遣在场的每个人，包括她的学校老师；她能让修车匠家的孩子把小车子让给她，还能让他们拉着她到处跑；她只消站在商店的橱窗外，就能把蛋糕和棒棒糖骗到手；她能让不肯出力的懒人抱起她，能让木讷的人和她聊天，能让严肃的人和她嬉闹；她兴之所至，几乎无所不能；她的魅力简直令人无法抗拒。她最吸引人的地方是她满怀爱意，无所顾忌，而且她坚定地相信人人都心中有爱，宽容大度。当这个可爱的小姑娘跑到你的身边，把她漂亮的小手放在你的手心，满怀欣喜地望着你，对你说"快来！"你怎么可能拒绝她，让她失望呢？你一定会和她一起，完全身不由己。她的魅力同时也来源于她非凡的容貌。她的个性和拿破仑有许多相似之处，就连宽厚、结实、挺拔的身形也和他如出一辙；她有着世界上最修长优美的四肢，有着纯正英国人的肤色；一张圆圆的脸，总是笑眯眯的，泛出红晕和日晒的健康色泽；一双蓝色的大眼睛，顾盼生辉，还有一头棕色的鬈发，总是一副灵动活泼的样子。她举手投足间自有一种帝王的风范，站着的时候喜欢把手背到后面，或者交叉叠在胸前；有时候，她如果感到有点儿难为情，就会双手十指交叉放在脑袋上，摁住她那一头柔亮的鬈发，那个样子真是可爱极了！没错，莉兹就是我们村子里的女王！在她的疆界中，唯一可以与她匹敌的是一只名叫五月花的白色格力犬，这只狗更像是她的朋友，和她在容貌、力量、活泼和智慧程度上势均力敌，旗鼓相当，五月花在动物世界里的统治地位就像她在人类世界里的一样。她们两个今天都和我在一起，莉兹和莉兹"可爱的五月花"。我们已经沿着这条街走到底了，前面有一条岔路，有一个位于椵树和橡树树荫里的制绳厂，还有一汪凉爽而清澈的池塘，池塘的边上环绕着几棵枝叶低垂的榆树，再往前就到山脚下了。街角处还有一栋房子，最尽头是周围景色如画的修车匠的店铺。这栋房子相比之下显得更为讲究。看看那精致雕花的百叶窗，镶着纯铜门环的绿色大门，再看看门口那个略显拘谨但礼貌至极的人，他正在送一个干活儿的人出门，不停地招呼"先生"，并且行礼致意，礼貌周到得足以接待王公贵族了。这栋房子是助理牧师的租住之处——他的房东太太可能更愿意把这里叫作公寓；他和自己的家里人住在四英里之外，但是每个礼拜都会往这里跑一两趟，在这个整洁的小客厅里写布道词，根据情况需要，主持婚礼或者葬礼。他的房东和房东太太都是难得一见的诚实而善良的人，自从他们觉得自己和教会结了缘，日常便有了一份从事神职工作的自持自重，这种意识对他们无疑是一种教化——他们行事因此多了一份得体、庄重和一丝不苟的礼貌。哦，瞧那可敬的修车匠，礼拜天的时候总是跟在自家租客的后面，帮助理牧师捧着教士长袍，他把妻子送他的最好的手帕别在身上，打扮得多么整齐漂亮！——或者去听听他是如何斥责号啕大哭的孩子，或大声吵嚷的妇人的，简直让人肃然起敬！那位助理牧师在他面前也相形见绌。他足可以永久担任教区的堂会理事了。

我们现在必须穿过岔路到阴凉的制绳厂这边。正对着我们的是一栋漂亮的白色小屋，它自成一体地位于村头上一座开满了花的花园里。小屋的主人是我们的石匠，村子里最矮的男人，和他漂亮、高挑的太太。石匠虽然是侏儒的身型，却有巨人一般洪亮的嗓门；他开口讲话的时候，会把人吓一跳，人们会误以为他在通过大喇叭喊话。他太太来自一个园艺世家，家里的兄弟、父亲和祖父都是园艺师，她本人的园艺也毫不逊色。我要尽量宽宏大度才能不憎恨她，因为在我最擅长的那些方面，在种菊花、大丽菊，还有其他类似的鲜艳花卉品种上，她总是技高一筹。她侍弄的花草都长势喜人；我弄的总是显露出一些蔫萎的迹象，或许是因为我的关爱"过分，而不明智"，照顾得过于周到，反而害死了它们。沿着山坡向上，半山腰的地方还有一座孤零零的小屋，里面住着一位军官和他美丽的家人。他们家里最大的男孩此刻正靠在大门口，眼巴巴地望着我的莉兹，眼睛里满是孩子特有的艳羡的神情，他的模样足可以做丘比特的原型了。

山路随着山势蜿蜒向上，路两边有宽阔的绿色植物带和密密匝匝的树篱，走在被绿色包围的山路上，多么惬意舒适！夕阳沿着被开掘成沙地的山坡缓缓沉下去，金色的余晖洒在山顶的农家小院上，一派安宁祥和的景象！有个人正从山上走下来，夕阳在他的身后，清晰地映出他的身影，勾勒出他如浮雕般的轮廓！那是可怜的园丁约翰·伊万斯——大约十年前他曾是位出色的园丁，可是在他妻子不幸亡故之后，他就疯了。他被送到了圣路加医院，回来的时候说是治好了，但是他之前的本事和力气都没了；他再也无法胜任打理花园的工作，更受不得管束，也无法承受日常劳作的辛苦，因而他只能去了救济所，在那里帮忙，照顾那些需要救济的人，干些零碎活儿，成了村子里的勤杂工，他能干的事也就这些。他时常会心不在焉，耽于一些异想天开、不切实际的计划，还会恍恍惚惚地对着眼前的事物发呆；然而，他对谁都没有恶意，不会伤害任何人，充满了孩子般的天真，总是一副面带微笑、心满意足的样子，最让人感动的是他有着一副感恩心肠，只念别人的好。每个人对约翰·伊万斯都是和善的，因为他总是让人心生怜悯。他待人一片坦诚，毫无戒心，总是让人忍不住要待他好一点。我不知道还有谁能勾起人们如此深沉又柔软的恻隐之心，他能让周围的每个人都变得更好。他同时也是个有用之人，在他力所能及的范围之内，他愿意竭尽全力，当然他最喜欢干的还是园艺活儿，他依然为自己修剪果树和种黄瓜的老手艺感到骄傲。眼下他算得上最幸福的人了，因为他在照看一片瓜圃——一片瓜圃！——呵！其实就是巴掌大的一块地儿，种了三棵瓜苗，也好意思称作瓜圃，实在是虚张声势、像煞有介事！约翰·伊万斯胸有成竹地认为这几棵秧苗会瓜果飘香。我们不妨等着瞧：就像那位大臣所说，"我不这么看"。

我们现在正好走到近顶的山脊处，山顶上的房子和它美丽的花园已经近在咫尺了。道路一侧的山坡顶上，沿着院子栅栏的外侧，长着一丛有些年头的荆棘——真是蔚为壮观的荆棘！长长的花枝上缀满了雪一样的白花，冰清玉洁，婀娜多姿，虽是一片淡雅的素色，却让人觉得明亮鲜艳，丰腴繁茂。若是能有一方水塘置于其下，映出它更为可爱的倒影，那该何等美妙！花影颤动摇曳，如一蓬羽毛轻轻抖动，比实际的颜色更白更绿，融于蔚蓝的天色中则更显明艳。那里确实应该有一处水塘；不过，在那华美的犹如被白色羽冠覆盖的高坡底下，深绿色的草地之上，有样东西起到了相同的作用——莉兹和五月花正在追逐嬉闹，她们"给荫翳处带来了阳光"。莉兹在草地上打着滚儿、嬉笑、拍手，像一朵玫瑰一样明艳夺目；五月花围在她的身边玩耍，像夏日里的闪电一样飞驰疾走，时而急停转身，时而蹦跳腾跃，时而主动出击，时而落荒溜逃，看得人眼花缭乱。她穿梭往返于那个可爱的小姑娘身边，如燕子掠过水面一般轻盈，带着同样迅疾如飞的敏捷，同样的自在、矫健和优雅。她们构成了一幅多么美妙的画面！她们使周围的美景都黯然失色，成为画面里的背景和陪衬！弯折而下的山路上，有一个和牛津的主街上一样平缓的弯道，一辆四轮马车正缓缓地爬上来，一个人骑在马上从它身边疾驰而过——（啊！莉兹和五月花一定会撇下你去和那匹良种马玩上一阵！）山路下到一半，恰好在弯道处的就是那位上尉军官的红房子，房子上面爬满了葡萄藤蔓，俨然一幅闲适与富足的画面。再往下，路的另一边，是小个子石匠家的白色小屋；接着就是椴树林和制绳厂；村子里的街道在树木的掩映中隐约可见，透过集簇的树冠，只能看见几根烟囱，各家样式各异的屋顶，还有东一处西一处的墙角；再远处，便是 B 城优雅的小镇了，那里竖立着不少老教堂雅致的塔楼和尖顶。灰白色的远山连绵起伏，将整个画面环绕其中，画面的每个角落都点缀着绿树，树木如此繁茂，以至于整个画面看上去就像是一幅林区的景色图，有林间空地和村落错落其中。这些树种类繁多，颜色参差，主要是榆树和橡树。榆树树形优雅，树的绿色明亮而厚重，树冠高处的枝条自然垂落，整个树顶看起来蓬松极了，又有着花环一样丰富的层次；橡树姿态庄重，阳光下新生的叶片熠熠生辉，把整个树都装点得耀眼夺目。

转过身继续朝山上走，我们会发现自己正置身英式田园风光特有的景致之中：眼前是一大片被道路分开的公共绿地；右边一侧的绿地被篱笆和树木环绕，其间不规则地分布着小屋和农舍，尽头是两列高大的橡树夹成的林荫大道；左边一侧景色更加迷人，清澈的水塘罗列其中，间杂着如岛屿般的房子和屋后花园，沿着山坡往下逐渐过渡为玉米地和草场，其间有一处古旧的农庄，房子上有尖尖的屋顶，还耸立着一簇烟囱，农庄背靠着绿树葱茏的山坡，坐落于一片开满了花的果园之中。这片绿地本身就是周遭景色中最亮眼的部分，其中的一半被低矮的荆豆花丛所覆盖，金色的花瓣尽情地反射着落日的最后几抹余晖，成群的牛羊在草地上漫步，还有两组正在玩板球的人。其中一组是年轻人，被一群观众围了起来，观众们或站或坐，或躺在草地上，都兴致盎然地关注着这场比赛。另一组是与他们相隔不远的一群小孩子，对于这些欢快的男孩子来说，他们还不怎么会玩板球，因而他们欢叫着，跳跃着，纵情地玩耍嬉闹。但是，这些板球运动员和乡下孩子都是我们村子里不容小觑的重要人物，不该作为风景中的身影而被一笔带过。他们值得单辟一章来介绍——一篇专门写他们的文字——而且我的确会为他们写一篇。所以，请不必担心，我不会忘了这些每天散步途中都会遇见的欢乐面孔的。

乡间漫步

霜降

一月二十三日——今日午间我和我的白色格力犬五月花出门散步。我们走进了一个美丽异常的世界——有点像一个无声的梦幻国度——一个由无与伦比的魔术师白霜所创造的天地。之前刚刚下过雪，地上的万物都还是银装素裹，但雪过之后，树上的积雪在慢慢滑落，正当树篱抖落了身上蓬松的雪被之际，又被裹上了一层晶莹剔透的雾凇。万物都笼罩在一片怡人的静谧之中，虽然温度很低，但周遭一片柔和的景象，甚至感觉有些温暖；空气中没有一丝风，倒是充满了几乎可以被触碰到的安宁。天空的颜色，与其说是蓝的不如说是灰的，正好凸显出村子里被白雪覆盖的屋顶，和耸立其上的挂满雾凇的大树。阳光有些黯淡，太阳像是隔着一层纱，放射出些许浅淡的光亮，看起来就像月亮一样，不过略微明亮了些。我们站在窄小的家门口，朝着安静的街道望去，四下里一片寂静，也像极了月色中的幽静。人们像在过安息日一样，放下了工作，孩子们也不出门玩耍，这在工作日实属少见。听不到任何响动，只有结霜时发出的悦耳的嚓响，那种单调低沉的声音或许是生活和自然能够产生的最接近绝对安静的声响。那些从山上下来的马车，一路沿着结了冰霜的松软泥路滑行，如同影子一样没有什么声音；即使是五月花，虽然兴致高昂，欢快地奔驰跳跃，但脚步落下的时候也像是雪落在雪地之上，悄然无声。

　　不过，我们马上就能听到足够大的响动啦：五月花已经来到了莉兹家的门前；莉兹原本坐在窗台上，红扑扑的小脸儿透过窗棂笑嘻嘻地朝外望着，她一看见五月花就从窗台上消失了。她马上就下来了。不！钥匙在门里面旋转，不祥的声音透过锁孔传了出来——莉兹一声声坚定的"让我出去"，"我就要去"，混合着她对着五月花和我发出的尖叫，并穿透了一连串低声的唠叨说教，这一大段说辞的主要内容就是道歉、冻疮、滑雪、骨折、棒棒糖、棍子还有姜饼，都出自莉兹素来小心谨慎的母亲。"别在门上乱抓，五月花！别这么喊了，我的莉兹！我们回来的时候再来找你。""我现在就来！放我出去！我就要去！"这是我们听到的莉兹小姐的最后几句话。天哪！如果我能做到，我绝不会纵容那孩子！但是，我真的认为她的妈妈应该让那个可怜的小家伙今天和我们一起出去走走。溺爱对孩子实在是有百害而无一利，而锻炼无疑是对付冻疮最好的办法。况且，我相信她不会有任何——像滑雪时摔断骨头这样的闪失，我猜公共绿地上压根儿就没有滑道。我在心里不停地念念叨叨，完全没意识到我们已经快要到山顶了。我们正从那块明亮耀眼、雾气缭绕的公共绿地旁边经过，绿地上白雪皑皑，簇拥在一起的几座小屋正升起炊烟，烧着泥炭火的炉子一圈圈地往外吐着烟，芳香的气味也随之飘散开来。紧接着就传来了孩子们的欢声笑语，阵阵欢腾雀跃的声音似乎就来自我们的脚底下。啊，莉兹，你的妈妈真是英明！他们的欢呼声就来自那个不规则的水塘底部，水塘结了冰，上面有两条狭长、光滑且笔直的滑道，六七个衣衫破烂的小顽童正欢呼着，摇摇晃晃地从上面滑下来。我们没走几步就来到了位于他们正上方的山坡上。五月花再也按捺不住要和朋友们一起玩耍的冲动，因为这里大多数的顽童都是她的老相识，特别是带头滑冰的那个——他戴着一顶无檐儿帽，古铜色的皮肤，浅亚麻色的头发，和平常人肤色浅发色黑的样貌正相反，这使得他扁平而滑稽的五官看起来很是奇特，活像一个外国人。这个淘气包名叫杰克·拉普利，是五月花的亲密好友。五月花此时正站在陡坡的边缘，黑色的眼睛紧紧地盯着他，似乎正打算跳到他的头上去以示友好。她跳了，纵身一跃，朝着他的身上扑去，但杰克·拉普利也不是那么容易就被扑到的。他看见了五月花，就在她起跳的一刹那，他熟练地一闪身，从滑道跳到了粗糙的冰面上，扶着他后面那个家伙的肩膀站住了脚，而他后面那个可怜的家伙没留神他这么猛地插过来，一个趔趄朝后跌去，把队列里后面的人像纸牌屋一样挨个儿撞倒了。所幸没有造成什么伤害，但是大家伙儿都跌在了地上，有的哀号不已，有的乱踢乱蹬，还有的趴着站不起来，出尽了洋相。可杰克·拉普利和五月花，这场灾难的始作俑者，站在人群的边上，一个撒娇，一个爱抚，亲昵地靠在一起，互相称赞着对方；看着大伙儿倒霉的样子，他们两个都憋着笑，五月花忽闪着她黑色的大眼睛，杰克的阔嘴巴抿成了一条线，撇到了耳朵边，脸拧得像猴子一样。我想，五月花小姐，你最好还是跟着我继续走，让拉普利大人来替你善后。他肯定能全身而退。他可是村子里的机灵鬼——像罗宾·古德菲洛①一样的人物——整个教区里就数他最爱惹是生非，整天游手好闲，鬼点子最多，但也数他最心地善良；调皮捣蛋一流，但也总是助人为乐。村子里的智者都预测杰克·拉普利命途多舛，因此有时候在这些睿智之士面前，我难免要略带羞涩地承认，我对他颇有好感（对其他的顽皮孩子也是一样），我喜欢听他和五月花说话，就像五月花那样喜欢。"过来，五月花！"她只要一听到这声音就会跳起来，欢快得像只小鸟。路上此时已热闹了起来，轻便马车和邮递马车，披着红色斗篷的姑娘，还有远处看上去像个玩具一样的四轮马车，都从我们身边匆匆而过。坐车的人远不如步行走路的人快活——尤其是那位被冻坏了的先生，和那位看不见脸、一直在瑟瑟发抖的女士，他们是那辆宽敞的四轮马车上仅有的乘客。尽管那位女士裹着头巾，遮着面纱，戴着呢帽，但是只看她那样子就知道，要是把这些摘掉，她一定是一副惨相。

接下来又有一个水塘，又是孩子们嬉闹的声音。也是

① 罗宾·古德菲洛（Robin Goodfellow），也叫帕克（Puck），英国民间传说中的人物，是个自然精灵、恶魔，喜欢恶作剧和冒险活动。

在滑冰？哦，不！这是一种更有雅兴的活动。我们的芳邻，那位上尉军官正在溜冰，他家里可爱的男孩们，还有两三个四岁左右的机灵鬼，都站在场边看得如痴如醉，满怀着欣喜和赞叹！哦，多么幸福的观众！多么幸福的表演者！他们对他充满了仰慕之情，而他就是他们仰慕的对象，他们心中洋溢的热情和真诚，是所有的方阵舞曲和优雅的大一字舞步无论如何也激发不出来的。他确实滑得不错，我很高兴自己走了这条路，因为，尽管他心中满是作为父亲的欢快得意，但有一个之前观看过溜冰的人在这个孤独的水塘边充当他的观众，一定可以满足他对于自己技艺的自豪感。

现在我们才终于来到了树林——这些树真是美不胜收！它们从未像今天这样美。想象一下，一条差不多有一英里长的林荫大道两侧，有两列笔直、等距的橡树夹道而列，橡树的枝干伸展交错，在头顶搭出一道弯拱，在远处交会成纵向的景深，像教堂的屋顶和廊柱一样，而每一棵树的每一条枝干上都缀满了透亮晶莹的霜花，像雪一样洁白无瑕，像雕刻的象牙一般细致精巧。多么美丽，多么整洁，多么多姿，多么饱满，多么让人赏心悦目——更重要的是，多么让人感伤！这赤裸无色的美景中蕴藏着一种简单的力量，它摄人心魄，让人为之一颤，让人顿生敬畏，它就像死亡的想象悄悄降临——纯净，荣耀，带着微笑——但依然是死亡。雕塑总是能带给我同样的震撼和想象，但绘画从来不会。颜色就是生命。我们现在已经走到了这条壮丽大道的尽头，来到了一个陡峭山坡的顶上，在这里可以将四个郡的景色尽收眼底——一幅江山雪景图。有一条纵深的小路沿着山势陡然而下，那其实是一条狭窄的供小车走的车道，车道两侧是覆盖着蕨类、荆豆花和低矮的金雀花丛的高坡，上面是茂盛的树篱枝条撑起的绿色华盖，这里因为夏日里馥郁的百里香而闻名。此刻的高坡甚是可爱——高高的野草和荆豆枝条都裹上了一层霜花，被牢牢冻住了，白霜还爬上了翠绿多刺的冬青，还给耷拉着叶片的黑莓和去了梢的橡树上的深橘色的树叶都镶上了一道银边！哦，这才是最美的雾凇景象！冬青树上还零星残留着一两颗莓果，透过晶莹的冰凌，"露出自然绯红的靓色"，也能见到一颗遗落的野蔷薇果或是山楂果，那是给一直在此处出没的鸟儿们的。那些可怜的鸟儿，它们如此温顺，温顺得让人难过！此时灌木丛的中间正停着一只美丽而稀有的金冠鹪鹩，塞尔伯恩的怀特把这种鸟称为"鸟之影"，这个可怜的小东西，还像在无霜的冷枝上那样安卧着，试图寻求它注定无法找到的温暖。再往前，就在高坡的下面，有一条清溪，溪水依旧在透明纤薄的冰层之间流淌，仿佛一样活物——溪水的边上，有一只颜色绚丽的翠鸟，正贴着岸边疾飞短停，它姿态轻盈而迅捷，红蓝两色的华丽羽毛在阳光的照射下熠熠发光，宛如某种鲜艳的热带鸟类。它是来这条傍山的小溪里找水喝的——但即使是生着它这样的长喙和小头，也还是很难够到水，那些有着像花环一样美妙花纹的冰层边缘，距离下面孱弱的溪流实在是太近了。能如此近距离、长时间地观察这只羞怯的美丽小鸟实属难得，看着它在自然且自由的状态下展示它的身姿和美貌，实在是一桩乐事，这也是观察鸟类唯一的方法。过去，在还没有搬到街上去住的时候，我们总是会在寒冷的天气里，在客厅窗户的外面固定一块小木板，并在上面撒上面包屑。看着这些美丽的小东西克服它们的羞涩，放下心中的忐忑，走过来吃食，总是让我们感到由衷的快活。最先来的总是那些更为活泼的鸟类，"知更鸟和鹪鹩"一开始会小心翼翼、异常警觉地叼起面包屑就飞走，明亮而锐利的小眼睛紧紧地盯着窗户；接着它们会停下来啄两下，之后就会一直留在那里直到吃饱为止。那些更为怕人的鸟儿会学着它们的样子，紧随其后飞过来；最后来的是那只有点儿冒失的乌鸫——一副沮丧又贪吃的样子，会在两分钟之内把板子上剩余的东西一扫而光——还会用它黄色的喙啄啄窗户，想讨要更多。我们都爱极了那个耿直的家伙，还有它无所畏惧的自信心！它当然也很喜欢我们。我很纳闷，这种做法为什么不常见到了。"五月花！五月花！调皮的五月花！"她吓走了那只翠鸟；这会儿，她正把雪往我身上扒，以表示她的歉意，寻求我的宽待。"来吧，漂亮的五月花！我们该回家了。"

消融

一月二十八日——我们经历了雨水、降雪、霜冻和又一次降雨，已经整整四天没有出门了。现在冰雪消融，到处汪洋一片，但是我们松软的沙砾土壤、乡下人的靴子和乡下人不怕苦的性格，会帮助我们熬过这一切。到处都是湿答答的，真是让人难过的一天！就像十一月最后那几天一样：看不到太阳，也看不到天，不管是灰色还是蓝色的天空都看不到，一大块云低低地压在头顶上，暗暗的，让人感到压抑，就像伦敦的雾一样。五月花还是出门溜达去了，莉兹去上学了。没关系。再到山上去！我们必须出去走走。回首一看，到处都是汪洋的水世界！泰晤士河，肯尼特河，洛登河——都泛滥了；我们那些著名的小镇，原本处在内陆，此刻都变成了威尼斯一样的水城；中央公园犹如一座孤岛；从 B 地延伸至 W 地的大面积草场，此时成了一个里面长着树的、奇怪的巨型湖泊。哦，真是一片水汪汪的世界！我再也不想看它了。我要继续走下去。马路上又开始热闹了。噪声重又回来了。马车吱扭吱扭作响，马蹄啪嗒啪嗒飞溅着水花，货车辘辘而过，穿着木套鞋踩过泥坑的时候，会发出比平时更响的踢踏声。公共绿地上还像往日一样分布着好看的绿色和棕色色块，还像往常一样聚集着各种各样的动物，马、牛、羊、猪，还有驴。水塘并没有结冰，只有几块正在融化的冰块阴郁地漂浮在水面上，嘎嘎叫的鹅和呱呱叫的鸭取代了上尉军官和杰克·拉普利。林荫大道笼罩在一片寒寂和黑暗之中，灌木丛在往下滴水，小路上的水能没过膝盖，整个大自然都处于一种"消解和融化"的状态。

第一枝报春花

三月六日——三月里的好天气:万物萌动,生机勃勃,刮风和下雨的日子多了起来,常常是疾风伴着骤雨;然而,云被大风卷走,天空便呈现出醉人的蓝色,还透着些许阳光,明亮、清澈、健康。尽管不时有零星的阵雨,但路面上都很干爽。总的来说,天气宜人,十分宜人,让人蠢蠢欲动。那片可爱的公共绿地四面开阔,眼下并不适合散步,但是山脚下那些被遮蔽起来的小路却是不错的选择,那里背风向阳,没有强劲的大风,阳光也很充足。先经过我们的老房子,到那些蜿蜒的小路上绕一圈,再到救济所那边,穿过牧场,再回到公路上来——这就是我们今天的线路。我们出发了,五月花和我高高兴兴地走进阳光里,风吹起来的时候越发觉得神采奕奕,因为它给了我们一种强烈的存在感。清新的风拂面而来,让我们热血沸腾、精神焕发。如果只说身体上的享受,几乎没有什么能比得上坐在一辆套着纯种马的轻便马车里,让马儿拉着,顶着这样的风全速疾驰,所带来的爽快感觉。散步只能退居其次,但散步并不像前者那样奢侈,那样让人精神亢奋,并不会让人产生飞翔的幻觉，或者产生在热气球里被带上天的感觉。

　　无论如何，散步依旧是一件美事，特别是走在这种南方的灌木树丛之下，大自然正从那里的枝头上复苏。长春花开出了星星点点的蓝色花朵，衬着它油亮的长圆形叶片，给灌木丛戴上了一道花环；忍冬和接骨木上长出了鼓胀的花苞，草皮和苔藓正呈现出丰富多样、深浅不一的棕色和绿色。我们此时正走到一个四条小路会合的地方，或者说是一条可以通行的石头沙砾铺就的路与一片不能通行的、美丽却潜藏危险的草坡交叉的地方。那里有一座白色的小农舍，比一间小屋大不了多少，后面还有一个堆着草料的院子，院子拾掇得整整齐齐，显得舒适又有序，但也让所有人都猜不透主人到底藏着多少家底。他是如何变得如此富有的几乎一直是个谜。因为农场固然是农场主巴纳德自己的，但是并不大；虽然他平素里总是谨慎又节俭，但他绝不是个吝啬鬼。他的马、狗和猪都是整个教区里养得最好的——五月花，虽然她的美貌因为肥胖而遭到折损，但还是忍不住羡慕他家那只母狗弗莱的境况。巴纳德妻子的裙子和围巾比村里人的普遍要贵上一倍；他家里举办的宴会（当然并不是很多）上摆出来的好东西有平常的两倍多——两对鸭子、两盘青豆、两只火鸡雏、两条熏火腿、两份梅子布丁；而且，他还有一辆一匹马拉的轻便马车，并捐资兴建了一座卫理公会的小教堂。然而，他依然是这一带最富有的人。他不管干什么都干得有声有色。钱就像雪片一样朝他飞来。他看起来就像个有钱人，四四方方的脸庞，宽阔结实的身板儿，性格开朗，又有毅力，是一位在地方上有头脸的人物。他从不夸耀自己的财富，或者无端地摆架子，但是，每个在集市上或是教区委员会碰到他的人，都能一眼看出他是那里最有钱的人。他们没有孩子来继承家产，但是有位过继过来的外甥，是位意气风发的少年，或许将来有一天，他能够将这份厚实的家产很好地传承下去。

现在我们转到宽阔的大路上，沿着路一直走到开阔的公地，那里有像庄园里一样修剪整齐的树木，有美丽的溪流，蜿蜒流淌，还有极具乡村风情的桥。我们在这里再次转弯，经过另一所白房子，房子在屋前几棵大榆树的掩映下忽隐忽现。啊！那里并不是财富的栖息之所，却有着仅次于财富的第二等美妙事物——一种饱含勤劳和乐观的清贫。二十年前瑞秋·希尔顿是这一带乡里最漂亮、最快活的姑娘。她的父亲，原先是位猎场看守人，退休之后在村子里开了一间酒馆。他那里的好啤酒，他热情随和的性情，还有他黑眼睛的女儿，为他招揽了不少生意。当年追求瑞秋的人不胜枚举，但是约瑟夫·怀特，一个家境殷实的农户家的儿子，风度翩翩又充满活力，最终赢得了美人的芳心。他们结了婚就住在这里，现在他们还住在这里，和以前一样快活，不过多了十四个大大小小、年龄不一的孩子，大的十九岁，小的才十九个月。他们比教区里别的人家更加勤劳，也更会享受生活。我敢说全英格兰也没有几个家庭像他们家这样吃苦耐劳，这样充满欢声笑语。她是个无忧无虑的快活主妇，当初的美貌被岁月放大成了现在的秀美风韵；他瘦瘦高高，结实健壮，肌腱像鞭绳一样有力，声音洪亮爽朗，脸庞轮廓清晰，带着饱经风霜的沧桑。每当谈话谈得尽兴时，他的眼睛和嘴唇就会流露出笑意，脸上散发着光芒，深深地感染着周围的人。他们很穷，我常常希望他们能变得更有钱，但是我不知道——或许那样反倒会打扰到他们，让他们心神不宁。

　　紧挨着农户怀特家的是一间破败的小屋，曾经粉刷过一次，现在处于不新不旧的尴尬状态。疏于管理的花园里晾晒着袜子和衬衫，被风吹得鼓胀起来，表明这里住着一位洗衣妇。眼下住在这里，过着幸福的独居生活的是贝蒂·亚当斯，她的丈夫是位园丁，有时会帮助我们打理花园。我从未见过任何人像她一样，每次见到都让我想起那位尽人皆知的麦格·美瑞利斯夫人[①]；一样的高挑，一样的花白头发，一样的庄重，一样的黝黑皮肤，一样的吉卜赛人长相，连穿衣戴帽都和她的原型人物一样，说起话来也几乎总是一副讳莫如深的样子。不过，她们的相像仅限于此。亚当斯太太是个非常诚实的人，勤勤恳恳，任劳任怨，通过洗衣和打扫卫生挣了不少钱。这些钱她都花在了比保洁更为奢侈的方面——绿茶、杜松子酒，还有鼻烟。她的丈夫住在十英里之外的一个大户人家。他是个一流的园丁——或者说，他会成为一个一流的园丁，假使他不那么野心勃勃的话。他什么都尝试，但一事无成。然而，他能说会道，看起来一副很懂行的样子，再加上力气大、能

---

① 麦格·美瑞利斯（Meg Merrilies），英国历史小说家沃尔特·司各特的小说《占星人》中的人物，一位吉卜赛老妇，能通灵，能预知未来。

干活儿，每次都能蒙混过关。如果能让他喝上几杯，碰上一个对头的主顾，他一个人能顶四个人的工。假使能让他适得其所，全力以赴，他是不会出半点差池的。

啊，五月花飞奔到前面去了！她只要一看见老宅，那颗傻傻的心脏就会加速跳动——不过，说实在话，我也一样。那是多么漂亮的一个地方呀——或者说我觉得那里是多么漂亮呀！我想，我会把任何一个我度过了十八年快乐时光的地方想成这个样子。可是，它是真的漂亮。那是一座结实的大房子，白色外墙，样式极为简单，四周环绕着挺拔的橡树和榆树。高大繁茂的植被荫蔽着下面一块美丽的草坪，草坪上有蔓长的野生灌木丛、枝叶成荫的合欢、蓬乱的多花蔷薇、一丛丛隆起的山茱萸，还有葡萄牙桂樱和月桂，上面垂挂着金链花和稠李；给画面当中引入光亮的是一道长长的流水，它看起来就像一条自然的溪流，岸边野蛮生长着稠密的灌木，间杂着金雀花、荆豆花和黑莓，还有几棵去了梢的橡树，上面爬满了常春藤和忍冬；所有这些都被一道破旧的长满了青苔的庄园栅栏围了起来，阻挡了这一块绵延生长的茂密草坪继续蔓延的趋势。这就是老宅的真实样貌，三年前，当我离开这个家的时候，心都要碎了。那种撕心裂肺的感觉，就好像被连根拔起！从那之后，我一直对甘蓝类蔬菜、芹菜，还有所有可以移植的植物都充满了怜悯。尽管和它们，还有别的蔬菜一样，搬家移种后最初的痛苦已经过去，我已经在新的土地上深深地扎根，牢牢地挺立住，但我无论如何都不想再次被连根拔起，哪怕是要把我安置回曾经深爱的故地——就算它的美没有丝毫的折损，更不用说实际情况远非如此。这三年里，老宅已经三易其主，每一位继任者对这里的改进，都无一例外地遭遇了厄运。有人为了阻挡湿气而填埋了水道；有人为了视野开阔而砍伐树木，又有人为了有所遮挡而重新种树；有人为了让室内的光线暗淡而封死了窗户（这样使得房子的一角看起来就像黑桃八不幸丢掉了角上的一颗桃心）；又有人为了更加敞亮，而大刀阔斧地砍去了树木、黑莓灌木、常春藤、忍冬、庄园栅栏和杂乱的灌木丛，之后又修建了廊柱。这个可怜的地方已经变得面目全非，倘若它能重新找回自己旧日的镜子，那道流水，它一定也认不出自己的样子了。可我还是喜欢在附近转转，五月花也一样。她最喜欢去的地方是一个塌陷的坡地，上面满是兔子洞，她会慢慢地把自己柔软的头和脖子伸到里面去，然后徒劳地抓划着她那漂亮的爪子。我最喜欢去的地方生着一丛向阳的灌木树篱，它们看起来暖融融的，也在同一个少有人去的偏远地带，这一片树篱以早开的花儿闻名。再没有别处有如此多姿多彩的花儿了：黄色的报春花、白色的丁香、深浅不一的紫罗兰、黄花九轮草、樱草、白星海芋、红门兰、野生风信子、金钱薄荷、三色堇、草莓、蝴蝶花，这些构成了这个野生树篱植物群落的一小部分。这些花儿在向阳的开阔小山坡上恣意生长，遍布了整个山坡，山坡上还长着一棵被称作"林中淑女"的垂枝桦——我常常被在这里出没的一条棕色小蛇吓到，它早早地从冬眠中苏醒，看起来很无辜的样子。它似乎和我一样喜欢这里，绕早开的花丛蜿蜒爬行，或者穿梭于落叶丛里，发出沙沙的声响。

报春花的花枝上已经长出了叶子和绿色的短芽，但还没有开花；即使是在盘根错节的荆豆花丛中也见不到一朵花，它们若是开起花来总是一朵挨一朵，像是开在一个花篮里。不，我的五月花，没有兔子！没有报春花！我们还是穿过那道门，到树木葱茏的蜿蜒小路上去吧，它会带我们回家。

我们正沿着路往回走，路边的老榆树庄严肃穆，此时已经枝叶稠密，在头顶撑起一片浓荫，遮天蔽日。据说这个深潭边游荡着一个幽灵——一位无头的白衣女士。我不敢说曾经见到过她，尽管我常常在深夜里沿着这条小路徘徊，聆听夜莺的歌唱，观赏萤火虫的明光——但是，就在那里，比遇上一千个幽灵还要稀罕，还要美好，比夜莺或萤火虫还要亲切的，是一丛报春花，这年开得最早的一丛。那一丛花就在远处幽静的角落里，从一棵老柳树长满苔藓的树根上萌发出来，又在清明透亮的潭水中投下鲜活的倒影。哦，它们是多么美丽——三朵盛放的小花，两朵含苞待放的花蕾！我真开心自己走了这条路！它们所在的地方无法靠近。即使是热爱挑战困难和不可能的杰克·拉普利在这里也束手无策：五月花在那样陡峭的岸边也站不住脚。不过这样更好。谁忍心去打扰它们呢？它们在那里守着自己纯净又芬芳的美丽，没有风雨的侵袭，尽情在阳光下雀跃，看上去似乎它们自己也正享受着这种幸福。谁会去打扰它们呢？哦，我真开心选择了这条回家的路。

采撷紫罗兰

　　三月二十七日——阴沉而昏暗的早晨，空气湿润；清新，但没有风；清凉，但没有寒意。这对于一个刚刚从伦敦回来的人正合适，远离那里的温热、光芒和喧嚣，投入远僻乡村的迷宫之中，重新获得头脑的休憩、内心的安宁，找回那些在巨大的巴别塔[①]中遗落的东西。我必须出去采些紫罗兰——这是必需的——而且我必须独自前往：任何的响动，即使是我的小莉兹的声音，或者五月花脑袋亲昵的碰触，甚至是她富有弹性的跳跃，都会打扰到我梦寐以求的安宁的感觉。我只能只身前往，带着那个编得像蜂巢一样的小篮子，那可是我的心爱之物，因为那是她赠予我的，我只用它装紫罗兰和其他我喜爱的东西，而且我要尽早离开大马路。现在我不想碰到任何人，即使是那些平日里我最想见到的人。

---

①　巴别塔（Tower of Babel），也称通天塔，据《圣经·旧约·创世记》第十一章记载，这座直插云霄的高塔惊动了上帝，为了阻止人们继续修建高塔，他混淆了人类的语言，这座塔的修建于是半途而废。这里借指喧嚣而浮华的伦敦。

哈！——这不就是他们一行吗——一位绅士骑着一匹骏马，一位女士姿态轻松而优雅地与之相随——看，疾行掠起的风将她的面纱轻轻吹动，更让她显得妩媚动人！还有一位快活的骑士少年，骑着一匹健硕的白色阿拉伯纯种马，在他们身边立马扬鞭，随时准备奋蹄向前，跑到他们前面去——如此有骑士风度的一行人可不就是 M 先生和 M 太太，还有亲爱的 R 吗？不对！仆人的衣服不是他们家的。这一定是某个公爵之家，还有他们家里在伊顿公学读书的小少爷。我得继续走了。我现在不会碰到任何人了，因为我已经远远地离开大路，正沿着一条小路穿过草地。小路是羊群踩出来的，蜿蜒于荆豆花、欧石楠和低矮的金雀花灌木丛中——小路上有斑斑驳驳的草皮，踩上去软绵绵的，即使在这个季节，也能闻到百里香的味道和甜甜的香气。

我们有幸生活在一个没有圈地的教区，或许应该感谢那两三个固执的农场主明智的坚持，也幸亏没人愿意理会那位大吵大嚷、意气用事的领主大人，我们才得以留住了这些肥美的绿色草地，它们如同被耕地包围的荒野孤岛，却不经意间构成了英格兰风光独特的美。我正在经过的这片公地——人们都管它叫草地——正是这些得以幸存的绿地中最可爱的一块。这是一处被遮蔽的景致，远离村庄，似乎与世无争。它是凹陷下去的一处低谷，如果说四周的高地是山丘未免太言过其实了；此处一边临着一条热闹的大马路，还有另一条马路横贯其中；四周风景如画，环绕着草地、茅屋、农场和果园；它的一角有一方巨大的水塘，明净清澈，实属罕见，水塘使整个画面都变得欢快、明亮起来。燕子常常在池塘边聚集，孩子们也是。此刻那里就有一群欢快的孩子，我很少见过这里没有孩子的时候。孩子们喜欢水，尤其是清澈、明净、闪闪发光的水；水让他们兴奋，满足他们的好奇心；水就是活力和生命。

我踏足其上的小路通向一个不那么欢快的地方，通往公地一侧一座庞大厚重的建筑，它坚固的两翼从主体部分伸展出来，占据了方形地块的三个边，使整个院子看起来冰冷、阴森。房子的一侧是一个晦暗的花园，有一位老人正在里面挖土，花园里笔直而齐整地排列着一畦畦的绿叶菜、土豆、甘蓝、洋葱和豆子，都种在黑黝黝的土壤中；菜畦都翻了土，散发着腐臭的气息，宛如新掘的坟墓。没有一株花或者开花的灌木！既没有玫瑰，也没有醋栗丛！全是些精明实用、让人打不起精神的东西。哦，和那些农家小院的花园真是大相径庭，那里长长的土地没有固定的形状，却长着一束束喜气洋洋的西洋樱草和番红花，他们的桂竹香会隔着窄窄的篱笆格子送出阵阵甜香，他们的醋栗丛长得枝叶丰茂，青翠欲滴，鲜活的绿色看在人眼里就像花儿一样美丽！哦，真是截然不同啊！这所阴郁住宅的另一侧是一片草坪，草地呈现出死水一般浓重、暗淡的绿色，四周是等距间隔的柳树，和花园一样，与那块公地之间隔着一条宽阔的、护城河一样的水道。这就是教区的救济所。与之相关的一切都牢靠、结实、有用——但都那么枯燥！冰冷！黑暗！院子里有孩子，可他们没有一丝声响。每次来到这里，我都要加快脚步走过去，仿佛这是一所监狱。囚禁、疾病、年老、赤贫、悲痛，这些都是我无力消除，也无力缓解的——然而，每次看到这里的围墙，这些念头和感觉就会不由自主地冒出来；虽然并不确定，但或许，围墙的里面并不像它所引发的病态想象一样，充满了如此极端的悲凉景象。那里应该井井有条，干净整洁，应该有食物、衣服和温暖，应该为无家可归之人提供庇护，为患病之人提供药品和照顾，让年迈的老人得到休息和满足，让人们获得同情，真诚而令人积极的同情，就像穷人对穷人，或穷人对不幸的人所展露的那种同情。或许还会有比教区的救济所更为悲惨的地方——但我总是要匆匆走过。那种感觉，那种看法，总是会不受控制地冒出来。

那个阴郁花园的尽头是一条浓荫蔽日的小路，蜿蜒延伸，如同一条溪水，在绿色的草地中间温柔地"曲折透迤"（借用一下威伯福斯先生[①]描写亨利小镇上泰晤士河的词语），草地上活跃着成群的牛羊，美丽的羊羔正享受着大好春光，颇为自得地摇摇晃晃，走来走去，憨态可掬。那些可耕种的田地上，更是洋溢着勃勃生机，有一大批人正弯着腰种豆子，都是女人和孩子，穿着各式各样、五颜六色的服装；男孩子们吹着口哨，和那些赶车的老把式推着犁和耙，从地里走过。他们的活儿缓慢而沉重，是这个忙碌季节里最主要的工作。种豆子真是一件累人的活计呀！人正好和区别于他们的田间牲畜调换了位置！想一想吧，他们一天当中有六个、八个甚至十个钟头都要弯着腰，用

---

① 威伯福斯先生（William Wilberforce，1759—1833），英国议会议员（1780—1825）、慈善家、废奴主义者。

小棍子在地上钻出洞，然后再把豆子一颗一颗地放进去。他们按照种豆的多少来领取报酬，曾有些可怜的妇女因为重复播种而受到谴责，也就是说，她们在一个洞里放了不止一颗豆子。在我看来，考虑到所要抵制的诱惑，不重复播种实在是在践行人类美德的最高标准。

沿着小路再转过一个弯，我们就来到了被几棵高大的榆树环抱的老房子前——这座老旧的农舍，总是毫无来由地会把我的思绪带到莎士比亚的时代。这是一座狭长、低矮的不规则建筑，房子一角多出来了一个房间，上面爬满了长着细密的白色叶脉的常春藤。主屋的二楼向外凸出，下面有橡木的梁柱支撑，楼下的一扇窗户，其古旧的窗棂和细长的窗格围成了半个浅浅的六边形。门厅走廊里摆着几个座位，顶上是带尖塔的屋顶，还竖着几根烟囱，这就构成了一幅完整的画面！唉，它几乎就是一幅风景画了！然而，在一位粗心的房东和一位破产的租户手里，这房子的外墙已经剥落，快要朽坏了。

又往前走了几码，我就来到了坡地上。啊！我闻到了它们的味道——细腻的香气丝丝缕缕地在湿重的空气里弥散开来。穿过这道小门，沿着这块绿色麦田的绿色南坡，它们就映入眼帘，可爱的紫罗兰，真是可爱至极。地面上满是紫白相间的紫罗兰花，它们给那些挂着露珠的矮草涂抹上了一层珐琅彩釉，其色泽在昏暗阴沉的天空之下更显得鲜艳夺目。那里的紫罗兰有成百上千株。早些年里，我已经习惯了看着它们从嫩绿色的小芽慢慢长大，而后在不知不觉间开出一两朵花。我还从未见过它们以如此绚烂的姿态，如此纯粹的美丽，在我的眼前突然呈现——我真应该感谢纷扰杂乱的伦敦，让我此刻能享受这纯粹而又真挚的快乐！它们栖身在这陡坡之上，构成了一道亮丽的风景线，长满了新叶的枝条在它们顶上招摇，早春的蜜蜂聚集在此处，飞来飞去，将它们身上花蜜的甜香和更为细腻的紫罗兰的香气混合在一起。那些枝条是如此透亮、光滑，透着勃发的力量，满含着生机和活力！那边，在长满苔藓的老树根旁，还有一丛茂盛的报春花，一只黄蝴蝶在上面翩翩起舞，宛如飘浮在空中的一朵花。坐在这样葱茏的山坡上，将我的篮子装满鲜花，是何等幸福啊！真是让人神清气爽，宛如新生！如果能在这样安宁、甜美的风景中安家，人一定会重新变得像孩子一样无畏、快活和温柔。很快，思绪会变得如诗章一样美妙，感受会像信仰一样指引你。接下来，我们就会成为幸福而善良的人。哦，如果我的一生能这样度过，随着喜悦和纯真的心境起伏漂泊，在宁静与感激中安享大自然的寻常馈赠，并对让生活如此美好的简单习惯和有益身心的性情心怀莫大的感恩，该有多好！啊！谁会敢于奢望如此幸福的人生呢？但至少，我现在可以紧紧抓住，并延长这转瞬即逝的快乐感觉。我可以在篮子里装满纯洁的花朵，在心里装满纯洁的思想；可以用花的芬芳让我的小家充满喜悦；可以把我的珍宝与一个亲爱的人分享，一个未找到它们的人；在我闭上眼睛，进入梦乡时会梦到它们，看见它们。

灌木林

　　四月十八日——冬天一样的寒冷天气,实在让人难过,东北风呼呼地刮着, 明晃晃的太阳让人睁不开眼睛, 却没有带来丝毫的热度;干燥的空气致使嘴唇和手都皲裂开来,如同遭受了十二月的霜冻;雨下起来如万箭垂落,冰凉刺骨, 像一月里的冰雹;自然界一片死寂,仿佛陷入了停顿;花园里没有一颗嫩芽,树篱中没有一片新叶,田野里见不到任何一朵摇着铃铛一样花筒的黄花九轮草,幽谷中不见夜莺的身影,大池塘的水面上没有燕子飞掠的痕迹,到处都见不到布谷鸟。(可千万别让我错过那个蛮横的十四行诗人!)然而, 在这个冬日一般的早春,在这一场倒春寒里,也有别样的风景。如果开花时钟必须停摆一个或两个月, 还有比停在此刻报春花和紫罗兰盛开之际更好的时候吗? 我从不记得(我的记性, 虽不大能记得住那些明智和有用的事, 但在这些琐碎闲事上还是可以信任的)它们中的任何一种能开得如此繁盛, 或者说能延续如此长的花期。报春花季将是这一年留在我脑海中的印记。篱笆上,沟渠里,草地上,田野间,即使是小径和马路上都随处可见它们的身影，但它们主要的聚集地是在大约一英里之外的一个灌木林里。它们在那里铺展蔓延，像地毯一般，我罔顾一位成熟女士所应有的矜持，频频前往那里观赏。今天下午我正要到那里去，五月花和她的伙伴儿也一道前往。

我的五月花是个相当奇特的动物。她的本能和直觉几乎接近理性，这让她常常有惊人之举。她看到我们做什么，就会模仿着做，其灵活程度不亚于猴子，而且比猴子还要一本正经，还有更明显的目的性。她会先把坚果砸碎再吃；会采集醋栗，能把它们干净利落地从枝干上捋下来；会把苹果和梨偷摘下来，大口大口地嚼着吃，在果园里差不多和一个熊孩子一样有危害性。她会嗅闻花香，会在见面时冲人微笑，会用甜美活泼的声音搭腔（真可惜是用一种我们听不懂的语言！）；她在和我们的谈话中具有巨大的优势，因为她对我们的意图一清二楚；——所有这些，还有许许多多让人忍俊不禁的本事（更不用说她那犬类特有的绝活，会把猎物径直交到主人的手上，绝不会让别的人得逞），都是我这只漂亮的格力犬无师自通的，她靠的只是单纯的模仿和灵活的头脑。五月花，在狩猎季结束的时候，失去了两个玩伴。一个是她的好朋友，我们的老猎犬布拉什；另一个是玛瑞特，一只蓝色的格力犬，既是她的战友又是她的对手。这两只是四脚动物中的佼佼者，他们暂时被送走寄养，等到夏天狩猎季的时候才会回来。五月花因此品尝到了孤独的难受滋味，开始在左邻右舍找朋友。碰巧的是，狩猎季的暂停不仅使我们小户人家的狗由三只变成了一只，也使得这一带一个狩猎大户家的精良犬只遭到了遣散,他家的三只健壮幼崽来到了我们村的马轭匠家"散闲"(这是打猎的行话)。于是,五月花在落了单的那天早上(在此之前她一点儿也没有注意到她的邻居,尽管他们早就在街的北头住了有两个星期了),自以为这些近在咫尺的小狗崽是专门给她送来的及时安慰,便大胆地走过去,叩响了他们已经半敞着的、方便来去的狗舍大门。那三只狗走了出来,他们很警觉,也很英勇,但五月花显然不想进入他们的领地,于是把他们带到了她自己的地盘。这种演练每天都在重复,只有一点发生了变化:这三只狗,第一只身上有斑纹,第二只皮毛是黄色的,第三只是黑色的,只有前面两只获得五月花的准许,可以与她一起散步,相伴左右,而最后一个可怜的家伙,我看不出他有任何不对,或许仅仅是因为五月花的任性独断,不仅被这位窈窕淑女驱逐,就连他过去的伙伴们也嫌弃他——可以说是直接被打入了冷宫。在获得认可的这两位追随者中,那只名叫萨拉丁的黄色绅士狗毫无疑问是更受宠的。他简直就是五月花的影子,不管我愿不愿意都会跟着我散步。除非我把五月花小姐也丢下,否则绝无可能摆脱掉他;——可是没有了五月花的乡间漫步,就好比是堂吉诃德的冒险没有了忠实的扈从桑丘的陪伴。

我们出发了,五月花和我,还有萨拉丁和那只斑纹狗;五月花和我走起路来,总是带着与我们的性别和年龄相符合的沉稳和端庄(她今年已经满五岁,马上要六岁了)——那两只幼犬,萨拉丁和斑纹狗(毫无冒犯的意思),实际上比狗崽大不了多少,总是欢蹦乱跳,尽情地嬉闹。

我们行走路线的最初一段，是沿着通往我们老宅的那些荫蔽安静的小路前行。每次走在这段路上，我的心头总会涌起特别的归家似的感觉，脑子里总是会回想起那时候的欢笑悲苦。但现在，我们并不是来怀旧感伤的；——即使是聪明的五月花也听不懂那些伤感的话。我们必须继续往前走。今天已经是四月十八日了，可是树篱还是一副冬天的模样！报春花当然已经开了，每一朵都闪闪发光，宛若地上的星星，可是它们是那么孤单落寞，那么枝叶稀疏，看起来是那么寒意萧瑟！冷风在褐色的枝条间呼啸着，就像冬天一样。那些带着春天的气息、早早萌发的嫩芽，看起来还是褐色的；忍冬上的嫩叶，虽然也无畏地冒出了头，却是一副凄惨的模样，颜色发紫，如遭了霜冻，就像雪天早晨挤奶女工的胳膊肘。那些本该成双入对、忙于垒窝筑巢的鸟儿，看上去都瑟瑟发抖，局促不安，还有它们的巢！——"哦，萨拉丁！离开那片灌木丛！难道你看不出来，把你迷惑得上蹿下跳的就是一个知更鸟的鸟巢吗？你难道没看见那些漂亮的带着斑点的鸟蛋？你难道没听到那只可怜的雌鸟正哀鸣着求救？快点到这边来，先生！"还算幸运，萨拉丁（虽然是个异类，但品性还算不错）总算在碰到鸟窝之前，或者应该说在他的伙伴斑纹狗——两个当中更难管教的那个——还没有瞅见鸟巢之前，乖乖回来了。

接着我们在拐角处转了弯，过了桥，看到公共绿地上有一条清溪从榆树林中蜿蜒而过，一派宛如庄园的景致。那边穿着鼓鼓囊囊的裙子和斗篷的女人是谁？她宛如一架马车一般，迈着缓慢而泰然的步子朝我们走来。那是，那一定是沙莉·米尔应夫人，就我所知的农妇（我可以在语言上有此创新吗？①）而言，她无疑是其中最为典型的代表。没错，就是她。

我最初认识沙莉·米尔应夫人的时候，她和她的父亲（一位九十岁的耄耋老人）就住在我们原先的住所附近一处面积很大的农场里。那里很早之前是一处大庄园或者宫廷住宅，那时候依然是一幢庄严雄伟、宽敞气派的建筑，高挑的厅堂，宽敞的房间，即使是用作普通办公室，也是一派富丽堂皇的气象。墙上的镶板和巨大的几乎到天花板的雕花烟囱盖板上，都还依稀可见镏金的痕迹；大理石桌子和嵌花的橡木楼梯依然诉说着当初宫廷的奢华。沙莉夫人尽管不怎么喜欢这里的威严气势，却和整栋房子的年代感很相称。她是一个彻头彻尾的老派人物，对于年轻一代怀着深深的不屑：她每天四点起床，无论冬夏，六点钟吃早饭，十一点钟接近正午时分吃午饭，下午五点钟吃晚饭，很有规律地在晚上八点之前上床休息。除非是割草季或收获的农忙时节，她不得已要坐到太阳落山之后，尽管这是少不了的，但她总要不管不顾地抱怨一通。她总是毫无例外地要把整个教区里发生的不幸或者祸事都归咎到新派做法上，归咎于不规律的作息，归咎于白围裙、棉质长裤和平纹细布手帕这些现代罪恶（沙莉夫人本人总是穿着黑格子呢和一种她习惯称之为"丝织"的黄色混纺布料的衣服），

---

① 这里指"农妇"原文 farmeresses 一词。

还要归咎于条播犁、脱粒机和其他一些新式农业机械的发明。最后提到的这项发明尤其让她义愤填膺。哦，她一边用结实的右臂挥动着连枷，一边夸赞它的种种优点，她从年轻的时候就知道这些（据她说，别的农业机械和脱粒机一样也会造成骨骼和肌腱的严重退化），只要听听她这一番话，就足以让那个机器的发明人毁掉自己的机器。她甚至会操起自己最爱的这种农具，在空气中来回捶打，来证明自己的观点；而且，说实在的，在这个日趋没落的时代，没有几个男人能像六十五岁的沙莉夫人那样拥有如此结实、强壮、肌肉发达的臂膊了。

尽管她极力反对耕作工具上的进步，但她在宫廷农庄上的日子过得还算不错。好心的地主，轻松的租金，不间断的劳作，持之以恒的节俭，还有好的年景，确保了她不算丰厚但稳定的收益。她的生活一如既往，不断地抱怨，也不断地兴旺，不停地发达，也不停地埋怨，直到两桩不幸的事一起降临到了她头上——她的父亲去世了，而她的租约也到期了。尽管她的父亲一直卧病在床，而且已经年过九十，原本在世间流连的光阴也所剩无几，但他的去世对于这个女儿依旧是个巨大的打击。她已经上了年纪，开始担忧起自己以后的生活，再加上早已习惯了照顾这位善良的老先生，悉心关照他的饮食起居，因而，她就像一个母亲牵挂自己病痛中的孩子一样怀念父亲。租约到期是另一桩完全不同的伤心事，也颇伤脑筋。她的地主应该很愿意留住这位出色的租户，但是租赁合约不再基于原有的五十年来从未变过的条款了。因而，可怜的沙莉夫人不幸地发现租金上涨的同时，农产品的价格却在下跌——这实在是政治经济学中可怕的矛盾悖论。然而，即使是这样，我也相信她原本会挺过来的，而不是放弃那座房子，毕竟她就降生在那里，那座房子造就了她的生活方式和理念；可是她偏巧碰到了一位自命不凡的管家，他对创新与改革的痴迷，就好像她对于惯例和通行做法的坚持一样执着。那位管家坚持要在契约里约定，让她同意在每块地里都撒上一定数量的石灰。这项大胆的革新立刻就让她打定了主意，因为宫廷农庄的农场和田地，还从未因为哪种新式肥料而变得雪白一片。她把草拟的契约丢进了火里，不到一个星期就搬走了。

她将搬到何处去住引发了众多猜测，成了村子里许多人茶余饭后的消遣话题。当然，一位年近古稀的老妇人原本可以不再理会有关阶层门第的条条框框，但是沙莉夫人向来恪守品行操守，是个老古板，要坚决远离"大老爷们儿"（她一贯这样鄙夷地称呼他们），因而当发现她和她的小女仆搬到了耿直的老光棍儿——"草地上的乔治·罗宾逊"——家的农场时，我们都大为震惊。罗宾逊家的农场相当宽绰，沙莉夫人她们就住在农场一头的一间土屋里。农夫罗宾逊厌恶女人的名声在外，就像沙莉夫人看不上穿着紧身衣裤、犹如褪了毛的两足动物的男人一样，因而，那一带的人们都颇为惊诧，免不得到处说笑。这位率直的农夫很快就让他们闭了嘴，他告诉那些打趣的人，他已经严正警告过他的租客，别人愿意怎么说是别人的事，他是铁了心的绝不会娶她，所以她要是打着这个主意，趁早搬到别的地方去。不得不说，这项声明远不够客气恭敬，倒是格外直截了当，然而，声明并没有影响沙莉夫人给人的印象。她搬到了农场的住处，现在依然住在那里，陪伴她的是她的小女仆、她的虎斑猫、一只老弱的牧羊犬，还有她在宫廷农庄积攒下的一些无用杂物，那是她无论如何也无法割舍的。她在那里延续着她一贯的做派和作息习惯，既没有动过结婚的念头，也没有受到情事绯闻的干扰（就我所知），几乎没有什么烦心事，除了她和她的年轻女仆偶尔会找不到工作（即使是白镴盘子也不需要时时擦拭），和时不时要发作的风湿病。

她走过来了，宛如老去时光里的美好遗迹——尽管她有种种任性和偏见，但再也没有比她更好、更心善的女人了——她过来了，红色斗篷的帽兜罩在围得紧紧的黑色系带帽子的外面，帽子的丝绸材质曾经风行一时（可以想见），即使是现在也不算过时。她健硕的身体被五花八门的衣物包裹得严严实实，一层又一层，加厚的衬裙、罩衫、围裙、披肩和斗篷——这些衣服的重量也只有打谷子的人才有力气撑得起来，穿着走来走去——她过来了，还是原来那样方正又正直的脸庞，还是那样率真的大嗓门儿。我们聊得很开心，不着边际地什么都说，一会儿说到风湿病，一会儿说到刚孵出的小鸡，一会儿又说到坏天气和衬着羽毛的帽子——最后这个极其令人不愉快的话题是可怜的简·戴维斯（沙莉夫人的一个侄女）引发的。她放学回来从我们身边经过时，停下来摘掉她那顶海狸皮的帽子向我们致意，结果在礼貌问题上挨了姑妈好一顿训。简是个温柔、谦逊、总是微笑着的姑娘，差不多有十二岁，常常遭到她这位德高望重的亲戚的斥责，但她一向毕恭毕敬、言听计从。如果说这些斥责后面会跟着一笔遗产，我一点儿都不会吃惊的：我真诚地期盼会是这样。最后，终于到了互道再见的时候，她问我要到哪里去，当听说我要到那个占地十英亩的灌木林（那是她一直掌管的那个庄园的一部分）去时，她便讲了一则骇人的故事劝阻我，说六十年前，有两个偷羊贼被发现躲到了灌木林里，他们负隅顽抗，后来大伙儿费尽了周折，克服了种种困难，才将他们捕获，还有一位文职警官因此身受重伤。"求您千万别到那里去，小姐！看在上帝慈悲的分上，千万不要去冒险！想想看，只怕他们会杀了您！"这就是沙莉夫人最后的话。

我对她的关心和善意深表感谢！但是，即使我素来不莽撞行事，我也不会去害怕六十年前的偷羊贼。即使他们逃脱了犯罪招致的绞刑，我也非常怀疑他们会再度以身试法。所以，我们继续向前：沿着那条不长的林荫小路，出来就到了那片村子外的绿地，四周都是田野和树篱，我们必须穿过去才能到达灌木林。今天这个绿色的角落是如此生机盎然，有一半的草地都被牛群、马群和羊群占了！那些格力犬别提有多开心了，平日里坚硬的沙砾马路换成了这片欢乐的短草草坪，他们撒了欢儿地跑跳、嬉闹，似乎这块草坪就是为他们的玩闹而准备的！他们尽情玩耍的样子真是美极了，或者绕着圈互相追逐，一圈比一圈小，步步紧逼；或者进行各种角度的猛冲急转，在五月花的身边来回穿梭，还试图引诱她放下从容镇定的姿态，加入他们的追逐嬉闹中；或者公然挑衅对方，欢快地互相打闹、围堵；或者追逐母牛和小马驹；或者一跃而起，假装去捕捉飞行中的乌鸦；这些全是他们无害又单纯的游戏。"啊，淘气鬼！恶棍！捣蛋鬼！四脚小恶魔！小疯狗！萨拉丁！斑纹！"他们去追羊了——"萨拉丁，我叫你呢！"——他们已经把那只漂亮的斑点羊羔给孤立出来了——"小畜生，看我抓住你怎么收拾你！萨拉丁！斑纹！"此刻我们自己就要被当成偷羊贼给抓起来了。他们已经把那只可怜的小羊羔撵到了沟里，还站在高处盯住它，把它给围住了。"啊，小坏蛋们，我可逮到你们了！丢不丢人，萨拉丁！闪开，斑纹！看看五月花多乖。你们这两个小畜生，走开！丢人！真丢人！"我气势汹汹地挥舞着一条手帕，尽管它很难被当成一件有效的管教工具，但还是成功地把这两只狗崽给赶跑了。毕竟他们并没有恶意，只是为了玩儿，虽说玩得有点儿过头，差不多要赶上那个有男孩和青蛙的古老寓言①里所说的情形了。五月花跟在他们后面，可能是去责骂他们了：整个过程中她像一位法官一样严肃，非常鲜明地和我站在一起，完全没有参与他们的恶作剧。

这只可怜的美丽小羊羔！它躺在坡地上一动不动，我猜它一定是快要被吓死了，当然，那些小淘气并没有碰到它。它没有任何动静。还有呼吸吗？哦，是的，它在呼吸。它还活着，安然无恙。看啊，它睁开了眼睛，发现四周很

---

① 指《伊索寓言》。几个孩子在池塘边用石头砸青蛙玩，好几只青蛙被砸死了。这时，有一只青蛙从水中探出头来，说："孩子们，请停手吧。这对于你们来说是游戏，而对于我们却有性命之忧啊。"

安全，敌人已经不见了，它马上就跳了起来，一路小跑奔向妈妈，那只母羊一直站在不远也不近的地方咩咩地唤它。谁能想到这样一只小羊羔也有这样单纯的机智狡黠？我真的以为这个漂亮的小东西死了呢——而现在那只母羊又找回了它那个长着斑点的小卷毛，它该多开心呐！它们看起来那么激动！当然，这场冒险也让我惊慌失措；在一路担忧地追赶它们的时候，我敢说我的心跳得像那只小羊羔一样快。

啊！那个不知羞耻的小恶魔萨拉丁，这场混乱的制造者，此时又回来了，他把他那细长的鼻吻放到我的手里请求原谅，要与我重归于好！"哦，残忍的暴虐之王！最离经叛道的异端！真是恶魔附体！"然而，一个本性善良的小动物的忏悔是谁也无法拒绝的。我必须拍拍他。"好了，好了！我们现在去灌木林。我可以保证我们绝不会遇到比我们更坏的恶人了，好吗，五月花？而且，我们越早跑到看不见羊群的地方越好，因为斑纹似乎正在筹划新一轮的攻击。走吧，先生们，过了这道门，穿过草地，就到灌木林了。"

那棵挺立于山坡之上的巨大白蜡树真是蔚为壮观，光滑银亮的树皮，笔直挺拔的树干，和旁边那棵高大得不愧称为树的冬青，一起构成了一个绝妙的入口。我们这就来到了灌木林。啊！去年大约只有一半的树下灌木被修剪过，剩下的一半正恣意疯长：榛子、野蔷薇、忍冬、黑莓，形成了一片密不透风的灌木丛，而且几乎与其上方等距间隔的榆树、橡树和山毛榉树的低枝连成了一片。没有人能从那片密密匝匝、荆棘丛生的树丛中穿过去。然而，就在那个开阔的斜坡外侧，环绕着一条小路，小路、陡坡和灌木林的地面上长满了报春花，空气中溢满了清新柔和的花香。哦，这是多么妙不可言！地面上不单单有堪称花中瑰宝的报春花，更是一幅大自然的镶嵌拼花图，报春花只是其中的一部分。地上常春藤的枝蔓构成了一张巨网，上面点缀着淡紫色的花和色彩柔和的紫红色叶片，其间有繁茂的苔藓、珐琅彩色的野风信子、星星点点的白星海芋，而最重要的是，常春藤的藤蔓勾连起所有的花和比花还要美的叶片，把它们连缀成花环，常春藤的白色叶脉则似乎在一片浓绿或者参差错落的褐色中偾张——应该说，整个这一片土地都美丽动人！从未见过报春花长得如此繁盛、丰茂，也从未见过报春花和周围的环境如此相得益彰。那些花的颜色是专属于它们的可爱的黄色，是一提到报春花就会联想到的色彩，也是在它们上方翩翩起舞的蝴蝶（这是我今年见到的第一只蝴蝶！难道春天最终真的来了？）的真正的色泽——在它们中间散落间杂着一丛丛绛紫色的花簇，还有纯净的白色花簇，花朵颜色的不同似乎是由于土壤的偶然状况影响到了神奇又神秘莫测的自然操作，也就是决定花朵颜色的机制。哦，它们是如此馥郁芬芳！坐在这样一个浓荫蔽日的灌木林里是何等惬意啊！耳边有清风穿林而过的簌簌响动，那是最不可思议的声音；脚下有这般绚烂的彩色织锦；头上有林鸽在树梢间飞掠而过，用最原始的乐声唱出最深情的爱意。

是的！春天正翩翩而至。林鸽、蝴蝶，还有甜美的花朵，都是这四季中最甜美季节的标志。春天来了。榛子的茎鼓胀着，淡白色的穗头吐露出来；柳树上如绸缎般光亮的嫩芽，带着甜香，探出了头；最后几颗冬天的果子从山楂树上跌落下来，让位给如花儿一般绽开的鲜亮的嫩叶。

小树林

　　四月二十日——春天终于来了，天气突然之间全面回暖，像北方的夏天一样让人猝不及防。今天完全是暖春四月的天气——天空中有云朵和阳光，也有微风和阵雨；枝头上开着花，田野里长着草，池塘边聚集着燕子，树篱中蜿蜒着小蛇，杂木林里夜莺鸣唱，布谷鸟几乎无处不在。我的年轻朋友艾伦·G.会在傍晚的时候和我一同去采酢浆草。她从未见过这种优雅的植物，但她是位细腻的画家，这次我把这种花介绍给她一定会两厢受益的。艾伦会得到一个值得她动笔描绘的对象，而这漂亮的草则会在她的画里长存；对于一种像岩蔷薇一样生命短暂的花卉来说，这可是一个不小的恩惠；短暂易逝是酢浆草唯一的缺憾，艾伦将赋予它永不凋谢的生命。天气确实有点让人担忧，但我们是那种一旦有了明确的目标便绝不会在意天气的人；我们一定会去探访酢浆草，并且要带上五月花，前提是我们得甩掉她的小跟班儿。因为自上次追捕羊羔的事件之后，萨拉丁又和一只护雏心切的公鹅发生了冲突，公鹅在那场争斗中成了最终的胜利者。考虑到我们要去的那片树林

（当地的村民把它叫作响林）里有不少的野鹅，而胜利并不总是属于正确的一方，如果残暴苏丹（萨拉丁）再卷入一次这样的战斗，我一定会于心不安。所以这次我们除了五月花谁也不带。

说话的工夫，我们就出发上路了，沿着蜿蜒的小径，穿过嫩绿的树篱，我们就来到了大门那里，它边上是果树环抱的白色小屋，这些果树形成了通往响林的天然入口，不一会儿整片树林就展现在我们眼前了。

"这儿是不是很美，艾伦？"除了热情直接的"当然"，几乎不可能有别的回答。通常树林都是美丽的地方，但是这片树林——想象一片布满了林间空地和牧羊草场的小型树林，周围散布着错落的农家小院，果园中鲜花正盛开，一条清澈的小溪在草场之间蜿蜒流淌，一条马路从中横贯而过，使整个画面变得灵动，充满了光亮；这样你就能大致了解响林的样子了。这里可谓是一步一景，每走一步就会看到空地、小径和树丛新鲜变化的组合。风景中的点缀也在随时发生着变化。鸭子、鹅、猪和小孩子，随着我们向林中的深入，开始被羊群和森林马驹替代；而它们，在我们步入密林深处的时候，也消失不见了，我们的耳畔只剩下夜莺的鸣叫，眼前只有静默的花朵。

这里真是宛如童话般的仙境！头顶上高大的榆树刚刚萌发出娇嫩而鲜艳的绿叶，间或还有灰白色的橡树或者银色树皮的山毛榉，每一根枝条上都鼓出褐色的芽苞，与此同时，枝条上黄褐色的秋叶尚未全部落尽；高大的冬青和冬青下的山楂树，它们脆嫩而明亮的新叶和黑刺李的白色花朵混成了一片，又与忍冬花和野蔷薇的花冠缠绕在一起——真是仙境一般！

报春花、黄花九轮草、三色堇，还有五叶银莲花（或者称它们在汉普郡更为优雅的名字——风之花）一贯醒目的白色花朵，在我们的脚下铺展，厚厚一层，如同草地上的雏菊一般；但我们今天特地来寻访的漂亮小草却扭扭捏捏，不愿露面；艾伦开始担心我们是不是来错了地方，或是弄错了季节。最终她欣喜地在一丛冬青下面发现了它。"哦，快看！快看！我敢肯定这就是酢浆草！看那低垂的白色小花，形状如一片雪花，上面有紫色的花脉纹路，还有那美丽的心形三瓣叶片，有一些刚刚长出来，如此鲜亮柔嫩的绿色不免要使旁边榆树和山楂树的叶子显得暗淡无光；还有一些是更深一点的绿色，叶片中的叶脉呈现出丰富而多变的紫色！你还没看到它们吗？"我的年轻朋友显得有些迫不及待，她真是一个灵动的生命，一束欢跃的阳光，我为她的热情陶醉，一动不动地站在那里听她激动地讲述，她见我这样呆住，几乎要怪罪我，说——"你难道没看见它们吗？哦，多么美丽！而且这么一大片！如此繁茂！看那冬青的暗影正好衬托出花朵上的光亮和细腻的颜色变化！还有那边，有一片从老山毛榉根部的厚实苔藓中冒了出来！啊，让我们采一些回去吧。篮子在这儿呢！"于是我们开始迅速而小心地采摘，叶子、花、根，都要，因为这种植物太过娇嫩，容不得我们把它们分开；我们采的时候尽量动作迅速，小心翼翼，但还是碰到了各种各样的小麻烦：一会儿面纱被冬青树丛给挂住了，一会儿围巾又钩到了黑莓树丛上，但我们不停地采集，即使手指被划伤也顾不得停下，直到我们差不多把篮子都装满了，正说着准备要离开：

"可是五月花去哪儿了？五月花！五月花！找不到她可不能回家。五月花！她跑过来了，小美人！"（艾伦几乎和我一样喜欢五月花）"她嘴里叼了什么？那个毛乎乎的、圆圆的、棕色的东西，她那么温柔地衔在嘴里，那会是什么呢？一个鸟窝？真是个调皮的家伙！"

"不！千真万确，那是只刺猬！看哪，艾伦，它把自己蜷曲成一个刺球！丢开它，五月花！不要把它带过来！"五月花显然舍不得把弄到手的猎物松开，尽管它浑身是刺，让她费尽周折地叼着。在我看来，刺猬身形的变化比我所见到的任何事情都更让五月花感到迷惑，一般说来她的智商足以让她对发生的一切事情都了然于心。五月花最后还是放下了那只刺猬，却继续用她敏捷的猫掌一样的爪子拍打它，每次都小心翼翼地试探几下，每碰一下又突然而迅速地缩回来，仿佛她那可怜的俘虏是一块火红的烧炭。当发现这些试探性的拍打完全无助于解开她心中的疑惑时（因为那只刺猬在装死，就像那天那只小羊羔一样，看起来一动不动），她就用她漂亮的黑鼻子猛地推了它一下，不仅把它给翻了过来，还让它沿着草皮地面滚动了一段距离——那只机智的四脚动物在整个过程中都表现出完美的被动姿态，一副任人摆布的样子，这种完全不抵抗的做法实在让人钦佩。难怪五月花的判断出了差错，就算是我，如果没有意识到这个小东西的把戏，也会说，她像滚保龄球或者板球一样滚出去的这个毛乎乎的丑东西，是个无生命的死物，一个没有感觉和意志的东西。最后我可怜的爱犬完全被搞糊涂了，她筋疲力尽，彻底放弃了这场竞赛。她慢慢地走开，又忍不住一两次回过头看着这个让她倍感好奇的东西，似乎又想转身回去，再试着推一推。一只林鸽突然飞起，终于转移了她的注意力。艾伦饶有兴致地想象着那只刺猬逃走时的样子，直到我们的注意力被一个完全不同的事物吸引了过去。

就在我们要穿过树林，到达另一侧的一片高大橡树组成的开阔小树林时，耳边突然传来了有别于夜莺鸣叫的声音，那是伐木工人的斧头低沉而频繁的砍伐之声。从响林中出来之后，我们就看到了斧头所造成的一片混乱。绿茵茵的草地上横放着二十几棵最好的大树，它们都不同程度地遭到了破坏：有的被剥去了树皮，只剩下光秃秃的树干，等着装车运走，剥下的树皮在旁边堆了一大摞；有的正在被毁坏，工人们忙着在一旁剥皮、劈砍、削凿；还有一些尚未来得及砍去原本高贵的枝丫，树头上褐色芬芳的嫩芽依然新鲜，仿佛都还活着——这些高大伟岸的尸体，正是在今日惨遭了杀戮！这片小树林如同战场一般。那些给大树剥皮的年轻小伙子，还有那些拾捡碎木的孩子，都一脸敬畏，默不作声，似乎也意识到了身边正在发生的死亡。夜莺的歌唱微弱且断断续续——几声低沉、惊惧的叫声，宛若一首安魂曲。

啊！我们正置身谋杀现场，正目睹着那棵树被伐倒；他们刚刚用那些屠杀用的斧头削砍了树干，现在正准备把它锯断。总之，这是一项让人亢奋的精细活计，有关死亡的工作似乎一向如此。那个年轻人最后几下把树根砍断之后，似乎一下子如释重负；那把看起来软弱无力的锯，弯起来像丝带一样，可是却放倒了森林中的巨人，征服了那个鲜活的生命，将它彻底扳倒，这真是不可思议的结果！现在，他们已经锯开了树干的一半，那个伐木工人已经开始计算树会朝哪个方向倒下；他把一枚楔子朝着那个方向敲了进去；锯子又无声地工作了一会儿，接着又插进来一枚更大的楔子。看，树枝已经开始抖动！听，树干发出咔嚓一声巨响！巨大的斧头又在楔子上重击了一下，那棵树震颤着，似乎承受着巨大的痛苦，摇动着，倾斜旋转着，然后倒了下来。整个过程如此缓慢，如此庄重，又是如此让人不忍直视！与死亡，与人类最为壮丽的死亡何其相似！恺撒在元老院中[①]，塞内加在浴盆中[②]，也不会比这棵橡树倒下时更为肃穆庄重。

就连老天都仿佛对这场杀戮表现出了同情。云朵聚集在一起形成了一个又厚又低的云盖，黑沉、湿重，就像伦敦上空笼罩着的烟雾；落日在云盖底下放射出昏暗、血红色的光芒，绯红的射线从顶上散射而出，映出一幅火红色

① 公元前 44 年，恺撒（Gaius Julius Caesar，前 102 或前 100—前 44）在元老院被以布鲁图（Marcus Junius Brutus）和卡西乌（Gaius Cassius Longinus）为首的共和派成员刺杀。

② 塞内加（Lucius Annaeus Seneca，前 4—65），古罗马政治家、斯多葛派哲学家、悲剧作家、雄辩家。公元 65 年，因涉嫌参与谋刺尼禄，被多疑的尼禄逼迫自尽，割腕死于浴盆之中。

的、带着不祥之兆的壮丽画面，晦暗的红色暮光，就像地面上燃起的大火投射到天空中的光亮。那浓重的绯红渐渐退去，雨开始落下来。我们急匆匆地朝家里赶，然而心情沉重，早就忘了那些花儿、刺猬和身上淋了雨，只想着、念叨着那棵被伐倒的大树。

小山谷

　　五月二日——宜人的黄昏，阳光明亮，夏日的微风习习，天空中几乎没有一丝云彩，树丛中和田野里正是一派青翠欲滴的葱茏景象。这样的黄昏似乎正适合到我新近发现的去处走一遭。那是一处苔藓密布的山谷，是这一带最美丽的地方之一，就在我们无数次经过的那片田野的尽头。大约两个月前五月花在那里咬死了一只兔子，我们才碰巧发现了那个地方。从那之后，五月花便总是惦记着那里，我也一样。

　　我们就朝着那里进发了，穿过村子，沿着山路往上，一直到公共绿地那里，经过林荫大道，过了桥，然后沿着山脚下的路一直走就到了。今天晚上这一路上真是冷清啊！我们一个熟人也没碰到，除了可怜的瞎子罗伯特，他背着从树篱那边拔下来的一袋子草，还带着那个给他引路的小男孩。这是一种简单的分工合作！小杰姆把罗伯特带到长有长草的地方，告诉他哪边的草最茂盛；接着那位老先生就会把草齐根儿割断，他们俩一起把草装进袋子，拿到村子里去卖。街上一半的牛——因为我们的面包师、修车匠和鞋匠各家都有奥尔德尼奶牛——全靠着瞎子罗伯特的辛苦劳作，才长得膘肥体壮。

现在我们来到了通往小山谷的玉米地的入口处，这里视野极佳，可以将洛登河、磨坊、大农场及其如画的周边建筑，还有远处树木葱茏的远山都一览无余。不在这个入口处驻足停留是不可能的，这里的景色总是如此秀美，和眼下的时节也如此相称，明媚、快活，充满了春天的气息。可是五月花，她那个漂亮的小脑袋还在想着再逮到一只兔子的可能性，早就一路小跑直奔山谷去了，不过可怜的五月花整日忠实地追随我四处漫游，也该适当地放纵一下自己。因此，我们就直接去山谷了。

来到田地的尽头，也就是从公路上看上去似乎被一片浓密的灌木林截断的地方，我们突然间就到了一个峡谷的边缘。峡谷的一侧连着一片桤树、白桦和柳树混杂的低矮树林，另一侧则是苔藓和草皮，显得光秃秃的，偶尔能看到亮眼的正开着花的金雀花丛。有一两棵修剪过树冠的古树几乎遮住了通往谷底的蜿蜒小路，路边有一汪晶莹剔透的泉水，汩汩不绝，向下奔流。这个山谷其实是一块不规则的断裂地块，有的地方很深，当中还横亘着两三个同样地势不平的高坡，其间有的地方地势陡峭，寸草不生，如岩石一般；有的则被羽状柳树或者巨大的经年荆棘丛覆盖。地面上全是矮而细嫩的草，间杂着不同种类的柔软、美丽的苔藓，错落其上的是白星海芋斑驳的叶片和淡紫色的花朵，还有常见的淡色红门兰花、蓝釉色的野生风信子，它们在薄暮的光线中显得光彩夺目，此外还有大丛的樱草和黄花九轮草从矮草中冒出来，如一束束捧花。

　　山谷另一侧的地面比我们来时的那块田地低了不少，因而它独特的野趣和丰饶主要归功于这些高坡上如迷宫一般错综复杂的地貌。我们此刻似乎被这些绿色的断崖所包围，与世隔绝，抬眼望去只见这些绿莹莹的土丘和深邃的蓝色天空；在猛然间转身的时候，我们瞥见了一块与之相邻的草地，那里正有羊群在休憩，羊儿们躺在倾斜的坡地上，就好像夏日天空中飘荡的朵朵白云。那些温柔、安静的可爱生灵，它们是如此平静！那些爱凑热闹的便一个挨一个躺在一起，还有的是三个一组四个一群，另有一些则远远地分开。啊！它们当中还有小羊羔——美丽的、美丽的小羊羔——紧紧依偎在妈妈身边。温柔、安静、睡意沉沉的小东西！然而，这里并非阒静无声！有一群小羊羔毫无睡意，要多清醒有多清醒；它们一共六只，聚在一起玩耍，又蹦又跳，不停地舞动、腾跃，彼此用头抵撞，还奶声奶气地咩咩直叫，完全是成羊叫声的可爱迷你版。它们真是美丽极了，纯真的面孔上长着斑点，长着杂色的蹄子，卷曲的长尾巴，还有轻盈柔软的身体，跳跃的时候就像许多只小猫，但是特别温柔，还带着一种甜蜜又纯真的坦然，那是小猫，或者说任何猫咪都没有的。它们是如此全然、完美地享受着自身的存在！啊！小坏蛋们！你们吵闹的声音太大，把你们的妈妈都给吵醒了，有两三只母羊站了起来，其中一只迈着稳健的步子走到羊羔们中间，挑出了自己的孩子，温柔地抵了抵它的头，随后便快步离开了；那只受了指责的可怜小羊羔温顺地跟在后面，但总不时地停下来，回头朝着它的玩伴们投去羡慕的一瞥。余下的那些羊羔先是怔了一会儿，随后又开始了它们的玩闹。那只威严的母羊时不时地回头看看它的小羊有没有跟上来。最后它在草地上卧了下来，而小羊羔就紧挨在它身边。有生以来，我还从未见过如此美妙的田园景象。①

在山谷里又转了一个弯，我们就瞥见了它背后那片黑魆魆的灌木林，但我们和灌木丛之间还隔着一片长满灯芯草的沼泽地，那是泉水汇集而成的洼地，是红冠水鸡喜欢筑巢的地方。啊，正有一只红冠水鸡在急速地涉水而过；我能听到溅水的声音，和它在灯芯草中拍打翅膀的声音。这里就是这个荒野山谷最深的地方。地面上可谓是沟壑纵

---

① 我曾见过更让我动容的一幕。那次我和教区里的一些年轻女士沿着教堂边的小路散步，我们遇到了一大群羊，和通常一样，羊群由牧羊人和牧羊犬护卫着。我们渐渐落在了羊群后面，在几乎已经看不到它们的时候，我们又碰到了一只掉了队的母羊，它时而快走，时而放慢脚步，总是时不时地停下来朝后张望，叫上几声。在它后面的不远处走过来一只跛脚的小羊羔，时不时地咩咩叫，似乎是在回应自己的妈妈，并尽力地想要跟上她。小羊的两只前腿都瘸了，膝盖弯曲着，似乎是在用蹄子的最前端踮着脚走，如果我能够这样描述的话。我那个年轻的朋友认为这是先天畸形造成的瘸腿，我却觉得是意外造成的，那个可怜的小东西正忍受着剧烈的脚疼。不管怎样，它每走一步都要经受痛苦和困难是毋庸置疑的；母羊此时心中的痛苦和疼爱，它看到羊群渐渐远去时的茫然，以及可怜的羊羔设法跑上几步的努力，还有它们互相呼唤，流露出的悲苦，都感人至深，艾伦和我尽管都不是轻易落泪之人，也都强忍着才没有哭出来。我们找不到能抱小羊的男孩子，而它对于我们来说又太大了，但我确信母羊绝不会丢下它；随着天色暗下来，我们俩都相信羊群入栏的时候，牧羊人一定会发现它们两个不见了，而转头来找它们；事实果真如此，我真是太高兴了。（作者注）

横！这些眼下完全被植被覆盖的深堑，就是之前采挖砾石的矿坑；几乎无法描述这片如迷宫一般的坑地，因为他们采石的时候就是这样变化无常、不着边际的，但是可以想见采石的数量是相当可观的。算了，这样猜下去会没完没了！我们已经涉足到了泉水之中，必须要掉头回去了。转过一个角落，那里的岩壁上长着红门兰和白星海芋，犹如仙境中的露台，我们突然间从未曾到过的山谷一侧走了出来，这里正对着我们的好邻居农夫艾伦的小农场。

这一处乡间院落，属于之前在这一带被叫作"小片地"的地方：有三四十英亩可耕种的田地，农场主和他的儿子们自己耕种，而他的妻女则帮忙饲养家畜，靠着奶牛场、禽圈和果园的产出贴补家用，有些微薄的收入。这样在土地上劳作的耕作者阶层正在消亡，但是他们所承载的英国品格中最优秀的部分——勤劳、节俭、通情达理和善良——却依然存在。农夫艾伦本人就是一个极好的例证。他现在上了年纪，一头长长的白发，一双明亮的灰色眼睛，依然开朗乐观，令人尊敬，而他的妻子甚至比他还要优秀。他们曾经历过艰苦的抗争才保住了这一份家业。他们操劳一生，现在总算能安享晚年，这多亏了他们之前经营有道，操持有方，再加上他们那个有出息的儿子的帮衬。那个儿子离开村子的时候，还是一个穷酸的小伙计，现在已经成为伦敦一家大公司的合伙人了。正是因为他，他们才能熬过最困难的时日，过上现在无忧无虑的生活，正像他们的至亲好友所期盼的那样。

啊！艾伦先生这会儿就在果园里。这真是个漂亮的果园啊，红白两色的花正开得热闹，白色的是珍珠白的梨花，红色的是珊瑚红的苹果花。这些花真可谓是云蒸霞蔚！它们沐浴在晚霞的柔光中，在黑色房屋和饱经风霜的谷仓的映衬之下，更显得明艳妩媚！地面的草地上落满了梨树和樱桃树如雪花一样的花瓣。艾伦太太就坐在树下，给鸡鸭喂食，她那三个从伦敦来的孙女，三个三岁到五岁不等的漂亮小仙女（最年长和最年幼的仅仅相差二十二个月），就在她身边玩耍。

艾伦太太，我亲爱的艾伦太太是位难得一见的美人，尽管她现在已经是一位老妇人了，但我还是要说她依然风姿不减。我为什么不能这样说呢？高贵的神态和甜美的表情不管是在暮年还是在青年，都同样让人感到如沐春风。她的面孔和身姿很像那位给每个见过她的人都留下不可磨灭的印象的伟大女性——西登斯夫人[①]。艾伦夫人脸部的轮廓几乎和她完全一样，但更为柔和，更加温婉，眼睛和微笑里有着更多女性的沉静。艾伦太太从未扮演过麦克白夫人。她的头发依然像她二十岁时那样乌黑，在她宽大的前额处中分，向后梳于她那顶精致整洁的白色帽子下面。她围着一条平纹细布的围巾，穿着一件灰色的织布长袍，外面再加一件白围裙，这就是她一身的打扮了。

她坐在一棵老的接骨木树下，树的枝条张开如同一顶华盖，夕阳的余晖照亮了她可敬的身影，给树叶也镀上了一层绿宝石般的光泽。她安详地坐在那里，面带微笑，手

---

① 西登斯夫人（Sarah Kemble Siddons，1755—1831），英国著名女演员，以其塑造的莎士比亚剧中角色麦克白夫人而闻名。

上拿着眼镜，膝头上放着一篮大麦，小姑娘们正把她们肉嘟嘟的小手伸进篮子里抓麦子，然后又带着无法言表的喜悦把麦子撒给鸭子和小鸡们。可是，那些不知感恩的家禽似乎并不高兴，也没有表现出应有的感激，它们并不信任这些年幼的喂食者。所有的家畜都不喜欢孩子，一部分是因为它们本能地害怕孩子们的调皮和莽撞，还有一部分，我猜，是因为嫉妒。把嫉妒这种悲剧情感与农场动物联系起来似乎比较奇怪，可是看看那只趾高气扬的矮脚公鸡（显然是最受宠的一只）吧，它对安妮给它丢过来的大麦颇为不屑，转身便走，半含着委屈半含着柔情悄悄走到上了年纪的女主人的身边，它难道不是像奥赛罗一样满心嫉妒？只有艾伦太太的关注和她手里的一把麦子才能抚慰它。看哪，她正在唤着它，给它喂食，现在它抖擞着羽毛，拍打着翅膀，挺起它那光滑的颈项，昂首阔步走了过去，咯咯地啼叫几声，啄上几粒麦子，简直是矮脚鸡中最骄傲、最幸福的一只，堪称所有家禽中集宠爱和荣耀于一身者！

与此同时，我自己的宠物五月花也回到我的身边了，她这一阵子每遇到一个洞就要窥探一番，不肯放过山谷中的任何一个角落和拐弯，满心希望能再找到一只兔子。她把她蛇一样滑溜的脑袋伸到我的手里，既是在请我给予她最喜欢的爱抚，又是在不失礼貌地暗示我，到了该回家的时候了。西沉的落日也给了我同样的警告；于是，不一会儿工夫，我们便穿过了山谷、田地、大门，经过了农场和磨坊，来到了横跨洛登河的桥上。

多么壮观的落日！多么灿烂！多么美丽！太阳正在

隐去，余晖将几条狭长的云带渲染得金光闪耀，晃得人眼睛几乎无法直视。那些云带几分钟之前还是横卧在地平线上的柔软的水汽条痕，而那些飘浮在它们上面的更为柔软的云层，则环绕、卷曲，变幻出千百种不可思议的形状，就像夏日里的轻烟一样缥缈，富于变化。此刻难以形容的耀眼光线勾勒出它们的轮廓，加深了它们的颜色，给它们镶上了金边，绘制出一幅壮丽的画面。一转眼的工夫，那一轮耀眼的光球就完全消失了，上面的天空每时每刻都在变幻，变得无比绚丽多姿，炫目的金色光芒与彤亮的红色、璀璨的紫色交织、融合，小的暗色黑斑点缀其间，这些色彩又一起融进如篱雀蛋一般的青空里。抬头仰望，可见辉煌灿烂的天空，低头俯视，又能看见清澈可爱的洛登河水中这幅恢宏画面的倒影，这样的喜悦简直无法言说，永难忘怀。在写下这段文字的时候，我不禁心潮澎湃，眼眶湿润，我想到了大自然无与伦比的雄浑壮阔，上帝无法言表的仁慈，他如此慷慨，不吝将这样纯粹、这样祥和又这样热烈的图景，展现在那最为卑微、渺小的生灵面前。

樱草花球

五月十六日——生活中总会有些时候，你毫无征兆或毫无缘由地情绪低落、难过，就好像不堪生存压力的重负。在这种时候，你会感到难以言说的沮丧，对自己的各种想法都感到厌倦，脑海中有许许多多挥之不去的画面——它们各不相同，但都和痛苦有关：物是人非，朋友变得疏远、陌生，或者故去；即使得偿所愿，心里却依然感到失落；毫无益处的悔恨，无力实现的愿景，怀疑和恐惧，自我怀疑和自我诋毁。那些对这样的感受有所了解的人（又有谁能快乐无忧从不经历这些时刻呢？），就会理解为何读阿尔菲耶里①会汲取不到力量，读傅华萨②会感到索然无味了；也会理解为什么即使是最有效的镇静剂——最能够纾解女性痛苦、能让她们平心静气的针线活，今天也无法给

---

① 维托里奥·阿尔菲耶里（Vittorio Alfieri，1749—1803），意大利剧作家和诗人，以写悲剧著称。
② 让·傅华萨（Jean Froissart，约1337—约1405），中世纪法国作家，其记录百年战争的散文体著作《大事记》被认为是十四世纪英格兰和法国骑士文学的代表作。

我带来任何安慰了。我打算在这个凉爽怡人的午后到户外走走，试试看能否让心情好起来。我想，锻炼或不管何种形式的拉练才是治愈神经敏感的良药。"不过掷出一枚小石块，那巨人就倒地而亡。"[①]我要到草地上去，那些美丽的草地！我还会带上给我制造幸福的材料，莉兹和五月花，还有一个采花的篮子，我们会做一个樱草花球。"我的小莉兹，你见过樱草花球吗？""没有。""那就跟我来吧；走快点！跑起来，莉兹！"

我们走在路上，疾步如飞！沿着公路，穿过草地，经过救济所，顺着大水塘的岸边，直到我们潜进那条深深的窄道，路边的篱笆几乎能够到水面，我们在小道的尽头顺利到达了小农场。"穿过农场院子，莉兹；跨过大门；别害怕那些奶牛；它们已经够安静了。"——"我不害怕它们。"莉兹小姐勇敢又真诚地说道，脸上露出不服气的骄傲神情，被人认为她会害怕什么让她颇为不快。为了表明自己的态度和行事作风，证明自己足够勇敢，她袭击了那群奶牛中块头最大的一头，用手拽了一下它的尾巴。"我不害怕它们。""我知道你不害怕，莉兹；不过还是别招惹它们了，也别去追那只雄火鸡。到我这儿来，亲爱的！"没想到，莉兹真的乖乖走了过来。

---

① 出自英国诗人马修·格林（Matthew Green，1696—1737）的诗作《脾气》（*The Spleen*，1737），格林在这首诗中提倡以乐观、锻炼和安适疗愈心灵的创伤，用词机智诙谐，妙语横生。作者引用的这一句典出《圣经·撒母耳记》，指牧羊少年大卫用弹弓掷出的石块打死了巨人歌利亚。

与此同时，我的另一个宝贝儿五月花也陷入了困境。她原本在追一头巨大、笨重的老母猪，没想到那头猪的哼叫声把一只身形更为硕大的动物——看守院子的纽芬兰犬——从睡梦中给吵醒了。他嗷嗷叫着从狗窝里面冲了出来，直竖着尾巴，摇晃着身上长长的链子。五月花的注意力立刻就从母猪转移到了这个新玩伴的身上，至于他是敌是友，她完全不在乎；从狗窝里冲出来的他，看到自己的进攻毫不奏效，并且身边没有丝毫威胁，于是便悠闲地观察起他这位美丽迷人的对手来。只见她在他周围跳跃奔走，总是处于他链子所能够到的范围之外，但是，她的性别所具有的自然而本能的魅惑，每次都会把他挑逗起来去追她，但她心里非常清楚，他只会白忙活一场。我从未见过比这个更有趣的调情了。最后，那只高贵的动物被折腾得筋疲力尽，便打起了退堂鼓，退守到狗窝的最里面，即使她就站在门口，也再不肯出来。"你已经玩够了，五月花。来吧，莉兹。穿过那片麦子地，马上就到大门口了。停下来！让我把你举起来。不要跳，别把你的脖子给摔断了，莉兹！"很快，我们就置身草地上了，远离尘世。即使是身处孤岛的鲁滨孙·克鲁索，也很难享受到比此刻更完整、更美妙的孤寂了。

　　这片草地由两排小型封闭的肥美草场组成，长度有一到两英里，从中间可耕种的高地顺势向两侧延伸，还有一条无名小溪在这些草场中间蜿蜒环绕，溪水清澈、湍急，流经的路线曲折变化，似乎是在模仿那些奔流的北方大河，相比我们慵懒的南方溪流，这条小溪更像是北方河流的微缩复刻。从未见过如此欢快奔腾的流水：忽而从光滑的鹅卵石上流泻下来，唱着欢快的乐曲在阳光下熠熠闪动，汩汩的水声和林雀的歌唱一样甜美，富有野趣；忽而静静地流淌，映出岸边郁郁葱葱的驴蹄草的金色倒影；忽而漫过一片丰美的绿草地，草地陡然升起的部分形成了一个高高的、类似岬角的土坡，而其他柔软下沉的部分则构成了一个小小的水湾，其间的流水清浅而宽阔，渴望冒险的莉兹信心满满地认为自己可以不弄湿衣服，安全通过；忽而在两侧的沙岸中间左突右奔，形成一道深而窄的激流，五月花可以一跃而过；忽而如沉睡一般，半遮半掩地潜藏于两岸丰饶而多样的植被之下，从桤木、山楂树和野蔷薇的树丛之下淌过，而溪水的表面则被鸢尾①、百合和其他一些水生植物遮盖得严严实实。说实在的，这真是一条美丽的

---

① 一两年前一个明媚的午后，应该是比这个季节更晚一点的时候，我在沿着草地散步时，有机会捕捉到了自然历史中颇为有趣的一幕。我当时正站在溪水边，注意到一大片鸢尾丛中冒出来孤零零的一簇花。它看起来就像是簇到一起的几束花，下面的叶片发黑，但是呈透明状，与一些颜色鲜艳的管状物混在一起，那些管子主要是亮眼的蓝色和晶莹的绿色。在更为仔细地观察了这个现象之后，我才发现那是凑到一起的一群蜻蜓，它们刚刚破蛹而出，薄膜般的翅膀还是湿漉漉的，因而它们都无精打采的，一动不动。半小时之后，我们又回到那个地方时，它们都不见了。我们看见它们的时候，正是它们美丽的身体发育完成，而活力尚未被唤醒的时刻。在那之后，我在宾格利先生的书里找到了对于这个有趣过程的相似描述，那本书名为《动物传记》(Animal Biography, 1802)，是本相当好看的著作。（作者注）威廉·宾格利（William Bingley, 1774—1823），英国牧师、自然主义者、作家，《动物传记》是他最广为人知的作品。

小溪，是一条沃顿[①]本人来了也愿意坐在它的岸边，并且会爱上的小溪，因为水里有鳟鱼。我们看见它们溯流而上，还会在听到扑通一声时被吓一跳，那是它们猛地跃出水面捕食夏日里的蝇虫时发出的声音。艾萨克·沃顿应该也会爱上我们的小溪和这片安静的草地，因为这里的气息正是他内心祥和的精神写照，那是一种沉入灵魂的、舒缓的静谧。没有路能横穿这片草地，一条也没有。我们就算是花上整整一个春日的时间在这里闲逛，也不会发现任何有人烟的地方。草地属于几个小产权者，他们出于纯粹的好心和邻里间的照应，互相允许对方进入他们各自的领地。谁也没有滥用这种特权：水面对岸的田地，只是经由一块粗糙的木板、一棵被放倒的树或是一些类似的简易桥梁与此岸相接。我们拥有这其中最美的一块。因此，在这片迷人风景所具有的种种魅力之外，我们还体验到了一种财产带来的奇异乐趣，这几乎是一种本能。自己的娃娃即使是破了，莉兹也会爱不释手；五月花即使是啃着光溜溜的骨头，也乐在其中，因为那是她从自己胆怯的崇拜者——那只纽芬兰犬——的狗窝里偷来据为己有的。这真是一种奇妙的乐趣，越是像我这样的穷人，越是能感同身受！或许，只有穷人才能深刻地体会这种乐趣，富人反倒没有这样强烈的感受——他们的乐趣太过分散，被冲淡了，就像金叶一样，扩展得太大只剩下纤薄的一片。穷人那点儿微不足道的财产不仅更加珍贵，也更能给他们带来快乐，就像这片

---

① 即下文提到的艾萨克·沃顿（Isaac Walton，1593—1683），英国作家，代表作是《钓鱼大全》（*The Compleat Angler*，1653）。

长着花花草草的土地，有长满植被的圆丘，有一丛丛的灌木，有爬满常春藤的去梢的老树，还有明亮的、潺潺的流水，对于我来说是心头的挚爱。但我一定是对这片草地倾心已久，它是如此清新、舒爽、赏心悦目，走在其中让人心旷神怡，远远看去都是黄花九轮草和各色春天里的花。当我们踏足其上的时候，禁不住要吟诵起莎士比亚的《春之歌》：

> 当杂色的雏菊，紫罗兰，
>
> 银白色的碎米荠，
>
> 和黄色的疆南星一片一片，
>
> 将欢快的色彩铺满草地，
>
> 布谷鸟就会栖上每棵树的枝头……[1]

"布谷！布谷！"莉兹叫了起来，清亮的童音打断了我的吟诵，随即，仿佛是听到了她的召唤，真的有一只鸟在邻近的树上（这些草地上散布着一些大树，像庄园里一样）应和着我可爱的小姑娘，"布谷！布谷！"我对这位"春天的信使"怀有偏见，这种偏见与那些田园和诗意的表达大相径庭（我也是不由自主，这类的偏见还有很多）。布谷鸟的叫声非常单调，带着忧伤，男孩子们都争相模仿。不管是在肮脏的大街上，还是在烟熏火燎的房子中，你总是能听到"布谷！布谷！"的声音。这种鸟也因此受到诟

---

[1] 出自莎士比亚剧作《爱的徒劳》（*Love's Labour's Lost*，1598）第五幕第二场。

病，但这并不是它的过错。然而，在品位上的偏见、喜好或是憎恶，并不能随着理智的介入而被纠正。因而，为了躲避树上传来的乐曲声，它注定还要延续相当长一段时间（那永恒的歌唱一旦开始，便会像嘀嗒的钟表一样没完没了）——为了躲避这种噪声，我决心要激发另一种噪声，于是便挑战莉兹，要和她来一场采樱草花的比赛。这是一项考验技巧和速度的比拼，看谁能在最短的时间内把自己的篮子装满。我的这项策略完全奏效了。莉兹一边在地上摸爬，一边尖叫大喊，别提有多开心了！就算是二十只布谷鸟的叫声也会被淹没，因为她一边摘自己的花儿，一边还要从我的篮子里偷，又是大笑，又是尖叫，嘴巴一直说个没完。

最后篮子终于被装满了，莉兹宣布了获胜者，于是我们在溪水边坐下来，头上是一棵枝叶舒展的山楂树，枝条上刚刚冒出来珍珠一样的白色花蕾，周围开满了野生风信子那珐琅彩色的各色花朵，有蓝有白，我们就在这里开始做樱草花球。每个人都知道做樱草花球的程序：先在花茎最顶端往下一点的地方掐断花头，然后把几枝一簇的花头稳稳地卡到一根丝带上，直到做出像花环一样的长长一条，最后把花头攒在一处，结结实实地扎紧。总的来说，我们进行得异常顺利！所谓的顺利是相对而言的，就像人们说起一位年轻女士学画画，或是法国人说英语，或是女人写出的悲剧，或是一个可怜的没有手指的侏儒做的活计，或者是灵巧的水手用脚指头写的字，这种大体上是在条件相当艰苦的情况下去完成的任务。准确地说，我们还是碰到了一些意外。首先，莉兹掐花头的时候留的茎秆太短，基本上她所有的樱草花都浪费了，所以只得又重新采了一些；接着，五月花打翻了我满满一篮子的花，使那些花像精灵的信物一样，在溪水中顺流而下，漂走了；再后来，当我们进展得相当顺利，做出了一个超级花环，正准备要扎起来的时候，攥着丝带的莉兹突然瞥见了一只褐、红、紫三色相间且异常美丽的蝴蝶，于是就丢开手，跑去追新发现的事物了。因而，我们的花重又散了一地。不过，最后，借助于取代了莉兹的一棵桤树的树枝，又把花篮挂在一棵去了梢的白蜡树上，不让五月花看见，樱草花球才总算是完工了。樱草花球将花香和花的美丽融合在了一起，真是馥郁芬芳，美丽异常！金色的花朵，甜蜜的香气，浓艳得简直让人难以承受！它看起来是如此缤纷，摸起来如此娇嫩，闻起来是如此浓烈！莉兹完全被迷住了，拿着这件宝贝就跑开了，狂喜之中不知如何是好，她就躲到了树丛里，似乎不想被任何人看到，影响她天真无邪的欢喜，包括我。

就在莉兹欣赏樱草花球的同时，我坐在那里静静地聆听，不是听我的敌人布谷鸟的叫声，而是听由一群夜莺唱响的一场音乐会，这期间几乎没有任何过来打岔的鸟，仅仅是夜莺彼此间用短促甜美的声音进行的唱和、赛歌，这歌声如此悦耳，就如同玫瑰悦目一样。这些可爱的声音片段在我们听来真是如闻仙乐。我一边听着，一边开始愉快地浮想联翩，我几乎是无意识地就开始吟诵福特《情人的悲哀》①中鲁特琴手和夜莺之间的美丽故事。就是下面这段。在英国诗歌中还能找到比它更美的片段吗?

从意大利到希腊,

远古时代的诗人们,

为了颂扬他们的神庙,

所编撰的种种传说,

让我心生宏愿,

渴望能到天堂一游。

我来到了塞萨利,孤身一人,

除了我旧日的心头所爱,

我的所思所想,

再没有别的能与我为伴。

日复一日,我徘徊于

幽静的树林,寂寞的小路,

直到一天清晨,遇到奇事一桩:

我听到了最为美妙、最让人陶醉的争执,

那是艺术和自然的精彩对决。

我听到一段动人的音乐,或者说

触动我灵魂的音乐;我被那乐曲吸引,

悄悄地靠近,只见一位年轻人,

脸庞白皙的年轻人,正在他的鲁特琴上

演奏着让人惊奇的变奏和和弦,

---

① 《情人的悲哀》(*The Lover's Melancholy*,1629),英国剧作家、诗人约翰·福特(John Ford,1586—1639)早期的一部悲喜剧作品。

动听的旋律，似乎是，一纸勇敢的挑战书，

给林中嗓音清亮的合唱者，那些鸟儿，

它们正聚集在他的身边，默不作声，

惊叹于它们所听到的美妙乐声。和我一样。

一只夜莺，

自然界里技艺最为精湛的音乐家，

接受了挑战；那个英俊的年轻人，

每次在指尖奏出几段旋律之后，

她都亮起歌喉，将他比了下去。

不管年轻人在他颤抖的琴上，

奏响的旋律如何变化，

总是不及夜莺应和他时，

唱得那般婉转多变。

如此过去一阵子之后，

年轻人恼羞成怒，

那只鸟儿，

从未学过什么音符和乐理，

竟能和他一较高下，他可是

耗费了大把的光阴，

才将技艺锻炼至纯熟。

为了决出胜负，

他像进入迷狂状态一般，

开始在琴上飞快地弹奏，

完全是即兴所致，迅疾如电，

乐曲显得奇特而巧妙，

嘈杂中包含着和音，

不同方法弹奏的乐曲，

都融进欢快的主题。

那夜莺（注定要成为音乐的第一个殉难者）

拼尽全力去模仿其中的几种声调；

可任她歌喉婉转，最终也力不从心，

她满含悲愤地跌落在他的琴上，

心脏停止了跳动。

那个得胜的人竟伏在她的身体上，

声泪俱下地唱出了一支挽歌，

这真是一种奇特的悲痛。

他看着自己以技艺赢得的奖杯，

不禁恍叹，不禁落泪，

他又恍叹，又落泪，

"啊！可怜的生灵，我就要为你报仇，

惩罚这残忍的始作俑者。

从此以后，这把沾染了无辜者鲜血的鲁特琴，

将再也不会打扰祥和的宁静，

直到时间的尽头。"

悲痛之中，

只见他操起琴砸向一棵树，

我慌忙现身，走了上来。

当我把这一篇精彩的诗作背诵完，整个下午一直昏暗

低沉的天空开始变得越来越阴沉，黑色的云层如同黑色烟雾织就的花环，从铅灰色的天空飞掠而过。草地上刮起了更冷、更湿润的风，几滴大而重的雨滴砸在了水面上。"我们要赶上暴风雨了。莉兹！五月花！你们在哪儿？快，快，我的莉兹！快跑，快跑！再快点儿，再快点儿！"

我们撒开腿快跑。莉兹对于淋雨的想法并非完全不开心，说实在话，淋雨对于她就像对于鸭子一样是家常便饭；五月花则不然，她抬头瞥了一眼这糟糕的天气，颇为沮丧地动了动她漂亮的耳朵。在所有动物当中，除了猫，就数格力犬最讨厌下雨了。她本来可以躲过去的，她那灵巧的四条腿原本可以在大雨降下之前就把她带回家，但五月花的忠诚不允许她这么做，她是一位真正的伙伴，非常清楚什么是风雨同舟的伙伴精神，所以她一直等着我们。当然，她是一路小跑向前，然后停下来，朝后张望着，频频示意，黑色的大眼睛里流露出对我们行进缓慢的些许不屑。我们则尽量往前赶，一边鼓励着对方，一边又对彼此感到不满。"快点儿，我的莉兹！哦，真是个跑不快的！"——"快点，再快点！哦，真是个跑不快的！"我的冒失鬼应声重复道。"你吃得太胖了，莉兹，根本走不动路！"——"啊！还不知道谁胖呢？"小可爱反诘道。她妈妈说得没错，我把这孩子给宠坏了。

到了这个时候，我们三个全被雨淋透了。那是一场瓢泼大雨，瞬间就浸透了我们轻薄的夏日衣裙和五月花光滑的皮毛。等到我们都湿透的时候，太阳出来了，真的是太阳，它似乎就是来看我们的笑话的；接着，更让人恼火的是，等到云消雨霁、太阳光辉灿烂的时候，一个女仆和一个男孩赶过来接应我们，他们带的斗篷和伞具足够我们抵御一整天的降雨。算了，我们还是接着赶路，而且越走越快；莉兹只能被人抱着走，这看起来有些不雅，但那是因为她不幸地把一只鞋子丢在了泥里，我们请那个男孩来处理它。

　　我们终于到家了——浑身都湿漉漉的，可是情绪高涨，笑个没完，完全没把我们的遭遇当回事。五月花，这只颇有灵性的狗，随即就爬上狗窝里的床，这会儿应该舒舒服服地把头埋在干草中睡大觉了。莉兹也到床上去了，连哄带劝才让她接受这个明智的建议，还允诺了她要送来茶和吐司，可以一直待到明天再回家，还可以听一个小红帽的故事。而我则换上了干衣服，在暖融融的炉火旁尽情享受着这份惬意。说实在话，偶尔淋一次雨并不是什么坏事，但最好别穿华美的衣服，因为没有人愿意糟蹋掉一件新的毛皮大衣，或是一顶精致的羽毛饰帽。可如果没有这种顾虑，只是一件白色长衫和一顶草帽，就像今天这样，那我倒是更乐意淋雨。受点儿凉能让人头脑清醒，而随后享受到的温暖和干燥，更是让人舒服得无以复加。除此之外，那种刺激和劳累对于头脑和身体都有裨益。早上的时候我是多么抑郁难过啊！现在我又是何等快活啊！没有比淋一场大雨——一场真正的大雨，就像我和莉兹还有五月花经历的这场一样，更能治愈你低落的情绪了。试试看，我亲爱的读者，如果你也感到紧张压抑——我敢保证这个办法一定能奏效。

阿伯雷的老房子

六月二十五日——一个多么明媚、灿烂的日子！正值盛夏时节，中午的时候太阳明晃晃、光灿灿的，深邃的蓝色天空上飘着几朵白云，太阳时而被云层遮住，时而又穿破云层放射出耀眼的光芒。今天可不能出门散步，装装样子也不行，只是听到"散步"这两个字就让我们害怕。可是，没准儿我们会在回家之前忍不住去溜达上一大圈儿。我们打算乘车到阿伯雷的老房子那里去，在芬芳的杉树树荫下，茂盛的蔷薇树丛中，河水充盈的洛登河河畔，度过一个上午。"别指望我们能在六点钟之前回来。"我在出门的时候说。"最早六点钟！"我那个迷人的同伴又补充了一句。我们乘着家里的一辆轻便马车出发了，原本拉车的是小马驹，现在是我们家的老母马，车夫是一位好脾气的愣头小伙子，斯科拉博家的下一代，亨利的继任者，在家里负责照看马匹、马车、奶牛还有花园。

与我同坐这辆不起眼的代步工具的是一位年轻的小姐，她出身高贵，天资更高，坐这样的马车出行对于她本就是件新鲜事，再加上她天性率真自然，品味朴素，更让她觉得这是件无法言表的乐事。坐上马车的时候，她故意颠了几下，看到马车上下晃动，她像个孩子一样开心得笑个不停，就算是莉兹也不会比她这样更开心了。她一路赞叹着马匹和车夫、走过的道路和沿途的景色，尽情地享受着在最甜蜜的时节、最好的天气里在乡间出游的乐趣。我对这一切也很享受，因为这条路不管从哪个方面看，都让人感到愉悦，它时而蜿蜒于窄巷，时而穿行于高大的榆树下，时而出现在开满花的忍冬和蔷薇树篱间，空气中弥散着豆子开花时的诱人香气。我很享受这一切，然而，我相信，我最主要的乐趣还是来自我的这位旅伴。

能与艾米丽一世结识是一种荣幸。她就像是老一代诗人笔下的人物，会让人误以为是莎士比亚或者弗莱彻①所描述的女性走进了生活中，她和她们一样温柔，一样俏皮，一样优雅，一样善良。她也相当聪慧，非凡的头脑既清晰又灵活，轻易就掌握了那些精心实施的教育所教授的所有知识和才艺，再加上有良师益友为伴，她的学识与技艺愈发炉火纯青了。但是，人们很少会想到她有如此的造诣。人们之所以喜爱艾米丽，是因为她迷人真挚的性情、体贴可人的举止、真实广博的怜悯之心、敏锐的判断力和热烈的情感。她有爱尔兰血统，有着趋于完美的温柔嗓音，以及柔和、舒缓的口音，那是她们那里美丽的女性同胞独有的特质。此外，她长得很美——我认为她很美丽，所有见

---

① 约翰·弗莱彻（John Fletcher，1579—1625），詹姆斯一世统治时期最高产、最有影响力的剧作家。他的声望在王政复辟时期达到顶峰，与莎士比亚齐名。

过她的人都这么认为——但也漂亮，相当漂亮，全世界的人都必须承认；或许这两者的区别在于，相比美丽那种"光鲜亮丽的状态"，漂亮很少会引发他人的嫉妒，却更有让人羡慕的意味。她的漂亮是最为高级的一种漂亮，其主要特点是青春靓丽。她身形娇小可人，优雅而匀称，一张白皙的脸庞泛着红润，透出智慧与和善；她还有着世界上最漂亮的一双小脚和最白皙的一双手，这就是艾米丽一世。

她和外祖母住在一起，那是一位受人尊敬的老太太，因为得了中风，身子骨没有以前那么硬朗了，她们两个在一起（她们非常喜欢与彼此为伴，因此很少看见她们分开），她们是我见过的最为可爱的青年和老年组合。每一次看见她们，对于她们祖孙二人的尊重和爱戴都会增加一分——她们之间一直维持着最温柔、最美丽的自然关系——理查森[①]对此深有感触，因而在他那本无与伦比的著作中对其进行了巧妙的运用。我猜想，雪莉一定也是一位像 S 夫人那样受人尊敬的老太太，而我们可爱的艾米丽——哦，不！哈里叶特·拜伦连她的一半也比不上！在整整七卷书里，根本没有可以和她相提并论的人物。

---

① 塞缪尔·理查森（Samuel Richardson，1689—1761），十八世纪英国著名小说家，其代表作有《帕米拉》（又名《美德受到了奖赏》，*Pamela: Or Virtue Rewarded*，1740）、《克拉丽莎》（又名《一个年轻女士的故事》，*Clarissa: Or the History of a Young Lady*，1748），以及《查尔斯·格兰迪森爵士传》（*The History of Sir Charles Grandison*，1753），文中"无与伦比的著作"应该指的就是《查尔斯·格兰迪森爵士传》，因为后文中提到的雪莉、哈里叶特·拜伦都是该书的主要角色。

啊，我们一转眼已经来到了桥上！我们必须在这儿下车了！这就是洛登河，艾米丽。多么美的一条河，不是吗？河水漫涨，和堤岸齐平，如此清澈、平缓而宁静，倒映着岸边绿色的景致和蔚蓝的天空。明净的水面上漂浮着雪白的睡莲，那是百花之中最为圣洁的花，它端坐在清凉的叶片之上，犹如一位君王，看起来又仿佛是贞洁的化身，就像《科马斯》①中的那位贞女。那如女王一般的花朵变成流水，那些如仪仗队一般顺流而下的高贵天鹅也是如此，就像那些

> "圣玛丽湖上的天鹅，
>
> 浮水游弋，对影成双。"②

我们必须在这里下车，让理查德在树荫里照看我们的马车，而我们则要步行走过去：瞧，就在那儿！我们必须得踩着这些梯磴跨过去，没有别的路。

翻过这些篱笆墙我们很快就来到了一个原本环绕着大庄园的车道上，这里还留存着一些旧日的风貌，尽管庄园早就被分割，变成了可耕种的土地。在这里可以看到整个大宅的样貌，那是一栋詹姆斯一世时期的美丽建筑，那些

---

① 科马斯（Comus）是古希腊神话中的欢庆之神，约翰·弥尔顿（John Milton，1608—1674）在其同名剧作（Comus，1634）中塑造过一位受到科马斯诱惑和胁迫却坚守忠贞的贞洁女士。

② 出自英国浪漫主义诗人威廉·华兹华斯的诗作《未到耶罗》（Yarrow Unvisited，1803）。

没有玻璃的窗户和破旧的门扇，与富丽雄伟的建筑正面所展现出的力量和完整性，形成了让人感伤的巨大反差。

这片废墟——它的确如此——的故事一直对我有着独特的吸引力。那是一个古老又显赫的家族的衰亡史，记录了它从荣耀的巅峰逐渐衰落到贫困窘境的过程。宅邸和庄园，还有周边的一小块地产，由一个远房的表亲继承，而且其产权不能转让。已故的房屋主人，也就是他的姓氏和家族里的最后一位成员，与债务和困厄进行了长期的斗争，他自己耕种土地，像小福斯卡里[①]一样执着坚守着这个宏伟的家，尽管他对这个地方爱之深切，但最后也只能无奈放弃，退隐到一个无名小镇上的一间无名小屋之中，二十年前在那里郁郁而终。他的继任者对于这个地方没有丝毫的眷恋之情，理所当然地认为，相对于业已萎缩的地产来说，这里作为住所未免太大了，于是便果断卖掉了这里的豪华陈设，并准备把整个房子都拆掉，只是后来在尝试了一番之后，发现这里的砖石结构太过坚固，实在不值得费这么大的力气。然而，房子一边相当大的一块已经被扒开，那些精美的房间，连同里面的雕花和镏金装饰，都暴露在外，经受风吹日晒雨淋——已经成了过往辉煌的悲伤纪念。这块地基幸而被仁慈地忽视了；这个庄园，事实上已经破败不堪，草坪被用作公共的秣草地每年被收割两次，避暑的洞室坍塌成了废墟，鱼塘里则长满了芦苇和水生植物，被堵得密不透风；但是灌木丛和开花的树都没有

[①]　小福斯卡里出自古老的威尼斯名门望族福斯卡里家族（The Foscaris），家族的权势在十四到十五世纪达到顶峰，之后日渐衰落。

遭到破坏，长得尺寸巨大，自有一种野性的美，就好像我们想象的它们在原来的森林里所能长成的样子。没有什么比它们长得更繁茂了，尤其是到了春天，当丁香、金链花和重瓣樱花竞相绽放、争奇斗艳的时候。在这样的废墟当中看到繁花似锦的景象会让人有一种甜蜜的感伤，这似乎是自然对于人类破坏力的一种胜利。更准确地说在那个时节，这整个地方都会弥漫着一种温柔而舒缓的悲伤，会让我不明缘由地想起夏洛特·史密斯[1]小说中描写自然景观的段落，那是我儿时读过的书，或许正因如此这种感伤才留在了我的记忆中。

但现在，在沿着平缓的草地走了一段之后，我们登上了一个陡峭的草坡，草坡向下一直延伸到河边，坡顶上长着巨大的冷杉和同样壮观的椴树。从这里望去，越过蜿蜒的水道，静悄悄的草坪被远处的森林紧紧环抱，一派甜美祥和的景色。空气中弥散着葱郁的冷杉和开花的椴树的气息，多么芬芳迷人！这香气真是馥郁！还有蜜蜂嗡嗡地在椴树上飞来飞去！这些长着翅膀的小家伙甚至在我们头顶上盘旋转圈！它们发出的声音如此悦耳！那是最为动听的繁忙之音，总是让人联想到一切美好和美丽的事物——勤劳和预言，阳光和鲜花。这些椴树中间没准儿藏着上百个蜂群，那浓郁的香气正是源自蜂蜜的味道，浓烈而甜腻，几乎让人吃不消。

---

[1]　夏洛特·史密斯（Charlotte Turner Smith，1749—1806），英国浪漫主义诗人和小说家，发起了复兴英语十四行诗的运动，帮助建立了哥特式小说传统，作品有小说、诗集和儿童文学作品。

艾米丽惊呼了起来，赞叹着我们所处的那片浓深、稠密、枝叶严实的树荫，后来等到看到沿途浓密茂盛的忍冬几乎铺满路面，长得和树一样高的蔷薇丛几乎挡住我们的去路时，她更是不由得连连赞叹。

"继续走，艾米丽！还有一段路呢！从那丛茉莉花那里挤过去——它会让路的；我来对付这丛顽固的白玫瑰！"——"你要当心！一定要小心！"我最美丽的朋友说道："让我来挡住这些树枝。"在付出了一些面纱和裙边损坏的代价之后，我们最终走出了这片区域。艾米丽停下脚步，对着那株高大优雅的灌木沉思默想，赞叹感慨，那株灌木长长的带刺的枝条向四面八方蔓延，曾一度挡住了我们的去路，此时却在我们的头顶上摇曳着它柔嫩的团簇的花枝。"我何曾想过，"她感慨道，"自己会站在一株白色玫瑰树的树荫之中！多么美妙的芬芳！多么美丽的花朵！如此淡雅、洁白、娇嫩，花瓣纤薄柔滑如丝绸一般！这是哪种玫瑰？"——"你不知道吗？难道你之前从未见过？我觉得这种现在很稀少了，似乎也更难见到，因为它只在盛夏最热的时候开花；但艾米丽，这就是麝香玫瑰——就是泰坦尼亚①提到的那种麝香玫瑰，真正配得上莎士比亚和那姑娘的花。不是吗？——不！不要凑上去闻；凑上去闻反倒没别的玫瑰那么香；但若是在花瓶里插上一枝，或是捧一束在胸前，一个大房间里都会花香四溢，夏天的空气就是这样被它染香的。"——"哦！那我们要折上

---

① 泰坦尼亚（Titania），莎士比亚剧作《仲夏夜之梦》中奥伯龙的妻子、精灵王后。

二十枝，"艾米丽说，"我真希望外祖母能在这儿！她经常提起，紧靠着她父亲家房子的一头种着一株麝香玫瑰。我真希望她能在这儿看到这一切！"

我们一边捧着这些或许是在莎士比亚的时代就种下的麝香玫瑰，一边聊着她的愿望，不觉间就来到了台阶之前。台阶通往一个俯瞰着河流的方方正正的夏屋，或许是一间供宴饮用的屋子，屋子的底下一部分是船屋，屋子突出的屋顶、外墙和小塔楼的尖顶上爬满了常春藤和忍冬，上面还有一丛丛的伏牛花、稠李、合欢，一串串雪白的花朵，还有其他下垂的绿植和开花的树木，将整个屋子都给盖住了。玫瑰后面还有两棵硕大无朋的白杨树，高高耸立在黑色高大的冷杉树的上方，如两根庄重肃穆的柱子，使得整个画面多了一分建筑上的、如庙堂一般的壮观。

我们现在离大宅已经很近了。不过它看上去显得悲伤而且荒凉，宅子的入口处长满了荆棘和荨麻，似乎想要阻止我们进入的脚步。那间夏屋，美丽的夏屋，则是四下敞开的，从那里高悬于河面上的没有玻璃的窗户望去，可以看见直至乡村磨坊那里的一整段河流。

我们就坐在那里，享用着我们带来的一小篮水果和自家做的蛋糕，等到把这些食物吃完，艾米丽突然有了兴致，想要从洛登河的另一侧看看这如此令她着迷的风景。"我必须，"她说，"给这个覆满了常春藤的船屋，这间可爱的房间，还有这扇美丽的窗户画上几幅素描；外婆可能永远也不能从大路上走过来，亲眼来看这个地方，但是她一定得看看它大概是什么样子。"因此我们就出发了，还没忘记带上我们珍爱的麝香玫瑰。

要到我们想去的地方没有别的路，只能重新折回。我们在一天中最热的时候，顶着酷热走了一英里，接着又在河对岸沿河走了差不多同样的距离。我们手里没有画素描的任何材料，只有一张用来包食物的皱巴巴的纸，还有我碰巧随身带着的一支没有头的铅笔。但是，这些小小的困难对于开心快活的年轻人来说不啻为一种乐趣。可爱的艾米丽完全没有把这些阻碍放在眼里，她像一头小鹿一样欢跳着，我紧跟着她，因她的快乐而快乐着。太阳躲进了云层后面，走路变得轻松惬意；水面上似乎有沁人心脾的凉风袭来，随风而来的还有冷杉和椴树的浓郁香气。我们找到了一个呈现船屋、河水、白杨、磨坊的最佳视角，可以将这些景物完美地组合在一起。那个草编的果篮被当作一个桌子，派上了大用场；那支铅笔被我们忠实的男仆随身带的一把锋利的刀子（乡下的男孩子从来是刀不离身的，那是他最主要的宝贝）重新削尖、磨利之后，完成了双份任务：在艾米丽灵巧的双手中，完成了一幅逼真生动的素描，这幅作品既如实记录了眼前的风景，也如实反映了艺术家的水准；接着又投身一项更为谦卑的工作，试着在下面一首十四行诗里记下了我自己的印象和感受：

那是夏天最火热的时候，

是一天中最为宁静的午后时分，

蔚蓝的天空中游荡着几朵浮云，

如一条格纹面纱轻掩着烈日的光芒，

以免它太过灼人，我们就在那时，

徜徉于平缓的洛登河畔，对面的陡峭高坡上

馥郁的冷杉和椴树高高矗立，如荣耀的王冠，

随风起舞的枝条如浅色的流苏，快活悦动，

常春藤的荫蔽之下（柱子般的白杨昂首挺立

其上）

隐藏着业已毁圮的船屋，其深沉的暗影，

倒映在清澈的河水中，如高塔一般。

我的艾米丽，切莫忘记这平静的时刻，

切莫忘记这迷人的景色，

正是因为你，它们才变得加倍的珍贵。

苦 夏

八月十五日——寒冷，多云，有风，潮湿。我们现在正处于一年中的三伏天，可居然像许多蟋蟀一样乐呵呵地围坐在温暖的壁炉旁，原本我们应该像另一种快乐的昆虫，像蚱蜢一样在绿色的田野里喳喳地叫个没完，而此刻却只能在英国雨神圣斯威逊①的淫威之下瑟瑟发抖。太阳难得一见，他偶尔现身的时候，我们都翘首注目，热切的程度就如同天文学家们观测彗星，或者普通人紧紧盯着气球一样。我们抱怨这寒冷的天气，就像我们之前埋怨天气炎热一样。"和去年实在是有天壤之别！"无论你走到哪儿，听到的第一句话都是这样。每个人都在谈论天气，每个人都在抱怨天气。然而，在我看来，这样的天气也有它的好处，或者至少有补偿的作用，就像自然界的万物一样，我们如果用心去寻找，总能找到其有利亦有弊的两面。

① 圣斯威逊（St. Swithin，800—863），生前为温切斯特的大主教，死后成为温切斯特教堂的守护神。传说如果在圣斯威逊的斋戒日，即每年的七月十五日，当天下雨，则雨势会持续四十天，因此他常常被视作能带来降雨的圣人。

尽管我们现在乐于坦承对这轮光球的热爱，但去年，太阳为数众多的热爱者之中，并没有一人敢于正视他：每天只有在他道过"晚安"之后，这个世界才多少可以忍受。那时我们才能活动活动：那时我们才开始醒来，开始一天的生活。整整一天在他的影响之下，我们都处于一种昏昏沉沉、如梦如幻的奇异状态之中，天气热得让人无法工作，无法阅读，无法写作，甚至无法交谈，只好一连几个小时一直坐在绿色的凉棚里，躲在树叶的浓荫之下，任由思绪和想象漫无边际地神游。不得不承认，这样的白日梦也有其可爱之处。然而，如果这世界上一半的人都要像林中的睡美人一样，在睡梦中度过整个夏天，那么世界的另一半将会是怎样的情形？

我在这炎热天气里要做的唯一一项不怎么耗费力气的工作就是给我的花浇水。我对于它们的境况感同身受，这份自然的同情心，迫使我必须要从事这项劳动。那些可怜的小东西一度枯萎、凋谢，日渐萎靡，它们几乎可以说是热切地渴望能喝上一口水。况且，如果我不亲自给它们浇水，我怀疑也没有别的人会这样做了，要知道去年这里的雨水珍贵得差不多要赶上葡萄酒了。我们地上的泉水都干涸了，水井也都干枯了，原本的深水池塘日渐萎缩，最后都变成了泥塘。每次我那忠实的男仆受了指派去打水来浇灌我可怜的天竺葵、风铃草和晚香玉的时候，鹅啊，鸭啊，猪啊，洗衣女工啊，都用嫉妒和狐疑的眼神盯着那可怜的几小桶浑水。我们迫不得已只能从我最忠实的追随者的地盘上，也就是狗窝那里把水偷运过来，以免邻里对我指手画脚，可是最后连这个水源也断了。我的花园，我那鲜花盛开的花园，我眼中的欢乐之源，也只能像隔壁的花园一样断了水，也像那里的花草一样渐渐萎缩，被太阳炙烤、晒焦。看到这种情形，我实在于心不忍。

房子另一侧的情形则更为糟糕。每当日落之后，天气凉快下来时，我们走进去发现那里简直就是一片尘土的世界！院子里的花看起来像是干花标本，植物版的木乃伊，就像是在炉子里烘烤过一样。曾经粉嫩的蜀葵变成了一身素衣的贵格教徒；丁香满是尘土的味道。哦，到处都是尘土！五月花看起来灰头土脸的，莉兹也不例外；村子里所有的房屋、窗户、小鸡、孩子、树木和猪也都一样。鞋子就更别提了。那些自称坚硬的马路上全是被碾碎的砾石，几乎成了沙砾的深渊，脚在里面走不了三步，就会被盖上一层四分之一英寸厚的尘土。哎，白色的长衫变得惨不忍睹！黑色长衫也是一样！你不管穿什么都变成了清一色的土灰色。

接着，等我们走出街道去爬山的时候，更是累得筋疲力尽，我们一路拖着疲惫的脚步往上爬，在路边的灰褐色草坪上几乎走不动，因为那里又滑又热，泥土硬得像石头一样！倘若在这个时候我们碰巧遇上了一辆从马路中间跑过来的马车——从那尘土深不见底的马路中间过来，我们简直是被卷入了一场沙尘暴当中！呛得人喘不过来气！几乎要被憋死！除了那些一路被卷入其中的旅行者所遭受的痛苦，再也没有比这更可悲的情形了。我永远也无法忘记去年八月份我们遇到一辆马车时所经受的灾难：整整过去一小时之后，马匹和马夫，马车和乘客，都还被笼罩在一片尘土之中。外面的人、拉车的马匹和马夫都无精打采，默不作声，似乎陷入了毫无招架之力的绝望之中。他们已经放弃了改善自己处境的努力，老老实实地待在这无望的境地之中，无声地忍受着这困厄的极端处境。那六个坐在马车里的人则恰恰相反，还在和他们的命运抗争，徒劳地挣扎着，试图改善他们的不幸状况。看得出，他们正埋怨着糟糕的天气，咒骂着尘土，拼命想让自己凉快些，反倒把自己折腾得像炉火一样热。我记得特别清楚，那个没穿外套的胖绅士，一边不停地擦着汗，一边把假发托起来透气，嘴巴里清楚地喊着那个英语感叹词，那是我们的国骂，是我们的语言在欧洲大陆最被人熟知的那个词。还有那个可怜的男孩，热得满脸通红，身上都要冒火了，他的妈妈已经把自己身上多余的衣服都脱掉了，正要帮他把围巾解掉以减轻他的痛苦——但这个行为遭到他全力的抵抗。我对他当时的样子记得特别真切，还有坐在对面的那个面色苍白的姑娘，她不停地用帽子给自己扇风，结果却热得像发起了高烧。他们没过一会儿就消失在了自己扬起的尘土中，但是即便此刻，我眼前还能清晰地浮现出他们的样子，这幅画面和贺加斯的《下午》相映成趣，对于那些还在抱怨夏天太冷的人是个现成的教训。

说到我自己，我着实喜欢这个潮湿的季节。它让我们都只能待在家里，诚然，待在家里的时间过长，已经让人有了憋闷的感觉；但是话说回来，至少我们还很清醒，并且相当活跃，当我们能够外出的时候，还会觉得外面的世界格外怡人。除了那些过分挑剔的两足动物，男人和女人，一切都很好。稻谷在成熟，青草在生长，瓜果都果实累累；偷吃瓜果的鸟儿不在少数，黄蜂也是这十来年里最多的。我的花园再也不用浇水了，而且比往年更加美丽，令我在这项古老技艺上完胜我的宿敌——小个子石匠的漂亮妻子。和我的花相比，她的那些花简直不值一提。看看那些蜀葵，像玫瑰垒叠成的金字塔；从那高高的柱子上垂挂下来的各色大旋花，组成一个个花环，好像花团锦簇的啤酒花藤；那些巨大的暗色丁香，闻起来就像是香料群岛；那些招摇的复瓣大丽花，那些艳丽的红色天竺葵，还有那些怒放的虎斑百合。哦，实在是美不胜收！况且，天有时会放晴——今天傍晚就是如此。于是我们欢快地爬到了山上，速度差不多像在冬天一样快，接着就沿着公共绿地上碧绿的草坪快步前行，后来被十来个年轻人清亮的嗓音和欢笑声所吸引，便在此逗留了片刻，看那些男孩子玩板球。

我必须承认，自己对乡下男孩，这个不怎么受欢迎的群体，怀有特殊的偏爱：我和他们当中的大多数都很熟，可以这样说，我知道他们当中的许多人都是好孩子，而坏孩子则没有。总的来说，他们是一群开朗、活泼、性情温和的人，随时准备去拥抱欢乐，避开身边环境中的险恶，他们这种获得幸福的能力是成年男女和小女孩所难以企及的。他们也很有耐性，坦然地接受替罪羊的命运（不管是什么样的错，总能怪罪到他们头上），不管是在家里还是外面，他们逆来顺受的本领都让人称奇，要知道针对他们的谎言层出不穷，而相对来说他们撒的谎却少得出奇。他们最让人诟病的一点，就是在成人之后，他们鲜少能实现年少时的志向。不过，那是以后的问题，或许也不会成为一个问题，不应该过早地操心。在那些比他们更优秀的人，或者他们认为比他们更优秀的人面前，他们格外懂得察言观色，见机行事，那股子机灵劲儿着实让人称奇。我说的并不是懂得用金钱、礼物、溢美之词，或者更为直接、常见的方式贿赂人心——他们更为敏感，更懂得如何讨人欢心。只消一句话，点一下头，一个微笑，或者只是叫他们的名字，就足以让他们对你诚心以待、为你效劳了。他们当中的五六个孩子，那些贫苦家庭中长大的淘气包，此刻已经跑回各自家里帮我们搬凳子去了。"谢谢你，乔·科比！你总是第一个，对，就放在那里，我在那儿什么都能看见。你上场了吗，乔？"——"还没有，夫人！下一轮我上场。"——"啊，我很高兴没错过，现在正好要轮到你。杰姆·尤思顿的这记投球真不错！我敢肯定一定会投进三柱门。快去，乔！他们正等着你呢。"根本用不着催促乔·科比更快一点。我觉得，除了赛马、格力犬或鹿之外，再没有比他跑得更快的了——他是最为敏捷、活跃的。乔是我的特殊朋友，是那些"毛孩子"的头儿，就像乔伊·布伦特是大孩子的头儿一样。他们两位都是靠着自己的本事获得这项荣誉头衔的，相对于乔伊来说，乔的情况更让人称道，因为乔比他的许多伙伴年龄更小（他们有些已经十五六岁了，年龄和个头差不多要赶上汤姆·库珀了），也是他们当中出身最为贫寒的。这一点不难推测，瞧瞧他身上那件打着补丁的肥大长袍，和脚上那双虽然没有补丁却破烂不堪的鞋子就知道了，要说有什么东西能妨碍他的敏捷身手，估计就是这双穿在脚上的鞋子了。可是，既然贫困从未对他造成困扰，我为什么要为此感到难过？乔已经十二岁了，在这个邪恶的世界上，他无疑是这些年来最为开心快活的人。忧愁根本无法靠近他。他红润的圆脸上永远挂着微笑，淡褐色的眼睛总是带着笑意，就是巫婆见了他，也躲得远远的。他在山顶那边的农场上打工，那里的人都知道他聪明伶俐，性情温和，总是把各种跑腿的活计都交给他做，除了完成分内的工作给车夫做帮手，他还要给女工帮忙，帮助女主人和男主人。他五点到七点在那里辛苦地劳作，然后到这里更加起劲地忙活，不过是以玩儿的名义——击球、投球、截球，就好像是为了生计而拼命，他一个人可以抵得上四个男孩子，必要的时候，他甚至可以抵得上十一个人的一整支队伍。国王的风琴手，已故的尼维特先生[1]，曾经一个人在哈利路亚的合唱曲中演唱二十个唱段，你会以为他的嗓子里躲着一窝夜莺，其实他和乔·科比是同一类人。他总是能无处不在；同时出现在两个地方对他来说易如反掌，而投球的时候，即使是面对威廉·格雷[2]本人，他也全然不放在眼里。球会像子弹一样击中目标。在八岁到十六岁打棒球的孩子里，他无疑是其中的王者，而且这并不妨碍他成为一个同样优秀的组

---

[1]　查尔斯·尼维特（Charles Knyvett，1752—1822），英国歌唱家、风琴演奏家。

[2]　威廉·格雷（William Grey，1508—1562），英国男爵、军事将领，曾在苏格兰战争和对法作战中屡建奇功。

织者。然而，即使是秩序完美的状态，也总是会有人抱怨，我们这儿就有一位和他对着干的杰姆·尤思顿。

杰姆·尤思顿是一个发育不良的十三岁男孩，大概是这个年龄吧，长得瘦瘦的，个子矮小，但是身体结实，十分活跃。他的脸长得出奇的丑，面无血色，形容枯槁，憔悴不堪，俨然一副老相，再加上头发的颜色太浅，看起来像是白色而不是亚麻色，因此越发显得像个小老头一般。他时常戴一顶蓝色的帽子，穿一件老式的大衣，那是他所就读的一所慈善学校的校服；他会一整天都呆坐在学校里，一到晚上就冲到球场上，精神抖擞，不知疲倦，随时准备大展拳脚，跟人吵上一阵，干上一架，或者冲人大声嚷嚷，不依不饶。他痛恨乔·科比，乔身上那种根深蒂固的温和性情、宽和的微笑、善解人意的点头，对于他这种性情暴烈的人来说，无疑是一种挑衅；而且他（除了极个别的情况，根本算不上一个伟大的板球手）还野心勃勃地想要成为这项运动的管理者。简言之，他生来就是一个蛊惑人心的煽动者，具备各种要在这个行当里出人头地的必备素质——声音洪亮，说话流利，能不厌其烦地反复说道，并且厚颜无耻。按照乡下的说法，他还是一个伟大的"学者"；他的"作品"，我们村里的校长用这个词来称呼一张花体字的书法习作，是既类似一张精美的贺卡，又像一张习字模板的东西，边上会用一圈彩色的小号印刷字体做装饰。我记得，他最近的一张作品，周围装饰的是刻版的摩西故事①，从他在芦苇丛中被发现开始，画面中法老的女儿穿着玫瑰色的长裙，头上插着蓝色的羽毛。他的作品不仅在学校里受人追捧，在教区里也被人交口称赞，圣诞节的时候他的作品被送去挨家挨户地进行巡展，可以从助学人士那里募集到半便士和六便士的硬币——就像迷你版的登山募捐②。摩西的故事大获成功，杰姆用募集所得购买了一副板球球拍和球，这副装备不仅助长了他与生俱来的傲气（这个小学究开始嘟嘟囔囔地抱怨被一个劣等生抢了风头，并公开挑战乔·科比，要和他在演算法或者十字相乘法上一较高下），还让他在板球场上，同普遍的穷孩子相比，获得了极其突兀的优势。他手上掌握着资源（因为，唉！寒冬给孩子们的球拍带来了一场浩劫，他们最好的球也是一只坏球）——他有了资源，就能够控制配给，他的队伍开始壮大起来，正在这时乔收到了两副球拍和一个球，这个礼物名义上是送给这些毛孩子的，但实际上是送给他的——杰姆的追随者立马就离开了他——他们那天晚上无一例外都背弃了他。尽管众叛亲离，这位头目依然毫不收敛，继续他装腔作势、飞扬跋扈的做派。他照旧和人吵架、打架，仿佛背后还有一帮兄弟给他撑腰，他不惜与双方为敌，不考虑后果和得失，非要把场上的所有人都数落

---

① 摩西（Moses），希伯来先知，传说为了躲避埃及人的迫害，父母将襁褓中的摩西置于尼罗河的芦苇丛中，后被来此沐浴的埃及公主发现并收养。

② 登山募捐（Montem），伊顿公学的旧俗，那时的学生会在圣神降临节后的第一个周二登山，进行募捐助学活动。十九世纪后该习俗渐渐废止。

一通。他这样吵吵嚷嚷地闹腾了十分钟，正要拿着他自己的球拍下场（他从来就没有屈尊用过乔的球拍）。这是个脾气暴躁的淘气精，不过他身上也有些无畏和执着的品格。我会想念杰姆·尤思顿的。

啊，这里还有一个被大家伙儿冷落的人！那是我的朋友小轻骑兵——我不知道他的名字，只是根据他的帽子和外套这样称呼他。他显得非常特别，今年大约八岁，是我见过的最为年幼的庄重而有尊严的人；他个子不高，身体结实，身姿挺拔，行事慢条斯理的，长着一张古铜色的扁平脸庞，五官俊俏，看起来就像是可以转换的宽脸酒吧和萨拉辛人头像酒吧招牌上的面孔，在 B 城这两间酒吧正巧是一墙之隔的邻居，据我所知它们似乎从未分开过。事实上，他的脸庞和任何一个大眼圆睁、一动不动的脸庞都很相像，就是那种男孩子的样子！他走起路来昂首阔步，两只手插在裤子口袋里，像一架机器；轮到他做外野手的时候，他总是悠闲地坐在那里，除了把滚动的球停下来，不会更多地参与到击球中去。在一片混战当中，唯一听不到的就是他的声音：我甚至真的怀疑，他是否会发出声音，这可能就是我记录下这个场景，对他表达敬意的缘由所在。他对杰姆·尤思顿忠心耿耿，不管情势如何变化，他都不离不弃，其执着的动力可能源自他对这位领袖本能的认识，知道杰姆·尤思顿口若悬河，能为他们两个人说话。他是唯一可以算作追随我们这位煽动家的人，也因此而得到他的器重。杰姆会为了他跟人吵架，斥责别人，跟别人推推搡搡；要不是因为乔·科比一贯的好脾气，和对于有罪者和无辜者公正的区别对待，杰姆这样的护佑每天能给这个可怜的轻骑兵带来十顿痛打。

可惜天色渐晚，太阳落山已经好一阵子了。可是看哪，西边天空上正要散去的云朵披上了多么炫目的光彩——天边仿佛燃起了一长排玫瑰色的光焰！明天将是晴朗的好天气，尽管我刚刚对炎热天气颇有微词，这依然是不容小觑的好兆头。我们现在要回家了吗？我们是否要沿着绿色的小径，走那条最长但是最美的路回家？沿着左边这条路，从公共绿地的一角转弯，经过威利斯先生的小屋，正前方就是我们要回家的路。那个小屋看上去多么温馨舒适！小小的院落生机盎然，有奶牛，有母马，有像母马一样大的小马驹，还有刚生下的小马和那只巨大的护院狗，都长得膘肥体壮！院子周围的干草垛、麦秸垛、豆秸垛将院子围得严严实实，院子后面有狭长的花园、宽敞的晾晒场、整齐的果园，还有一大块田地，分种着四种不同作物。这个小院看起来多么舒适惬意，而它的主人又是多么配得上享受这份惬意啊！他们是教区里日子过得最为红火的一对夫妇——女主人是洗衣工，揽到的活儿比她能干的要多上二十倍，在洗裙子的荷叶边和衬衫这样精细的活计上，没人能比得上她；男主人既是农场主，又是农场主的雇工，耕种完自己的田地，还去给别人种田；——他们给大家提供了一个例证：即使是在这个没落的时代，即使这个大集体中那么多举足轻重的成员都每况愈下，人们依然可以通过勤劳改善自己的境况。男主人出生在救济所，靠着教区的救济长大，现在他依靠自己的双手，已经跻身地主的行列，缴纳各种赋税，时而抱怨一番，被人称作威利斯老爷，这是仅次于先生的称呼，要知道莎士比亚也不过是这个称呼；对于一个人来说，夫复何求？他的妻子，除了是这乡下一带最好的洗衣工之外，还是一位长相秀丽的妇人。她正站在泉水边，为明日的洗衣活计汲水——那汪清澈、深邃、无声的泉水，正在开满鲜花的堤岸之下沉睡，红色是洋地黄高高挺立的螺旋茎秆和密密麻麻垂挂着的花冠钟，蓝色是美丽的勿忘我，那宝石一般的花朵，看上去就像是璀璨的绿松石和黄晶石。再晚一点就看不到它的美了。这里就是那怡人的林荫小径，高高的榆树遮住了仅存的一线暮光。啊，不过会有仙女们的明灯来为我们指路，它们是地上的星星——萤火虫！就在那儿，有三只聚在一起。你难道没有看见它们吗？有一只似乎在颤抖，不停地振动，仿佛站在草叶的尖端；另外两只潜在树篱更深处，某个绿色的窝坑里，它们的光洒在上面反射出翡翠般的荧光。我希望我的那些打板球的朋友不要从这条路回家。我出于不想说出口的原因，不希望这些美丽的生灵被抓走，在这件事上，我连乔·科比也信不过——男孩子们就喜欢把它们逮进帽子里。不过这是条小路，少有人走，只是一块田地通往另一块田地的通道。这个时候没有人会到这儿来。这些萤火虫还是相当安全的，明天我会再来这里看望它们。现在，就道一声晚安吧！美丽的昆虫，仙女们的明灯，晚安！

杂木林

九月九日——明媚的晴日午后。能再次出门散步是多么惬意的事啊——再次看见稀罕到不能再稀罕的大晴天！我们英国人常常被人诟病对天气谈论得过多，但是今年夏天的天气由不得人们不去谈论。夏天！我是这么说的吗？哦，这个夏天根本配不上这个甜美又明媚的名字！这是一个寒冷而阴沉的季节，阴云密布，雨水连绵！甚至比十一月还不如！因为十一月里白天短，在温暖的房间里闭门不出，让屋子里的太阳——灯——照亮房间，便可以舒舒服服地度过漫长的夜晚，不管外面是否狂风大作。然而，尽管我们可以，而且我们确实在三伏天里点起了火，却无法挡住外面的天光；雨一下就是十六个小时，噼噼啪啪地敲打在窗户上，滴滴答答地从屋檐上落下——十六个小时的雨，不仅听得到，而且看得到，一个星期七天，天天如此——即使是约伯和格丽泽尔①也会被折磨得失去耐心，尤其是当约伯是一位农夫，格丽泽尔是位乡下姑娘的时候。

---

① 约伯（Job），圣经人物，虽历经磨难，依然坚守对上帝的信仰；格丽泽尔（Grizzel），民间故事中以德行和忍耐著称的妇女。

这样的季节真是闻所未闻！干草泡在水里，牛群淹在水里，水果腐烂，稻谷发霉！还有顽皮的洛登河，从来不听河水之神帕夫的建议，"在堤岸之间流淌"，而是在乡间、田野、道路、花园和房屋之间肆意奔流，像疯了似的。这天气怎能不被说道。事实上，想谈论别的事情倒没那么容易。我一个朋友有一次给我写信的时候，觉得有必要为这天气赋诗一首，结果洋洋洒洒用巴斯体写了三页。我仿照着补上一段，摘录于此：

> 毫无疑问，水瓶座大人正统治着世界，
> 最近他的水罐发生了奇怪的倾翻；
> 也有可能，他误把滤盆当成了水罐，
> 并不停地拿它在某个巨湖里舀水；
> 尽管那并不是忘川——
> 有谁能忘却浑身湿透的苦楚？
> 我敢断言，那一定是在冥河的水中，
> 因为雨水淅淅沥沥，人们怨声载道。
> "明天确实下了雨"，成了合乎语法的说法；
> 小板凳和折叠椅被拿去劈成柴火；
> 我只能给自己留一条小小的平底船，
> 即使是睡觉时我也撑着伞，穿着木套鞋：
> 不管何时心血来潮，我都能划船穿过窗户
> 去拜访一位友人，并问候一句，"可会游泳？"

关于我的朋友①就说到这里。简言之，不管是白话还是诗文，每个人都在对天气抱怨个不停。但是，现在这些都过去了。太阳出来把世界烘干，泥糊变成尘土，河流退回自己原本的河道，农夫们不再抱怨，而我们则打算像往常一样出门散步，去往杂木林，那是大约一英里外的一片美丽树林。但我们此行的一位伙伴还不为亲爱的读者所知，我们理应把他介绍给大家。

狗，如果他们固执地按照自己的方式行事，有时会古怪得像那些没有皮毛和羽毛、两条腿走路、会说话，并通常被认为是具备理智的动物。就拿我那只美丽的白色格力犬五月花②来说，她几乎像这世上最讲究的小姐一样乖张任性。放下那些别的奇思怪想不说，她忽然对一只极其丑陋的流浪狗产生了强烈的好感。那只狗大约六个月之前出现在这里，并打算留在村子里过活，谁也说不清楚是怎么

---

① 我的这位朋友才思敏捷，天赋过人，倘若她不是天生丽质，家境优渥——也就是说，如果她困于生计，或渴望受人仰慕，只要受迫于这强大激励中的任何一个，再经受必要的痛苦，她都不可避免地会成为一位聪明的作家。事实上，她的随笔和"一挥而就"的"幽默小品"都文笔清雅，颇有见地。以下面的这张便笺为例。这是她去年米迦勒节附在一个封口的篮子上的标签，描述了装在篮子里的这份沉甸甸的礼物：

送给 M 小姐
人们常说
"睹物思人"；
因而，亲爱的朋友，
我送来了我的代表，
"什么？""一只鹅！"（作者注）

② 写下这段文字后不久她就死了，呜呼哀哉！（作者注）

一回事。他要么到蕾切尔·斯特朗，那个洗衣工那里讨巧，博取她的同情，她因为工作很自然地喜欢狗；要么到玫瑰酒吧，在那些脚步轻快、性情豪爽的少女那里蹭上一顿；要么后腿站立，巴巴地从那些成对的"推杯换盏的密友"，或者到酒屋外的长凳上，从谈论着晚饭或夜宵的孤独的赶牲口的人那里讨口吃的；或者是遇到了那些披着绶带、趾高气扬的绅士，他们在登上宝座——马车车厢——的时候，目光被他的丑陋所吸引，满怀鄙夷地丢给他一口吃的；或者去蹭鞋匠吉普老爷家的猪食；或者从便利店店主布朗老爷家的看门狗那里，衔来那些吃剩下的大骨头；或者偷韦勒太太的猫喝的脱脂奶。他被猫唾弃；遭到大狗的威胁；被猪追来追去；被太太们厉声呵斥；被鞋匠一顿痛骂；遭受便利店店主一顿鞭打；遭到所有孩子的嘲弄和教区里所有动物的排斥。可是，他挨过这些悲苦，容忍种种不幸，"因为苦难是他族群的徽章"[①]；而且他似乎从偶尔的一顿饱饭，一缕阳光，或者能让他可怜的躯体栖身其上的一束干草中，找到了这凄凉境遇中的些许温暖。

他正是在这样的困境中被五月花发现的，五月花，这只血统最为高贵、最有贵族气派的格力犬，将他从困境中解救了出来——把他带到自己的地盘——狗窝里；五月花抵制住了所有想要驱逐他的企图；不管女仆和男仆、女主人和男主人怎样不满，坚持把他安置下来；她用自己的保护行动和顽强的个人意志，战胜了所有人的反对；与他共

---

① 出自莎士比亚剧作《威尼斯商人》第一幕第三场，原句为"苦难是我们所有族群的徽章"，作者做了些许改动。

享一张床，以及自己乱糟糟的居住环境；最后，成功地把他变成和她一样不可或缺的家庭成员。

达什——他甚至还成功地让我们给他起了名字，在此之前他一直是个无名之辈——达什是一种西班牙小猎犬，至少在他混杂的血统中有些这种美丽犬种的特征。他长相丑陋，可以说是丑陋至极——准确地说，是最寒碜的样貌。除此之外，他还有一条腿跛脚，这让他走起路来会有朝一边歪斜的尴尬。他最大的优势是得到了五月花的宠爱，除此之外，他身上还有其他的优点可以来解释他目前的状况，那就是，他是我见过的最忠诚、最依恋主人、最重感情的动物，他在这些方面无可匹敌。这并非虚言。他似乎觉得有必要以额外的乖巧举动来弥补自己相貌上的丑陋，于是就用他的跛脚跳舞，摇动起他那难看的尾巴，这是每一个懂得享受生活的人都乐于见到的——因而，他现在可以说是依靠自己的本事站稳了脚跟。每当有陌生人到来，我们都替他感到害臊，觉得有必要解释一下他是五月花的宠物的身份，但是，在我们这些已经看惯了他的自己人面前，他已经完全依靠他自己赢得了大家的喜爱。我和那些聪慧的女人一样，有女性特有的弱点，那就是会爱上喜欢自己的人，不管是谁——因而，我喜欢达什。他的主人发现他找东西的本事一流，尽管他瘸了腿，但是能在野外搜索，辨识伪装方面能击败英格兰任何一只西班牙猎犬——因而，他喜欢达什。家里的男仆不容别人诋毁达什的容貌，和另一个比自己大的男孩打了一架，结果把那个男孩痛扁了一顿——因而，他喜欢达什；女仆们也喜欢他，或者是假装喜欢他，因为我们喜欢他——这个逆来顺受、亦步亦趋的群体向来是如此行事的。现在，不管去哪儿，五月花和达什都跟着去，就像我之前说的，他们正要跟我们一起去杂木林——或者说是去杂木林边上的木屋，去我们的小奶工汉娜·宾特那里预订牛奶和黄油，这是一项非常适合家庭主妇的工作，我们许多次愉快的散步都是为了到她这里来。

　　此刻，我们已经穿过了洒满阳光、尘土飞扬的乡村街道——一个月之前，谁能想到，我们会再次抱怨阳光和尘土！——沿着街角转弯，那里有两棵高大的橡树，树的枝叶优雅地伸展开来，掩映着其下清澈的深潭，潭水中清凉的绿色树影与明净的蓝色天空融汇在一起，不时还有白色的云朵飞掠而过。我们闲逛着就来到了车轮匠的店铺，那里总是别有韵味，店里的工具、制品、材料，形形色色，各式各样，颜色上却非常和谐；那里的声音，欢快的伙计一边敲打一边唱歌，也奏出一曲和谐又多彩的乐章。今天店铺里有点空，因为常在店里的人都在池塘那边的绿地上忙活——一个人正在装配一辆大车，另一个人在给马车刷油漆。随后，我们就远远地把村子甩在了身后，缓步沿着凉爽幽静的小路前行，小路两侧的树篱高大浓密，掩映着如翡翠般碧绿鲜嫩的草坡。

　　我原本想走快点的，可是未能如愿，因为他们今天在这里射击，达什和我都发觉了，他显得异常兴奋，因为枪对于他来说就像号角对于战马一样；我则颇为恼怒，强烈的程度和他不相上下，因为在枪声鸣响的那一刹那，我想我惊恐的程度毫不亚于一只鹧鸪，假使它碰巧没被杀死的话。达什的血管里流淌的血，显然比人们根据他的外貌猜测的更为高贵。他甚至跃跃欲试，想要冲进田野里，去追逐那些弄出巨大声响的作恶之人。但他毕竟是懂规矩的，我一句话就把他喝止住了。

啊！突然随着枪声传来了一阵刺耳的嘈杂之声——一阵之后，又陆续传来许多吵闹之声。我们还没有到达可以看见韦斯顿老爷的小屋的地方，那座小屋安然地躲在一丛榆树后面，但我们已经能清楚地听到韦斯顿太太的声音了，她声音很大，就是平常训斥人的声调。韦斯顿一家是最近才搬到这里来的，他们为人所知的第一件事就是妻子在治安官面前控诉她的丈夫殴打她：这是一项惯常的指控，她说的也挺像那么回事。韦斯顿太太让人们觉得她实在是受尽了委屈，她起先是柔声细语，后来就开始哭天抢地，痛哭流涕，激起了整个女性世界的怜悯和愤怒——怜悯是向着她的，愤怒是冲着她丈夫的——女人们遇到这种情况时总是满怀同情又义愤填膺。教区里的每位妇女都开始痛骂韦斯顿老爷，可怜的韦斯顿老爷在接下来的礼拜六就接到了法院传唤，让他对这项指控做出回应。这件事闹得沸沸扬扬，家里和外面都对他不依不饶，这个不幸的被告听说治安官要拿着拘捕令来抓他，就吓得逃跑了，接连两个星期都音讯全无。

两个星期之后他还是被人发现并带到了法院。韦斯顿太太像之前一样，又一次声泪俱下地讲述了她的故事。她并没有目击证人，之前作为控诉依据的伤疤也已经消失不见，而且现场也没有女人声援她的指控。不过即便如此，人们普遍还是指责韦斯顿老爷，他走上法庭的时候形势对他很不利，然而一个出乎意料的目击者为他挽回了局面。他的太太出庭时怀抱着一个十八个月大的小姑娘，本来大约是希望为自己博得同情的，因为一个怀抱着孩子的女人总是能激起人们心中美好的情感。那个小姑娘看上去既羞怯又紧张，在她母亲接受询问的时候一直安静得像一只小羊羔。可是一看到和她分别了两个星期的父亲，她就拍手，欢笑，大声叫着"爸爸！爸爸！"一头扑到他的怀里，搂住他的脖子，亲吻个不停，并一再叫喊着，"爸爸，回家吧！爸爸！爸爸！"——最后，她把小脑袋靠在他的胸前，一副心满意足的模样，享受着温柔和呵护，这是自所罗门王以来，任何打老婆的暴君都没有，也不能唤起的温情。我们的地方官本着那位犹太君王的精神行事，接受了人性的证据，撤销了这项指控。后来发生的事情证明他们的决定是完全正确的。韦斯顿太太不仅成了以谩骂（我们这一带称之为毒舌，这个合成词一定有其希腊源头）著称的女性典范，并且热衷于亲身实践家里两口子间的惩罚规范，她还乐于把这项罪名强加在她那倒霉的丈夫头上。

我们踩着梯磴翻过矮墙，现在正朝着杂木林所在的那片田野走去。这片草场的绿色看起来多么悦目啊！夕阳的余晖也格外迷人，从那片山毛榉、白蜡树和山杨树组成的小树林中透出来，像是落日的回眸！那片长着忍冬和野生蓝盆花（乡下人把它们称作吉卜赛玫瑰）的树篱多么可爱！啊，这不就是小多莉·韦斯顿吗，那位无意中成为关键证人的小姑娘！她脸蛋儿红扑扑的，活像一朵娇艳的玫瑰，正沿着小路蹒跚地走着去迎接她的父亲。这边是红头发的小顽童乔治·库珀，他正好收工回家，高唱着"家！可爱的家"。很快，他就发现调子太高唱不上去了，便打起口哨吹出曲调，等到过了那段调子太高的地方，又接着唱起来，"家！可爱的家！"虽说他只是个耕田的小子，但看起来似乎已经体会到了这句歌词的全部意蕴。不过，他的确懂得，因为他来自一个正派、善良又勤劳的大家庭。家和万事兴，这个耕田的小子总能在家里见到欢快的脸庞，感受到质朴的安慰——这就是他所学到的应该追求的一切。哦，如果能像乔治·库珀一样享受着简朴又纯粹的满足该有多好！他对于生活的全部奢求不过是一场板球比赛！因为他所有的愿望都能在"家！可爱的家"里得到满足。

今天所到之处都是吵吵闹闹的！他们正在清理农场主布鲁克的那一大片豆子地，大家伙儿都齐声喊着"颗粒归仓！"在此之前的其他声响——歌声、责骂声、枪声，都渐渐退去，变成了隐隐约约的回声。这真是让人愉快的吵闹之声！不过，为了耳朵，还是要赶紧走开。这里就是那片漂亮的杂木林了，此时正是树林最欢快的时刻，这里有宽阔的道路，有幽闭的深谷，有各色坚果和各种忍冬植物。在采了一束香甜的忍冬花之后，我们来到了汉娜·宾特家：对于其人其事，我们将在日后详细说明。

小记——可怜的达什也死了。我们并没能把他养上多长时间，事实上我认为他是死于从饥饿到饱食的过渡，这就像更为难受的从饱食到饥饿的过渡一样，对狗的胃和大多数的胃来说都很凶险。取代他地位的是另一个达什，他同样受到了我们的喜爱，和他的前任相比，他在举止上一样温顺可亲，在外貌上则要可称道得多，和我的朋友丁立老爷家的西班牙猎犬几乎一模一样；那只狗会从喜鹊那里偷骨头，也是这种狗当中第一只叫达什的狗。希望粗心的读者不要以为我把同一个名字赋予了三只不同的狗，是在对那位让"胡椒与芥末"①这名字永垂不朽的作家进行拙劣的模仿，这位作家是不可模仿的，这是其一；再者，可能有人认为我要么是缺乏创造力，要么是对犬种类别缺乏了解，才会如此编排。其实，我只是遵从平常行事的谨慎态度，使用了我恰巧觉得合适的名字。事实上，英国有一半漂亮的西班牙小猎犬都叫达什，就像有一半高大的男仆都叫托马斯一样。这个名字适用于整个犬种。去年夏天的一天，我在一处农家院子的门口坐在敞篷马车里，等候在里面处理公务的父亲时，看见一只高贵美丽的同种类犬，威严又悠闲地卧在台阶上，便一下子有了要结识他的冲动。和我有同样想法的父亲，在走过他身旁的时候，用手轻轻拍了拍他，叫了他一声"可怜的家伙"，结果没有引起他一丁点儿回应。"达什！"我大胆喊了一句，"好达什！高贵的达什！"结果他一下子站了起来，轻轻一跃就从门口跳到了马车上。当然，我猜对了。那位绅士的名字就叫达什。

---

① 胡椒与芥末（Peppers and Mustards）是司各特的小说《占星人》里提到的六只英国小猎犬，它们有着黄色和黑褐色深浅不等的皮毛，而被主人统一称为"胡椒和芥末"。后文提到的作家即指沃尔特·司各特。

采坚果

九月二十六日——秋日里让人心旷神怡的一天，空气、天空和大地都沉浸在一片清静之中，甚至比五月还要柔美，还要温和。我们出门散步，心情与此时的天气和时节颇为相宜，大家都一致同意要避开阳光大好的公共绿地和热闹的大马路，沿着那些阴凉的、少有人走的小路悄然前行，那里不大会遇着什么人，即使是那些可爱的家庭队伍也未必遇得上，前些年我们总是怀着极大的兴趣用目光追随着他们——那是从麦田里回来的父亲、母亲和孩子们。小孩子们抱着捆扎得结结实实的扎人的麦穗，还有他们自己搜集来的东西，或者抱着瓶子和装着他们的家常便饭的篮子；母亲通常怀抱着婴儿，哄着让他安静下来；父亲和大孩子们则带着摇篮，脚步沉重地跟在后面，他们看上去既疲惫又开心。我们今天不会遇见这样的家庭队伍，因为收割几乎已经结束了，田地里看不到人，到处都是一片寂静。除了知更鸟预示着冬天的歌唱，大自然里阒静无声。然而，这又是多么美好，多么温柔，多么祥和，多么丰富！雨水让牧草依然像在春天一样鲜嫩碧绿，树叶都还像在仲夏时节一样鲜亮，水岸上有圆叶风铃草，树篱间有忍冬，还有低矮的荆豆花丛：春天的时候被羊羔们啃食过，此刻又繁花满枝，一片金黄。

目之所及，皆是美景；或许因为周遭是一个像森林一样的封闭环境便愈加觉得其美丽。我们的视野极度受限，如同置身小径、岔路、普通的马车道所构成的迷宫之中，这些道路通往组成这部分教区的无数个小农场。不管是上山还是下山，行走在这些安静的林荫小路上，我们几乎没有机会瞥见外面的世界，除非是从大门里探出身去，我们可以看见由树篱围起来的某个小型围场，树篱中间密植着长势良好的乔木，以至于这样一个绿草茵茵的开口处看起来完全像是一片林中空地；或者有时能看见某处农舍，坐落于岔路口那一小片绿地的角落里，突如其来映入眼帘的民居总是让我们不免惊叹：在如此幽闭之处，竟然也有人居住。倘若我们这里再多一些丘陵和山谷，倘若我们的岔路再更为典型一些，我们教区的这一带就会像极了拉罗克－雅克琳夫人在她那本最有趣的书里对于旺达省的描写。[①]我深信那些分隔田地的树木，再没有比此处的更像样了。这里有一处漂亮舒适的山间农舍，茂盛的藤蔓植物将房子

---

① 对于此类美景同样有趣的描述可以在《旺达的女仆》这部英国小说中找到，小说的行文如图画一般简练传神，别具一格。该书的作者勒努瓦太太，是克里斯托弗·斯马特的女儿，她完全继承了父亲的天赋。她的作品值得被更多人知晓。（作者注）拉罗克－雅克琳（Marie Louise Victoire de Donnissan de Laroche-Jacquelin，1772—1857），法国作家，以记录自己在旺达生活的回忆录而著称。克里斯托弗·斯马特（Christopher Smart，1722—1771），英国诗人。

的正面盖得严严实实，并一直缠绕着爬上了烟囱的顶端；依着山坡而下的果园，里面果实累累——即使是这里，即使是这个漂亮安静的小窝也被树叶遮蔽了起来，几乎很难看到外面。啊！他们正在果园里采摘水果。瞧，有个小淘气正站在一棵布满了苔藓的老苹果树上——那棵老树被满枝金黄的果子压弯了腰——看哪，他不停地把苹果扔给树下的小妹妹，苹果又红又圆，就像妹妹的红脸蛋儿，妹妹撑着裙子想要接住苹果，她开心地笑着，只要有苹果在她身边落下，她就央求哥哥再抛给她；再看另外一个小顽童，表情像法官一样严肃，他手脚并用地在苹果树下爬来爬去，自顾自地①捡拾掉下来的苹果，并确实地把它们挨个放进草地上的大篮子里，篮子敞着大口被牢牢地搁在地上，里头满满当当的全是些带着褐色的青果子，这是老树边上一棵苹果树的果子；再看他们当中最小的那个孩子，像个婴儿一样坐在一边的草坡上，每只手上都攥着一只皱巴巴的、畸形的甜苹果，一会儿从这只手上咬一口脆甜多汁的苹果，一会儿从另一只手上咬一口——这难道不是一幅可爱的英国风情画？果园再远一些的地方，有一个勇敢健壮的小伙子，应该是家里的长子，他爬到了大梨树的顶上，攀上了一根高大笔直的旁枝（天知道他是如何做到的），稳稳地坐在那里，一副大无畏的样子，就好像坐在桅杆顶端的水

---

① 自顾自地（Deedily），我不确定这个词是不是规范的英语表达，但它是地道的汉普郡说法，曾被语言最为规范的女作家简·奥斯汀小姐使用过。它的意思是（该词的一大优点是没有确切的同义词）缓慢而持久地专注做一件事，全身心地投入其中。（作者注）

手一样，虽说坐得稳当，也难免让人揪心。他用力摇晃了
一下树枝，石头一样结实的王子梨便如一阵急雨一样纷纷
落下，他的父亲快速地把梨捡起，而他的母亲则因为母亲
特有的担忧几乎无暇顾及——这样的担忧只会让那个兴致
正高的孩子进行更大胆的冒险。这难道不也是一幅美丽的
画面吗？而且布鲁克一家，个个都长相出众。我不知道他
们家族里是否有吉卜赛血统，但他们确实有吉卜赛人的长
相：光亮的棕色皮肤，脸颊和嘴唇显得特别红润，头发是
贴着头皮的黑色小卷卷，白得发亮的牙齿——还有那迷人
的眼睛！那种美貌会让你的玫瑰和百合都黯然失色。即使
是白人孩子中最漂亮的莉兹，站在威利·布鲁克旁边也会
显得平淡无奇。威利就是那个冷静地捡苹果的小家伙，他
用自己胖乎乎的手捡起苹果，然后整整齐齐地码进篮子
里，旁边就是他的父亲，他可是种田的一把好手。"威利！"
他听到有人叫他，却看不见是谁，因为我们被一个高坡和
上面蔓长的山楂树丛给挡住了，不过我们在底下的枝条和
草地之间找到了一个望风口。"威利！"对于他来说，这
声音听起来就像是在虚幻的梦中，那双黑色的眼睛带着惊
诧，突然从地面上抬起，长长的如丝般的睫毛向上翻起直
到碰到上面精致的眉毛，棕色的脸颊上慢慢泛起一片绯红，
鲜红的嘴唇上浮起一丝微笑，浅浅地搁在两侧的酒窝里。
但是随即喊声停住了，这个安静的小男孩稍稍停下片刻，
又冷静地重新开始工作了。他的确是个特别招人喜爱的孩
子。我觉得有朝一日他一定会和莉兹结为夫妻。我愿意向
他们各自的妈妈去提亲，不过眼下他们都还太小，谈婚论

嫁对他们来说太早了——这位如意郎君，我猜，大概有六岁，而那位美丽的新娘才五岁，但至少我们或许可以依照王室的传统给他们举行一场订婚仪式，反正也没什么坏处。莉兹小姐，我可以肯定，一定会摆出一副端庄娴静、知书达理的样子，仿佛十几载光阴已经悄然过去，而那位可爱的威利会睁大他那双无辜的大眼睛，纳闷儿到底发生了什么事。他们会成为我们村子里的奥伯龙和泰坦尼亚[①]，那对仙王和仙后。

啊！眼前就是那道缠绕着长春花的树篱了，这里的长春花长得密集又繁盛，四季常青的叶子和香桃木的一样闪闪发光，上面开满了星星形状的蓝色花朵。很少能在英格兰的这个地区见到野生的长春花，但是我们确实遇到了，而且还开得如此繁茂喜人——它就是花中的知更鸟，寒冬之友。除非遇到罕见的对植物破坏极大的寒潮，否则长春花可以从九月开到次年的六月，比流连到最后的老鹳草开得还要久，比最早的报春花还要早，甚至比山地雏菊还要顽强——它们可以从雪被之下探出头来，可以在冰层之上顾盼生辉，可以笑对生命中的暴风雨，同时也会拥抱、享受阳光。噢，都应该活得像这种花一样！

树篱下方有一条小溪顺着山势汩汩奔流，而因为我们已经过了最高处，虽然察觉不到但现在开始下行，溪水也因势开始分流，肆意流淌，形成了各种不同的清澈水洼和水道，有的又细又窄，被水草塞满，即使是孩子也能轻易

----

① 奥伯龙和泰坦尼亚（Oberon and Titania），莎翁剧作《仲夏夜之梦》中的男女主人公。

地跨过去。树篱的样子也有了变化，不再是一堵紧实的植物墙，墙通常由山楂树、槭树和蔷薇组成，间杂着黑莓和忍冬，上面还有高大的榆树或是密植的树苗。不！更像是高高耸立在我们之上的美丽草地，后面有高高的灌木支撑并将其环绕，而我们这一面并不需要支撑防护，因为它自然形成了一个陡坡，上面点缀着一丛丛的金雀花，还有几棵缠绕着常春藤的去梢椴树，这里那里间或还有榛树的长枝条悬于水面之上。"啊！那根枝条上还有榛果！"立刻，我这位同行的伙伴就开心起来，像个小男孩一样兴奋活跃，用他的手杖钩住一根柔软的榛树枝条，把上面那一串褐色的榛果给摘了下来。接着，一眨眼的工夫，他已经爬上了陡坡，开始采摘起坚果来，一会儿把自己的收获从低矮的枝头装进绅士们随身携带的各种大口袋里；一会儿把高处的枝条弯到小路上来，用很大的力气把它们压住，这样我就可以够到它们，并亲身体验一下采摘到野果的乐趣。他知道这对于我来说会是一种莫大的享受。我把披肩拿掉，把裙边塞好，把我那顶草帽当作篮子，就开始了采集和攀爬——因为，不管你用什么方法，采坚果都免不了要手脚并用——那些枝条，不管你怎样用力地抓住那些新生的嫩枝和碧绿的叶片，总是会回弹、脱手；不过即使是这样也有乐趣，因而我们也不停手，攀爬、采摘，用尽了所有的力气，释放了所有的欢乐。哦，真是让人欲罢不能啊！我的一生当中，一直对这类潜藏着发现的寻找活动（我相信，人们对于野外活动的热爱，源自其头脑中的自然本能）保有热情，因而我喜爱采集紫罗兰，因而当我们有了一个像样的花园时，我总是喜欢采摘草莓，割芦笋，而最喜欢的莫过于在灌木丛中采集榛果，不过在这里采集榛果比以往的所有经历都更棒。和今天的采摘活动相比，之前的只是装装样子，没有惊喜，没有悬念，没有突发状况——与这种野外采摘活动相比，根本不值一提，就好像在资深的狐狸猎人眼中，从袋子里掏出一只狐狸根本不能和从地下洞穴中猎到一只狐狸相比一样。

哦，这次采坚果的经历是多么让人愉悦啊！采到的坚果居然有这么多，让人觉得仿佛整个教区里都没有一个男孩子，也没有一个年轻人，或是年轻姑娘——一篮坚果是乡下小伙子向姑娘们献殷勤时通用的礼物；我们那位美丽的姑娘哈丽特这一季至少收到了半打这样的礼物；但唯独没有人发现这里的坚果。而且，它们还长得如此饱满，我们弄丢了一半的果仁，因为果子太过成熟，稍微一动，果仁就从果壳里掉出来了。不过，就算我们弄丢了，也会被有些家伙捡起来。五月花就几乎和松鼠一样喜欢坚果，破开果壳取出果仁的熟练程度也和松鼠有一比。此刻她正扬起她那白色光滑的脑袋，盯着果子掉落下来。看哪，她的脖子像天鹅一样朝后甩出去，折起的耳朵因为热切的期盼而优美地颤动起来，她敏锐的眼睛始终追随着簌簌的响动声，她的脚轻快地舞动着，拍打着地面，迫不及待地一跃而起，几乎像是凝固在了空中，就像有一次布拉什[1]在树篱中搜索，而她从布拉什的探寻中察觉出里面正有一只兔

---

[1]　前文提到的一只老猎犬。

子，她当时就是这副模样。快看，她正巧在那颗坚果落入水中之前抓住了它；不过，就算是掉进了水里也难不倒她，她会从水底把它给捞上来；她会在盘结的草丛中搜索坚果，甚至会到我的帽子里找——她看到它们就是这么一副眼巴巴的样子！"哦，采坚果是多么有趣的事啊！对吗，五月花？可是口袋都装满了，充当篮子用的帽子也满了，而且那座明亮的大钟——太阳——告诉我们天已经不早了。毕竟，和那些可怜的小伙子抢夺坚果是不对的，对吧，五月花？"五月花优雅地摇了摇头表示否认，好像她听懂了我的问题似的。"我们现在必须得回家了，对吧？但是有空的时候我们还会再来采坚果，对吗，我的五月花？"

出　游

　　十月二十七日——一个可爱的秋日，微风和煦，蓝色的天空柔和、清丽，赏心悦目——天空的颜色是一种让大地的丰美看起来舒心的蓝色，大地在这个最为丰饶的季节被成熟醇美的色泽浸染，处处绚丽多姿。确实这样的秋天足够对英国气候中少有的南方的美好春日做个补偿，那样的春天常被诗人们谈起，我们却很少能享受得到。这样的秋天如同绚丽的薄暮笼罩在我们四周，这正是一年中的黄昏时分。我禁不住诱惑，让自己比往常有了更多享受的机会。这次散步（请允许我使用类似"爱尔兰公牛"[①]这样的含混修辞）实际上是乘着马车兜风。我的一位挚友讨好我，让我与她结伴，乘着她那辆漂亮的小马车去她四英里之外的家。她先行打发送她来的马夫回去报信，自己则一把揽过缰绳，赶起马车，我们就这样上路了。

---

① 爱尔兰公牛（Irish bull）或公牛（bull）用来指代自相矛盾的表达，或荒唐可笑、不合情理的说法，据说源自十九世纪都柏林三一学院的学者约翰·马哈发（John Mahaffy）的话"爱尔兰公牛总是处于怀孕状态"（An Irish bull is always pregnant）。

我这位美丽的同伴深受上天眷顾，不仅天生丽质，而且家境殷实，幸而她绝非怙恩恃宠之人。她容貌出众，引得路人总免不了要回头观望；她个子高挑，身材匀称，有着鲜明的罗马人的轮廓和样貌特征以及英国人的细腻肤色，自有一种卓尔不群的气质。她的美透着公爵夫人一样的高贵，似乎生来就是为了穿戴羽毛和钻石，为了彰显一种宫廷式的优雅和华美，而她举手投足间具有贵族气质的率真更能加深人们对她的印象。命运似乎格外地对她青睐有加。她的丈夫是一位出身高贵、事业有成的富裕乡绅，他们伉俪情深——并且膝下还有一个像她一样可爱的女儿。有幸与她结识的人都喜欢见到她，对于他们来说，她不仅因为性情温和、心地善良而招人喜欢，更因为她独特的爽朗和率真，使她在交谈中独具魅力。她像水一样透明。你能够看到她心灵的每一种色彩和微妙变化，那是一颗像她本人一样高贵而美好的心灵。与她交谈就仿佛置身德·让李思夫人①所描绘的真理殿堂，而且她的情感都饱含着善意，我们本性中微小的缺陷和怪癖在她看来都迷人至极，她对于同胞们的困顿、渴求、所思所想、喜怒哀乐都能感同身受，因而即使她心直口快，我也从来不知道她曾得罪过谁或者与谁反目。

　　但我们必须得继续赶路。要是她知道我正在把她写进书里，她会做何感想？我们必须朝山上走。啊！这完全不像是我们要做的事！这匹马，这匹血统高贵又美丽的马，

----

① 德·让李思夫人（Madame de Genlis，1746—1830），法国著名女作家。

被喂养得很好，膘肥体壮，毛色油亮，站在我们门口神气活现得完全是一副阿拉伯纯种马的派头，这会儿却突然间垂头丧气。他确实并没有完全止步不前，但是他移动的速度只是略微好过站着不动——迈着最缓慢、最无精打采的步子。即使是那些在葬礼上满面愁容拉着灵车，在黑色羽毛下踱步的马儿也比他走得快。对他挥鞭、勒缰、言语呵斥都没有用。这个无赖已经发现，此时驾驭他的是一双脆弱又温柔的手。哦，要是换作原来那位驾车的，也就是车夫，只要拉一把缰绳，挥一下鞭子，他就乖乖听话，跑得像飞起来一样了！可是现在那位车夫已经跑到我们前面一英里的地方了，喊也听不见，并且还在大步流星地赶路，把我们远远地甩在后面了。他刚刚上到了山顶；接着，一转眼的工夫，啊，已经看不见了，毫无疑问这一路都看不到他了，只能等到了铺着草坪的大门口再和他见面了。好吧！这样也没什么大不了，不过是延长了我们在这么美好的天气里一起欣赏美景的时间。一旦我们打定了主意不去理会我们的马走得有多慢，不去烦心，进行徒劳的努力，他的步伐对于我们来说就已经不是困扰了。可以断定他能在日落之前赶到家，这就足够让我们满意了。他毕竟是一匹高贵的动物，而且当他发现我们决定让他按照自己的方式赶路，他或许会心生怜悯，让我们也如愿以偿。他这一性别的动物总是要寻求控制权的，但是一旦他们处于不容争辩的地位，他们中的一些会变得足够慷慨，而放弃这一权利。我所认识的友人中，有两三位心思缜密的妻子，能把自己的丈夫管得服服帖帖，她们并没有什么高妙的绝招，靠的就是这种表面上的顺从依附。她们的例子在我们眼下的处境中更有意义，因为我们除此之外别无他法。

我们在这样的思辨之中到达了山顶，并且以"回眸"的视角观赏了身后沐浴在金色阳光中的美丽远景。考珀①曾经说过，要以写诗的豪情记录最为普通和平淡的感情，这或许就是他充满创造力的一大秘诀。

> 景色之美日日看日日欢心，
>
> 发现景色之新则可以摆脱
>
> 长久的认知和经年的审视。

我每天都要上山——每天我都会在山顶驻足，欣赏宽阔蜿蜒的道路和道路两侧与茂盛的树篱连成一片的绿色荒野；有两间漂亮的农舍，在远近不同的位置，但都恰巧位于道路拐弯的地方；远处的树丛中间有一处村落，远远地可以看见那里大片的屋顶和一丛丛的烟囱；在更远处，有农宅、大屋、教堂和小镇，它们似乎被一大片森林包裹了起来，又被蓝色氤氲的远山所环抱。每天我都会赞叹这美丽的风景，但它从未像今天这样美轮美奂。煌煌秋日里所有的色彩，橙黄、黄褐、亮黄、大红，都在碧绿的草坪上和蔬菜田里漫洒开来，让人目不暇接、眼花缭乱；而在我们的眼前还有那片公共草地，如画般起伏的地面上有聚集

---

① 威廉·考珀（William Cowper，1731—1800），英国诗人，擅长描绘日常生活和英国乡村景色，浪漫派诗歌的先驱。以下，以及后文节选的诗文均出自他的长诗《沙发》（*The Sofa*，1785）。

在一起的农舍，有分散开的水道，绿地的一边是田野、农场和果园，而另一边则是高大挺拔的橡树相夹的林荫大道。那块荒凉、分裂的大地，让余下地块上那些长势喜人的农作物看起来如此丰饶而不同！考珀曾替我描述过这样的风景。当我们在乡间漫步的时候，他描绘的生动画面总是会浮现在我的脑海中。这是他眼中的公共绿地，也是我眼中的。

> 公地上遍布着羊齿蕨，
>
> 还有凸出的、带刺的金雀花，
>
> 奇形怪状，容易扎手，
>
> 然而它开着花，用金色装点着自己
>
> —— 那一片草地
>
> 清香扑鼻，布满了芬芳的草药
>
> 和泥土里真菌的果实，
>
> 出人意料的浓郁香气，
>
> 又带给人莫大的欢愉。

　　这一段描述很准确。那边，左侧是我的板球场（考珀的公地还缺少这最后的点睛之笔），有一个小顽童孤零零地站在那里，似乎是在遥想着它过去和未来的辉煌，因为，啊，此刻，板球季已经过去了。啊，原来是本·科比，孩子王乔·科比的兄弟，或许还是他的继任者，因为自今年的米迦勒节之后乔就不在我们这里了！他从农场荣升到两英里之外的大宅里去了。他在那儿负责擦鞋、磨刀和跑腿，用他母亲的话来说，类似于当上了"男仆的学徒"。如果乔哪天出了师，当上了管家，我一点儿也不会感到惊讶。尽管我们对他喜爱有加，但他日后若有辉煌的前程，就足以弥补我们失去他的遗憾了。眼下，我们还有本。

本·科比比乔小一岁，和杰姆·尤思顿是同一所学校的同学和对手。当然，他的本事和杰姆截然不同：杰姆是个学者，本是个谐星。杰姆擅长算数和写作；本擅长扮鬼脸，搞恶作剧。他的校长提到他时说，要是学校里有两个他这样的学生，他准保就辞职不干了。而据我的观察，这位受人尊敬的老师绝不是信口开河。必须得承认，本是严肃庄重的头号克星。他极度反感权威和规范，对于颠覆权威、打破规范这样的事，有着让人叫绝的胆量和手段。他扮鬼脸的本事简直让人叹为观止。他"操控自己和他人肌肉的本领"几乎和李斯顿不相上下，而他本来的面孔，扁平、方正，脸形有点像中国人，皮肤细腻，呈古铜色，鼻子短小，嘴巴就像一条窄缝，这样一张脸几乎就和那位无与伦比的表演家的脸一样，充满了喜感。当这张富有喜感的面孔，搭配上本独特的活动五官的能力，他了然于心的眨眼、嬉笑、耸肩和点头，再加上他不露声色的机敏，妙语连珠的本事，以及插科打诨的非凡能耐，就完全成就了一个幽默的乡村男孩的完美形象，他堪称一位头角峥嵘的奇才。每个人都喜欢本，除了那些被他调侃的对象（这些人差不多占他朋友的一半），但那些人中没有人会像我们教区的小学校长一样，对他如此又恨又怕。这位校长是位让人敬重的老实人，本能让他在一天当中目瞪口呆二十次。

他在板球场上是个耀眼的明星，在这项运动上颇有天赋。他在球场上总是以一种特别的方式来展现技艺，就是故意装出很笨拙的样子——就好像小丑在哑剧表演中展现自己的柔韧性一样。他从不会失手。顺便说一下，他正是我们在眼下的困境中要找的人，在英国，没有哪一匹马是本·科比不能驾驭的。可惜我们现在离他太远了——而且说不定这样也好。我相信那个小无赖对我还是心存好感的，他应该记得，常与我一起散步的同伴乐于被他的机智逗乐，总是要施舍给他一些苹果和坚果。但不管怎样，他还是那个爱搞恶作剧的罗宾·古德菲洛，一个十足的顽皮帕克，对恶作剧的喜爱胜过其他一切事物。或许在他和这匹马之间，还是马更可靠一些。

今天林荫大道上很热闹。老婆婆们在捡拾树枝和橡果，而大大小小的猪正竭尽全力地帮助她们免除后一项麻烦；男孩女孩们正在远处的树丛中找寻山毛榉的果实；还有一群更小的孩子在尽可能多地收集枯叶，给篝火助燃，他们点燃的篝火正从树丛中冒出阵阵青烟——这类似于九天之后那场盛大篝火的预演；人们每年一度在这条林荫大道上庆祝盖伊·福克斯①之夜，为这个大叛徒点燃忠诚之火，与篝火相伴的还有爆竹，凡是男孩子们能要来的或是

---

① 盖伊·福克斯（Guy Fawkes，1570—1606），英国天主教徒，参与策划了1605年的"黑火药计划"，该计划预谋在1605年11月5日炸毁英国国会大厦，后他因计划泄露而被捕，并被处以极刑。英国民众在当年的11月5日点燃篝火、燃放爆竹，庆祝这一阴谋的破产。这项活动一直延续至今，成为深受孩子们喜爱的传统习俗。

借来的，更别说偷来的，都会拿到这里来燃放。本·科比在十一月五日那天可是个重要人物。孩子们攒了一个月的零用钱，私藏的半个便士，新版的四分之一便士，还有平日里带在身上的幸运便士，在那个晚上统统都会化作爆竹被点燃，消失不见。对我来说，我更喜欢白天的嘲讽戏。那里没有火药——让人讨厌的火药！没有额外的噪声，只听见小鬼们欢快的叫声，声音高亮，洋溢着幸福的气息；还有乌鸦的叫声，它们绕着大圈在头顶盘旋，不明白在它们的领地上正发生着什么——它们呱呱地高声喊叫，似乎是在询问在它们的老橡树中间袅袅升起的青烟到底意味着什么，青烟扶摇直上，似乎要与云朵相接。这群乌鸦聚在一起时是黑压压的一大片，它们的行径表现出一定的智力水平，尤其是它们的探寻。我猜想这是因为它们数量巨大，而且目标统一，类似于一种集体协作的智慧。鹅也是爱聚在一起的，可是它们看起来一点儿也不聪明。但是，毕竟它们是一种家禽，被我们给惯坏了。乌鸦是自然界里的自由公民，它们住在我们提供给它们的住处，寄居在我们的树林里和林荫大道上，但是从来不会梦想成为我们的臣民。

这条路真是如迷宫一般！我确信，从林荫大道到磨坊的短短半英里内，一共有四个转弯。正如我的伙伴所说，太遗憾了——遗憾的并不是我们这位善良、快活的磨坊主，老式英国自耕农的杰出代表，是如此富有，而是他如此富有的结果就是拉倒了原来倒映在洛登河上的最漂亮的一座磨坊；一起被毁掉的还有那座如画般美丽的、屋檐低矮、形状不规则的小屋，小屋有微微拱起的尖顶，顶上树立着一簇烟囱，永远都开着门，看上去就是一个既舒适又好客的居所。将这些推倒之后，原地建起来一座面积巨大、显眼又让人感到害怕的红砖磨坊，像工厂一样丑陋，后面还有一座与之相匹配的、同样巨大且同样是红色的方形大屋。原来那些老房子总是让我想起瓦利特①美丽的风景雕刻画《磨坊女工》中的场景。而要让眼前的这些房子入画还不知要等到何年何月，只要想想画面中的这一片红色，就让人受不了！这座房子简直就是一只煮熟的龙虾！福斯塔夫对巴道福②鼻子的描写相比之下实在是逊色多了。

前面就是那个庞然大物，一辆帆布大篷车，车上装着面粉，拉车的是四匹膘肥体壮的马。我正在想，不知道我们的马是否懂得规矩，知道避让。他要是不懂，我敢肯定我们也拿他没办法。那辆装在轮子上的巨船，陆地上的方舟，会像天神的马车一样从我们头上压过去。真的——哦，不！还好，现在总算是安全了。我应该记得在磨坊车队里赶车的是我的朋友塞缪尔·朗。他会照顾我们的。"谢谢你，塞缪尔！"而且塞缪尔将我们引上了正路，使我们安全地从他的马车边上过去，并护送我们上了桥。现在，他帮我们安全渡过了眼下的危机，友好地鞠了一躬，露出和善的微笑向我们道别，就像一个一贯友善又宽和的人会做的那样，但他的眼睛里还有一丝胜利的得意神情。据我观

---

① 威廉·瓦利特（William Woollett，1735—1785），英国雕版画家。
② 福斯塔夫（Falstaff）和巴道福（Bardolph）都是莎士比亚历史剧中的人物，福斯塔夫常常嘲讽巴道福有一个火焰般的大酒糟鼻，一张长满疖子的大红脸。

察，男人们，即使是他们当中最优秀的那些，当看到一个女人因为尝试原本属于男性的工作而陷入困境的时候，总是会流露出这种神情。不过，他帮了我们的大忙，就允许他小小地得意一番，体验一下这种优越感吧。他临行时用他巨大的鞭子打了一声震慑人心的响鞭，算是向我们那匹马致意，这个不听管束的家伙立刻变得精神抖擞。我们又跑起来了。我们经过了装玻璃工人的漂亮房子，房子有门廊，还有栽着榛子树的步道；两侧榆树夹道的小路上铺满了落叶，满地金黄；我们沿着这条路向前，经过那间小小的农舍，屋子门前种着七叶树，树上长着像橘子一样的橙色果实，闪闪发光；农舍的对面是刷着白墙的学校，那里的月季花开得正好；再往前，我们经过了公园、门房，还有克拉伦登伯爵曾经住过的大宅；现在这个老滑头发现塞缪尔·朗和他的鞭子已经远在一英里之外，又是女主人在驾驭着他，于是他的脚步又相应地慢了下来。或许就在此处他也感受到了这段路的美，故意放慢脚步，好好欣赏一番。当然，这段路确实相当美。公园的尖板条栅栏构成了道路一侧的边界，里面有一丛丛长势良好的橡树，还有各种姿态的鹿；道路的另一侧有一道溪水，水边生着一簇簇的桤木。转过一道弯，溪水弯折转道，接替而来的是一道低矮的树篱和一片绿色的草地；而另一侧的公园栅栏也换成了陡坡，坡上有一间安静的乡村小酒馆；再往上面一点，被森林环抱着的是乡间的小教堂，教堂的院子沿着地势向下延伸，有一座低矮的白色塔楼，从巨大的紫杉树林中露了出来：

巨大的树干！每一株树干上都生长着

缠绕的藤蔓，弯弯曲曲，

向上蜿蜒，盘根错节，难解难分。[①]

——华兹华斯

没有哪个乡村教堂的位置能比得上此处。教堂的围墙之内处处都是宁静与谦卑的所在。

啊！在我们的面前出现了一座更高的山，差不多算一座大山了。当我们沿着陡坡向上的时候，视野逐渐开阔，一派宏伟的气象！陡坡上野草丛生，长满了蕨类、欧石楠和金雀花，在这些高大的常绿灌木丛中，珊瑚红色的果实鲜艳夺目。多么辽阔的大地！可是我们现在没有时间驻足眺望，因为我们那匹倔脾气的马儿，在走了这么多平地之后，忽然来了兴致，我猜他兴许是想快点儿回到马厩里去，打定了让人捉摸不透的主意，开始小跑起来，而且是沿着这一带最陡峭的一座山。我们很快就到了山顶，接着在五分钟的时间里，我们就赶到了铺着草坪的大门前，置身艺术或者自然（我也说不清楚是哪一类）所造就的美丽杰作，山中游乐场之中。"先知先觉的品位之眼"还从未施展过如此有魔力的技巧来成就这样一片植物群。三十年前这个地方并不存在，那时这里只是一块不显眼的田地、草地和公地连起来的地方；现在这里俨然已经有了森林的样貌，目之所及是乔木和灌木的巧妙搭配，是树木的轮廓与

---

① 出自华兹华斯的诗作《紫杉》(*Yew-trees*，1815)。

树叶形成的难得一见的效果，绿色的林间空地，密不透风的幽闭之处，还有那似乎望不到头的绵延之态，让人眼花缭乱，既感到快乐，又觉得迷惑。这是园林改造地貌的胜利，在这样的秋日黄昏更显得美不胜收。夕阳的余晖照亮了泛着绯红的山毛榉、斑斑驳驳的悬铃木，为黑黢黢松林中密密麻麻垂挂着的松果镶上了一道亮闪闪的金边。道路在树叶的迷阵中蜿蜒穿行，优雅而迷人，不知不觉中将我们引向一片更为美丽的山坡。此刻，我们正处在一片花海中的大门口，天竺葵、康乃馨、茉莉都正开着花。啊！这里有一种花，比别的花更加可爱，有一种比知更鸟更加欢快的鸟，这只小鸟唱着"妈妈！妈妈！"的调子，活像一个活灵活现的仙子，两只小脚啪嗒啪嗒地跿着步，演奏出快活的乐曲，正是妈妈的小心肝弗朗西斯！跟随着她的指引，我们来到了那可爱的圆形房间，正赶上最后的夕阳晚照。沐浴在落日余晖中的壮丽风景，如一幅全景画卷展现在我们眼前，夕阳久久徘徊在长满老荆棘和低矮橡树的长岛上，那里是荒原里的绿洲，后来渐渐沉没在一排壮观的彩云之中。

十月二十八日——又是一个和煦、晴朗的早晨。但是今天的愉快经历必须长话短说，因为我没有多少时间来抒发感慨。

首先我们驾车去了小树林：林子里大片大片地种着橡树、榆树和山毛榉，主要还是和山上庄园的栅栏紧挨在一起的橡树，那里无疑是整个庄园之中最让人感到愉悦的地方之一。穿过树林的道路刻意保留了荒蛮的状态，这使得它们看上去就像是仅仅由马车碾出来的车道：地面被弄得凹凸不平，路上有陡峭的下坡，有向阳的斜坡，地势高低起伏，这边一个狭窄的山谷，那边一个陡然爬升的上坡，坡上自是风光无限，这样的路况使这条路颇具自然之美的冲击力，这种美感又因开路者匠心独运而得到了加强和提升。所有这一切，对我来说并不陌生，只是色彩让人耳目一新。我曾经在早春时节来过这里，那时柳树刚刚长出鲜嫩的新叶，榛子树上结着黄色的流穗，每一根枝条都生机勃发；我也曾在枝叶茂盛的仲夏时节一次次地到访这里，但从未在现在这个时候来过。此时浓绿的杉树正悬枝于高高低低如画般的栅栏之上，栅栏上间或还覆盖着苔藓和常春藤，与之形成巨大反差的，是山毛榉亮闪闪的、已经凋零过半的橙色叶片，零星几棵榆树上浅黄色的叶片，橡树上更为浓重丰富的色彩，还有被誉为"林中淑女"的垂枝桦光亮的树干。树下的植被群落也一样美如画。经年的荆棘生着带红点的叶片和更为红艳的浆果，黑莓丛结着猩红色的累累果实，高大的蕨类色彩斑斓，似乎要和地面上绚烂的多彩色块一较高下，地面上有的地方铺着枯叶，散落着松果，有的地方空出一小块，长满了各式各样的苔藓和多彩的真菌，热闹而欢快。今天的小树林是如此美丽丰饶！尤其是那条清澈如水晶的小溪，从那棵古老而"神奇"的榉树根部汩汩而出，细流淌过草地，明亮、沉静，就像五月清晨的露水。静谧的空气中落叶在簌簌飘落，与之相伴的，还有林鸽（它们刚刚从夏季的迁徙地回来，正在啄食常春藤的浆果）彼此间满含爱意的咕咕低语，透过这低语声人们仿佛能听见阳光和美。这片小树林实在是一个可以生死相许的地方。但是，我们必须得走了。我们沿着上行的道路重又回到外面的世界，路途上的风景秀美，经过了那些宛若隐匿在深谷中的小屋，那个悬于半山之中的果园，还有起伏不平的长满欧石楠的山坡。此处的风景自有一种蛮荒之美，高低起伏、大起大落的地势在整个英格兰地区都很少见，在这个富庶、可爱但是单调乏味的乡间更是难得一见。这里简直就是微缩版的瑞士。

接着我们翻过了山，去住在一所大屋的一家人那里进行晨间拜访——那是另一个好去处，在那里可以看到另一片乡野的秀丽风光。那个庄园微微沉落于山谷之中，园中散布着不少老树，树木葱茏，流水比比皆是，堪称园林景致中的杰作，不过这主要是参照达官贵人们官邸的常规样式来看，而绝非像我们刚刚去过的那个地方一样别具一格。然而，这座大宅的庭院里有一处独特的美景——那些环绕场地四周，为露台提供阴凉的、高大壮观的杉树，它们在夏天会散发出正宗塞巴香料的味道，而此刻在秋日斜阳的映照下，它们营造出了一种堪称神奇的效果，那些巨大的、缠绕着常春藤的红色树干，在黑色的暗影中森森耸立，如同一支巨人的军队。大宅的内部——哦，我可不能把读者们带到屋内，否则我们永远也出不来了！室内的阳光甚至还要更亮，因为在这样一个屋顶高挑、采光充足的房间里，坐着一位窈窕淑女，她顽皮又有趣，提香和委拉斯开兹①真应该再度投胎来为她作画，此刻正靠在一件和她一样闪亮而奇特的乐器②上面，吟唱着美丽的法国浪漫曲和苏格兰詹姆斯党③人的歌曲，还有各种我不知道来头的轻松欢快的滑稽歌曲——真是一位英国女即兴演唱家！比安诺·莱尔④还要快活！她的妹妹正在弹钢琴，她的美显得更为高级，嘴角时常带着真诚善意的微笑，令她的美更具感染力；她的父亲在演奏小提琴，琴声如诉如歌，真情流露，意蕴悠长，如此激昂有力的琴声，真是人间难闻，胜似天籁！哦，听着我的伙伴（我忘记说她正是那位配得上如此伴奏的歌手）在这两种乐器的伴奏下，演唱海顿优美的抒情曲《她从未诉衷肠》——她独特的嗓音，带着饱满的力度和自然的甜美，吞吐吸纳间收放自如，悠扬婉转，听到这样的诗歌，这样的音乐，这样完美的演绎，真是一种让人永世难忘的至高享受，简直无与伦比。那歌声至今还萦绕在我的耳畔。

经常漫步于乡野的人，到了蓬勃的春日，

---

① 提香·韦切利奥（Tiziano Vecellio，约 1488—1576），意大利文艺复兴盛期威尼斯画派的代表画家；委拉斯开兹（Diego Rodríguez de Silva y Velázquez，1599—1660），十七世纪巴洛克时期西班牙画家。
② 指一只鲁特竖琴。（作者注）
③ 詹姆斯党（Jacobitism）指支持斯图亚特王朝君主詹姆斯二世及其后代夺回英国王位的一个政治、军事团体，多由天主教徒组成。詹姆斯党在爱尔兰和苏格兰获得了广泛的支持，他们根据当地民歌改编创作的歌曲也广泛流传。
④ 安诺·莱尔（Annot Lyle），司各特小说《蒙特罗斯传奇》（*A Legend of Montrose*，1819）中的女主人公，以歌声动听而闻名。

眼前会自然浮现出美丽的春天图景，

闭上眼睛（赶在睡意袭来，

感觉困顿之前）就能看见，

绿色的草坡上甜美的花儿绽放，

东方染料浸染的樱草，淡色如洗的报春花，

还有蓝色的紫罗兰，带着露水娇艳欲滴，

映刻在脑海中的画面，不会遁去无踪：

我的耳畔也同样回荡着一段交响曲的乐章，

萦绕盘旋，绵绵不绝，那是一段人声，

和两种如人声的乐器浑然天成之曲！

那是来自天上，而非人间的天籁之音，

是灵魂在歌唱，可以媲美那段绝美仙乐，

抚慰老普洛斯彼罗①难解的愁思。

---

① 普洛斯彼罗（Prospero），莎士比亚剧作《暴风雨》中流落荒岛的米兰公爵，他用自己的魔法和精灵艾瑞尔策划了一场假面舞会，幻化出神仙降临、仙乐飘飘的场景。

汉娜·宾特

我之前可能已经说过，通往汉娜·宾特住处的杂木林，是一个乔木与灌木混杂在一起的美丽树林。准确地说，那片面积约有三十或四十英亩的土地上遍布着长势良好的树木——白蜡树、橡树和榆树，被间隔均匀地栽种着；其间间杂着大片大片的灌木林，榛树、枫树、山毛榉、冬青和山楂树，它们和黑莓、泻根还有野蔷薇的藤蔓，或者野生忍冬柔韧卷曲的枝条缠绕在一起，构成了几乎密不透风的树丛。林中那些没有灌木丛生的地方，大多只是被羽毛状的蕨类所覆盖，或者是被地毯一样的花朵覆盖，报春花、红门兰、黄花九轮草、金钱薄荷、老鹳草、羊胡子草、玉竹，还有勿忘我，它们大量地聚集在一起，密密麻麻，五彩斑斓，即使是在花园中我也很少能看到如此繁盛的景象。这边，野生风信子用鲜亮可爱的蓝色花朵给大地涂上了一层釉彩；那边——

> 裹着鲜绿色苔衣的老树根上，
> 长着叶子纤薄明亮的酢浆草，

心形叶片，三片连缀，它的根

如珊瑚珠串，默默无言；周围

盛开着树丛的骄傲，银莲花，

花蕊如金色的饰钉镶嵌在

象牙白的花瓣之上，精巧至极，

但最妙的是，四月花儿初开，

在洁白明艳、妖娆多姿之际，

由紫色彩云为它晕染一顶紫金之冠。①

那里花卉的繁多远远超出我所罗列的品种，主要因为地势起伏不平，时而缓缓隆起形成高坡，时而凹陷成山谷和空洞，每个地方的土壤都各不相同，以至于林中的植被变得非同寻常的丰富和完备。

然而，现在早已过了繁花似锦的季节，只有那些成片的忍冬能够在整个可爱的秋天持续开花，另外紫色的野豌豆上还留有一些不忍离去的花朵，围着树丛编出了一个花环，与黑莓丛泛着秋红的树叶，还有泻根藤蔓上挂着的白色小花连成一片。除此之外，没有什么能让人将视线从更具雄浑之美的树木上移开了——悬铃木宽大的树叶已经变得斑斑驳驳——橡树上沉甸甸地缀满了橡果——还有被称作"林中淑女"的垂枝桦，光亮细腻的树皮与冬青和山楂树的背景形成了强烈的对比。冬青和山楂树丛中点缀着红色的浆果，后面是老的山毛榉树，山毛榉的树叶已经开

① 出自夏洛特·史密斯（Charlotte Turner Smith，1749—1806）的诗作《滩头堡》（*Beachy Head and Other Poems*，1807）。

始变黄，深浅不一、丰富多样的黄色和褐色让它们成了最具观赏性的秋天树木，正像春天的时候，它们透明鲜嫩的新叶是树林中当之无愧的瑰丽饰品一样。

道路在几株高大的山毛榉边上猛然一转，就把我们带到了杂木林的边缘。从一扇简陋的门上探身望去，我们可以看到一片大约十英亩的开阔地带，四周被密密匝匝的林木包围了起来，那里的植物比我们刚刚来时的树林还要丰富，还要分散。作为一块五彩斑斓的田野，没有可出其右者。绯红色的石楠花，一方面与荆豆花的金色花朵形成了鲜明的对比，另一方面又与一片荞麦地相互映衬。尽管荞麦的种子已经开始成熟，但花朵尚未完全凋谢——美丽的荞麦——透明的叶片和茎秆透出一丝亮红，而娇嫩的粉白色花朵，如淡色的蓼草，像羽毛一样弯折，此时它们是如此丰盈、优雅，散发出沁人心脾的香气，就像五月黄昏里披着露水的山毛榉。那片无法进行耕作的山坡顶上长着晚生的洋地黄和庄严的毛蕊花；占据着荒地很大一块面积的牧场，绿草茵茵，如翡翠一般；一汪清澈的池塘，倒映着明亮的天空，为整个画面增添了一抹亮色；守林人的白色小屋从对面的矮林中露出一角，它的周围有一个美丽的洒满阳光的花园，汉娜·宾特爬满藤蔓的小屋就坐落在花园中央。

那些点缀在风景中的能走会跳的活物与周遭的景色浑然一体，显得快活又安宁。汉娜的奶牛正挨着守林人的小马驹安静地吃草；两只肥嘟嘟的小猎狗和一窝小猪崽闹得正欢；草地上散布着鸭、鹅、公鸡、母鸡还有小鸡；汉娜本人正从小屋的门口走出来，手里拿着牛奶桶，她的弟弟拿着挤奶工具跟在她后面。

我的朋友汉娜·宾特绝非等闲之辈。她的父亲，杰克·宾特（他终其一生也没能让人体面地叫他一声约翰，事实上在我们这一带他总是被人们叫作伦敦杰克），在他赶牲口的行当里享有很高的声誉。从萨里兹博瑞平原到史密斯菲尔德，没有人能像杰克·宾特一样，在他那只著名的牧羊犬"看守"的帮助下，如此娴熟地赶着羊群，克服种种困难，穿越小路和公地，街道和马路，艰难跋涉。"看守"有一张沧桑而淳朴的脸，黑色皮毛，口鼻处有一小片白色，一只耳朵也是白的，在大小市集上和他主人那张同样淳朴而饱经风霜的面孔一样有名。能锁定这两位，让他们为自己赶牲口的贩子都是幸运的；"看守"早已名声在外，路上他对羊群的守护胜过其他任何牧羊犬——杰克也一样，他总是能把牲口准时送达，牲口的状态也更好。没有人比他更了解夜里在哪里投宿更好，哪里可以让他的牲口吃到好的草料，哪里能让他和"看守"都找到好酒。"看守"和其他的牧羊犬一样，已经习惯了依靠面包和啤酒过活。他的主人，尽管不反对喝上一瓶上等的黑啤酒，但是更偏爱杜松子酒。他们那些在霜冻和大雾天里，沿着泥泞的道路艰难前行，累得筋疲力尽的人，毫无疑问更愿意享受一下让人感到温暖和振奋的刺激性饮品，不像我们坐在温暖舒适的房间里，喝水就够了，他们对于酒的感觉不是我们能轻易想象得到的。毋庸置疑，我们这位赶牲口的从来抵挡不了酒瓶的温柔诱惑，而且他素来无拘无束，生性快活、随和，也就是人们常说的老好人，总是乐于见到别人和他一样开心快活，所以他动不动就自掏腰包请大家伙儿喝上几杯，这固然使得他人气大增，可是他的财力却大受折损。

当他尚能保持收支平衡的时候，日子过得还是相当不错的，他凭着自己的勤劳让家里的那几口人过上了还算舒适的生活，可是有一年的寒冬，一场突如其来的风湿热找上了他，并最终使他的腿落下了残疾，使这个教区里最活跃、坚强的汉子，变成了一个实实在在的瘸子。这时候，他不计后果慷慨解囊的习性就开始让他吃苦头了。可怜的杰克，一个冲动但善良的家伙，一个最为慈爱的父亲，只能眼睁睁地看着自己三个没娘的孩子陷入悲苦的贫困之中，作为一个深爱着孩子的父亲，这种痛苦让他受尽了折磨。他可能完全没有料到，自己竟然从年幼的女儿，一个十二岁的姑娘那里，找到了智慧和心灵上的帮助。

汉娜是家里最大的孩子，自从两三年前母亲去世之后，她已经习惯了为家里大大小小的事操心，照顾两个弟弟，喂猪和鸡鸭，在爸爸经常不在家的情况下操持好这个家。她是一个聪明又机灵的小姑娘，天性乐观，性格坚韧，还颇有点傲气，总是担心会接受教区的救济，虽说现在农户能得到的救济已经一天不如一天了，但这毕竟构成了英国人百折不挠的独立品格最坚实的保障。这种精神在我们这位小姑娘身上得到了完美的体现。当她的父亲说起要舍弃他们舒适的小屋，搬到救济所里去住，而她和两个弟弟都要去做工的时候，汉娜做出了一个大胆的决定，她丝毫没有向生病的父亲透露自己的打算和担忧，而是在安置好他们的琐碎事物之后，立刻就开始实施自己的计划和设想。

　　尽管这个可怜的赶牲口的人看起来似乎不懂得为未来打算，但是他从未欠下任何债务，而且因为长期在一个互济会认捐，他得到了一份微薄的津贴。虽然他注定要与疾病和困顿相伴多年，但这笔钱多少给了他一点支持。这一点他女儿是知道的。同时，她还知道父亲健康遭损之时所效力的东家，是附近一个富有且慷慨的牲口商人，那位东家很愿意帮助一位忠心耿耿的老仆人，并且也确实曾过来说要给些钱帮他们一把。汉娜认为完全没有理由拒绝这样一位人士的帮助。来自农场主奥克利的帮助和教区的救济完全是两码事。然而，她向他索求的并不是金钱，而是对于他来说更为司空见惯的东西——"一头奶牛！随便什么样的奶牛！年老的，瘸腿的，不管什么样儿，只要是头奶牛就行！她保证会把它照料好，如若不然，他完全可以把奶牛再要回去。她甚至希望自己能慢慢地，通过分期付款的办法把奶牛给买下来，不过对此她尚不能给出确切的承诺！"这位富裕的农户既觉得好笑，又对这孩子的诚意颇感兴趣，便给了她一头，不是卖给她，而是作为礼物，送给她一头上好的年轻奥尔德尼奶牛。她接下来又去找了这块庄园的领主，凭着对他品行同样的了解，恳请他允许自己在杂木林的公地上放养奶牛。"农场主奥克利送了她一头上好的奥尔德尼奶牛，只要他允许在这块荒地上放养这头牛，她就能付得起租金，她的父亲就不用到教区的救济所里去了。"这位领主同样答应了，一半是出于真正善良的本性，一半是不肯在慷慨大方这一点上输给自己的佃户，他不仅应允了放牧的许可，还大大降低了租金，以至于仅仅所产的葡萄就足以抵得上这位仁慈的地主所要求的租金了。

现在，汉娜成了一名出色的挤奶女工，证明了自己当初的决策是多么英明。她不可能再找到一份如此稀缺或者需求如此巨大的工作了。这一带，最让那些小产业者头疼的一件小事就是，很难弄到或者说几乎不可能弄到牛奶、鸡蛋和黄油这一类的畜牧产品，而这些偏偏是日常所需最必不可少的东西。对于你们这些土生土长的伦敦人来说，在抱怨自己早餐的时候，一定以为香浓的奶油、新鲜的黄油和刚下的鸡蛋就是产自乡下的——是那里自然出产的东西——然而，在这个以牧场著称的地区，除了小牛和养牛的农夫能沾到奶牛的光，其他人都无福消受牛奶和奶制品，而且农夫们的妻子已经不再饲养家禽了，你们若是知道这些一定会略感安慰；我们这些不幸的村里人每天坐下来享用第一餐的时候，经常发现实在没什么好吃的，跟我们这里毫无建树的畜牧业相比，能吃上稀薄的牛奶和来自剑桥的黄油的人足以为此感到满足了。

汉娜的奥尔德尼奶牛使我们得以重获这种乡下人的特权。我们还从未见过一个如此干净的小挤奶工。她处理掉了家里那些花里胡哨的东西，那是可怜的杰克在家里日子过得宽绰的时候，为了取悦自己而给家里添置的，有陶瓷茶具、镶了金边的杯子、带花纹的托盘，汉娜把它们换成了制作奶制品的器具，并且很快就做起了稳定又赚钱的生意，买卖牛奶、鸡蛋、黄油、蜂蜜和家禽——他们可是一直都喂养家禽的。

她同样也把家里料理得井井有条。她的父亲，虽然腿
瘸了，但双手还是跟之前一样灵巧能干，开始编起了草垫
和篮子，而且编得漂亮又精巧。家里最大的男孩是个聪明
伶俐的小伙子，帮父亲割灯芯草和柳条，还在姐姐的指挥
下，给奶牛搭起了一个牛棚，开垦出了更大的花园（每次
都征得了她那位好心的领主大人的许可），花园里的植物
长得如此丰茂，里面的产出不仅能养猪，给家里提供近一
半的供养，而且还给家里这位不知疲倦的女管事提供了另
外可供买卖的商品。家里最小的男孩没有那么勤快活跃，
汉娜设法让他去上了慈善学校，他在那里取得了长足的进
步——不过，在晒干草、租干草的季节，或者他能帮上忙
的时候，他还是得留在家里，这让他的校长颇为恼火，因
为这孩子是他最喜欢的，他还为乔治申请奖学金的事情费
尽了心力（那些干起农活来慢吞吞的孩子，往往在拿起书
本的时候会变得才思敏捷）。大家普遍认为这个被大加赞
赏的孩子，假以时日，会被提升到助理的位置，而且将来
很有可能会成为教区里令人尊敬的老师。于是他的姐姐，
尽管还会时不时地拉他过来帮忙，但已经意识到乔治不在
她这里帮忙反而更好，而他的兄长汤姆，已经足以胜任一
个园丁副手的职位了，只是他在家里太重要了，难得有一
天的闲暇。

简言之，在汉娜·宾特掌管杂木林小屋的这五年里，
一切都很顺利。她的奶牛、小牛、猪、蜜蜂和鸡鸭，每一
种都依照各自的方式繁殖和增长。她甚至让牧羊犬"看守"

在喜欢重口味儿啤酒的同时，也喜欢上了黄油和牛奶，而且几乎说服了她的父亲（她对于父亲的需求和愿望总是格外上心），让他用牛奶取代杜松子酒。汉娜并非没有敌人和对手。怎么会没有呢？住在门房上的那位老太太，总是心怀叵测，看不惯新生事物，从一开始就预言汉娜搞不出什么名堂，后面又因为自己的预言落空而不肯原谅她；贝蒂·巴恩斯，那个酒徒农夫的邋遢遗孀，租了一块地，自己养了一头奶牛，却因为弄得太过肮脏不堪而受到大家的一致唾弃，她说尽了一个怨妇的恶毒心肠所能想到的诋毁汉娜和她的奶牛的坏话；不仅如此，就连她的邻居，守林人耐得·迈尔斯，也总是要抱怨一番：以前杂木林公地这一带都归他管，包括那些灌木林，当他发现一个小姑娘竟然在自己的地盘上占得一席之地，一头奶牛就挨着自己的马驹吃草，那些毫不讲理的公鸡母鸡对原本要喂给自己高贵的野鸡吃的荞麦虎视眈眈的时候，就算他是个热心肠、好脾气的家伙，也忍不住要抱怨几句。耐得堪称守林人的典范，身材高大魁梧，很有男子气概，一副让人感到亲切的面孔，眼睛含着笑意，脸上总是挂着善解人意的微笑，走起路来大步流星。他平常总是穿着绿色的外套，戴着金色蕾丝边的帽子，他那只高贵的纽芬兰犬"海神"（按照打猎的行话来讲是只寻回犬），以及美丽的西班牙猎犬"调情"总是和他形影不离。谁也没有想到平日里和善的他，在第一次发现汉娜和"看守"竟然在他原有的地盘杂木林公地上，同样可以掌管一方时，脸上竟会出现那样扭曲的表情。

没错！汉娜有自己的敌人，但他们正在渐渐成为过去。那个住在门房上的老太太已经去世了，怪可怜的；贝蒂·巴恩斯，自己也染上了酗酒的毛病，原有的几个朋友也都离她而去，她现在一副可怜兮兮的倒霉样儿，看上去好像也时日无多了！至于守林人嘛，嗯，他倒是没死，也不像快要死的样子，不过，在他身上发生了最让人意想不到的变化——当然，或许同样的变化也发生在了汉娜身上。

豆蔻之年一般说来是小姑娘们长得很漂亮的时候，可是没有几个十二岁的小姑娘能比汉娜·宾特显得更普通。她那时个子矮小敦实，瘦瘦的脸庞，五官有些突兀，脸色发黄，还顶着一头乱糟糟的枯黄头发，眼睛很亮，显露出对于她那个年龄来说让人意想不到的品质，她过分懂事，过于敏感，也太过聪明——十二岁时的她已经有了一个小个子老仙女的气质。现在她十七岁了，情况有了巨大的改观。她发黄的脸色已经消失不见，脸也长开了，个子长了一大截，体态轻盈，颇有乡间淑女的风范；她明亮而锐利的眼神温和了许多，甚至因为女性想要取悦于人的愿望而充满了柔情蜜意；她的鬈发现在梳得一丝不乱，发型精致而整洁；她显然格外留心自己的着装，尽量搭配出好看的效果，无论是样式和面料，都和她本人很相配，如果这不能算作仪态大方，至少应该被看作最高境界的卖弄风情。虽说女大十八变，但如此脱胎换骨的蜕变真是让人大开眼界。这姑娘俨然就是个美人了，耐得·迈尔斯显然也注意到了这一点。他就在那儿站着，这个愣头小伙子，就在她身边（在我们讲她的小故事的时候，他就过来了，现在挤

144

奶工作已经结束了！）——他就站着那儿，一手拎着她的牛奶桶，另一只手轻轻抚摸着"看守"，而她则拍拍"海神"的大脑袋，以回应他的美意。他们二人站在那里，要多像一对情侣就有多像，他脸上带着微笑，她则羞红了脸——在他们的一生当中，他从未显得如此英俊，她也从未显得如此美丽。他们站在那里，幸福得已经忘记了整个世界，眼睛里只剩下彼此，完全是这世上最幸福的一对儿。他们站在那里，就算是为了整个基督教世界的牛奶和黄油也不能去打扰他们。如果说他们是在商定结婚的日子，我一点儿也不会感到吃惊。

叶　落

十一月六日——今天风和日丽，平静、和煦，就像四月初的样子；或许秋日的午后和春天的早晨两者在感觉上确实很相像，即使是看起来，也比一年中任何两个时节都更相像。这两个时节里牧草几乎是一样的鲜嫩多汁，空气中有同样宜人的温煦，还有一样纯净可爱的蓝天，天上飘浮着羊毛一样松软的云朵。最大的不同是春天有百花齐放，秋天有落叶纷飞。十一月间的树叶是如此富丽多彩、绚烂多姿，足以抵得上春天里的繁盛花事，然而，田野和花园里所有的花都无法弥补树叶的缺失——树叶是大自然为大树粗糙的躯干披上的一件美丽而优雅的衣裳——那张绿色的织锦，风景正因为有了它才显得生动可爱，树林正因为有了它才满目华彩。

如果必须在这两个富有魅力的季节中选择一个的话，选择眼前的好时节一定不算是糟糕的抉择，不管这种权衡来自对过去满怀感激的回望，还是对未来满怀憧憬的前瞻。况且，毋庸置疑，在十一月里，再也找不到比今天更好的天气样本了——这是一个让人忍不住要去闲逛的日子。

沿着黄色的公地和桦树成荫的山谷，

还有树篱围起来的人迹罕至的小路；①

而且，再也没有比绿树成荫、阳光明媚的伯克郡更迷人的乡野可供我们散步了，这里的风光既没有过分宏伟，也没有太过荒蛮，让人感觉如此安宁，如此欢悦，如此多变，又是如此富于英国风情。

我们必须绕道到水边走一趟，因为我要给农场主赖利带个口信，而且实不相瞒，这绝不是让人感到无聊的苦差事。那里的道路干燥、平坦、僻静，正是人们所期望的那种乡间小路，但又不会让人感到太过孤单，女士们可不喜欢那种感觉。那条路沿途会经过洛登河——那满溢的、清亮透彻的洛登河水——足以像镜子一样倒映出这蔚蓝的天空，道路的尽头就是我们这一带最漂亮也最舒适的农庄之一了。

这条小路今天是如此迷人，得有上千种颜色点缀其间！道路是棕色的，两侧是青翠的树篱，其间散落着浅黄色的叶片，那是刚刚开始凋落的榆树叶；灌木丛中深浅不一的紫红色黑莓果在长长的藤蔓上显得分外耀眼；头顶上杉树还是一成不变的绿色，与之形成对比的是斑驳的悬铃木树叶、黄褐色的山毛榉，以及橡树干枯的叶片，微风吹来，树叶沙沙作响；虽然此时已是深秋，依然有几种常见的耐寒黄色花卉（不管是野生的还是栽培的花卉，黄色是

---

① 出自夏洛特·史密斯的诗作《滩头堡》。

最常见的颜色，而蓝色则是最罕见的）迎风而开，尽管品种不一，但几乎都是同一色调的黄色，这当中还可以看见红色的浆果，鲜艳夺目。这条小路真是要多美有多美！

道路开阔处的那座小山看上去也让人心生欢喜，路旁有成群的牛羊，还有乔治·何恩，我们这里的小邮差，他正在使劲儿地滚铁环，以便能让自己跑得更快一些，更早地完成工作，就当是自己正在玩儿呢！山顶这片带着水塘的公地也是如此美丽！玛莎·皮瑟家的孩子们正在水塘边玩耍，三个小精灵分别有三岁、四岁和五岁，从他们晒得黝黑的脸庞和破旧的衣服上还分辨不出他们的性别，他们正在用各自刷得锃亮的家用小水杯和一个棕色的豁了口的水罐舀水，打算把那只大水壶填满，可那只水壶如果灌满了水，即使他们三个合力也休想把它拎起来！他们三个都是红扑扑的小脸蛋儿，胖嘟嘟的小手，圆圆的乐呵呵的小脸，很像是画家眼中要入画的一组人物；背景中那个低矮的小屋，从葡萄藤蔓和月季花丛中露出一角，玛莎正站在门前，准备着要下锅的土豆，她的穿着朴素整洁，一边微笑着，一边看着那边舀水，然后往水壶里灌水的过程，这简直就是一幅完整的图画。

但我们必须得继续往前走。现在白天太过短暂，没有时间停下来获取更多的素描作品了。天气也越来越冷，我们必须得加快脚步赶路。达什在我们前面领路，不停地在草地边沿儿两道浓密的树丛中钻来钻去，他移动的速度表明有猎物正在活动，他的搜寻还搅落了树叶，它们像是遇到了严霜过后的东风，纷纷飘落。啊！山鸡！

一只漂亮的雄性山鸡！达什在追踪猎物方面的能力绝对不容置疑，不管是在树丛中还是在密林里，因为一只好的西班牙猎犬是不屑于到开阔的田野里去的；但我怀疑是一只活动的野兔惊动了山鸡，同时这只兔子也被山鸡扑棱翅膀的声音吓住了，就像那只高贵的鸟儿在听到猎枪的声音时一样。的确，我相信一只山鸡突然腾起的样子，会让那些年轻的猎手感到紧张（他们不会坦然承认这一点，但是据我的观察，的确如此）。直到渐渐习惯了那种声音之后，这种猛然间扇动翅膀的巨大响动才会让他们和达什一样变得兴奋起来。达什此时正在用尽蛮力在树丛间穿梭，叫声更加响亮，摇落树叶的速度也快了——这是因为他正陶醉在找到山鸡的骄傲之中，或许还对我没有开枪射击有一丝懊恼，至少看起来是这样，如果我是个男人，他早就生气了。达什毕竟是一只非常聪明的狗，而且他在猎场的四年时间里绝不会没有发现，尽管绅士们会开枪，但女士不会。

终于到了洛登河畔！美丽的洛登河！几乎每个人都会不由自主地在桥上驻足，倚靠在栏杆上，对着这美不胜收的景色凝神注目——那是大宅所在的风水宝地，密布着大片大片的椴树、杉树和前所未见的巨型杨树；对岸的绿色草地上点缀着橡树和榆树，清澈弯转的河流，最远处还有磨坊和如画般美丽的老房子；所有这一切在浓浓的秋色中更显绚丽多姿，又因与明净的碧空、此刻的安宁融为一体，多了些许柔美与甘醇。即使是每日都要过桥的农夫，也忍不住要在这桥上停留片刻。

但天色渐晚，寒意渐深。我笃信寒霜将至。毕竟春天才是最宜人的季节，即使眼前的景色美丽如斯。我们必须得走了。沿着那条宽阔但树影浓深的小路，进到庄园之中，四季常青的树木暗黑一片，其间有鹿穿梭而过，草地上牛羊和马正在高大的榆树下面吃着牧草；小路的一侧是一道荒坡，长满了蕨类和成片的荆豆花，上面则是浓密地结着浆果的荆棘丛和闪闪发亮的冬青；另一侧是一道如画般的老栅栏，其间有明亮的月桂和叶片如羽毛一般的雪松，两侧的景致各有千秋，争相竞美。沿着这条披着浓荫的小路向前，到了一个陡弯处突然开阔起来，有四条道路交会于此，其中一条庄严的大道通往那座宅邸。透过大道两侧的古紫杉树可以看见乡村教堂朴素的尖顶：我们此行的终点和目标、善良的农场主赖利宽敞舒适的家宅就坐落在此间，四周有果园和花园环绕，后面有谷仓和草垛，还有整个农庄的财富作为后盾。

我们相谈甚欢，传达了口信，又得到了回复，这个美丽的晴日渐渐消逝，寒霜浓重的夜晚已经来临；古老大道上榆树和椴树的树叶在寒风中瑟瑟作响，最后利落地从枝头飘落到地面，仿佛达什正在树顶搜寻山鸡；太阳透过薄雾发出惨淡的光芒，那点儿微弱的光和热与他美丽的妹妹月亮女士所能给的不相上下。我不知道有什么能比一轮冷日更令人感到失望的。我开始裹紧身上的斗篷，计算着距离自己家火炉的路程，心里一边收回我对于十一月的所有赞美，一边像一只快要被冻僵的蝴蝶，或者被寒霜打落的大丽花一样，期盼着春雨绵绵、花满枝头的四月。

哦，天哪！这到底是什么天气，我对它的印象居然难以维持超过半个小时！不过，我在怀疑，到底是天气的原因，还是我的原因，因为达什看起来好像丝毫没有在意天气的变化。或许等到明年春天我不小心被雨淋个湿透，心里又向往起秋天的时候，这件事就算扯平了。

图书在版编目（CIP）数据

我们的村庄：汉英对照 ／（英）玛丽·拉塞尔·米特福德（Mary Russell Mitford）著；张方方译．—南京：译林出版社，2024.4
（双语经典）
书名原文：Our Village
ISBN 978-7-5753-0020-9

I.①我… II.①玛… ②张… III.①英语 – 汉语 – 对照读物 IV.① H319.4

中国国家版本馆 CIP 数据核字（2024）第 005677 号

我们的村庄　　〔英国〕玛丽·拉塞尔·米特福德／著　　张方方／译

责任编辑　　陈绍敏
特约编辑　　张艳华　苑浩泰
装帧设计　　鹏飞艺术
校　　对　　刘文硕
责任印制　　贺　伟

出版发行　　译林出版社
地　　址　　南京市湖南路 1 号 A 楼
邮　　箱　　yilin@yilin.com
网　　址　　www.yilin.com
市场热线　　010−85376701
排　　版　　鹏飞艺术
印　　刷　　三河市中晟雅豪印务有限公司
开　　本　　889 毫米 ×1194 毫米　1/32
印　　张　　13.25
版　　次　　2024 年 4 月第 1 版
印　　次　　2024 年 4 月第 1 次印刷
书　　号　　ISBN 978−7−5753−0020−9
定　　价　　49.80元